MW00582074

"Nguyen Williams and Crandal provide a conci
will help children and adolescents adhere to cogi
ples in a manner relevant to them. A much-need
orders in these groups."

> —**Donna Roybal, MD**, director of Pediatric Consult-Liaison Services,
> divisions of child and adolescent psychiatry and mood and anxiety
> disorders, and departments of psychiatry and pediatrics, University
> of Texas Health Sciences Center at San Antonio

"Concise, well organized, scientifically based, yet easy to understand and utilize…excellent resource!"

> —**Rebecca Susan Daily, MD, DFAACAP, FAPA**, chief of child and
> adolescent psychiatry, and vice-chair of child psychiatry in the department
> of psychiatry and behavioral sciences at the University of Oklahoma

"This text offers clinicians an easily understood map for charting the therapeutic journey that might be taken with a wide range of depressed youth. The organization of core and supplementary skills provides the reader with a clear starting point as well as decision-making guidelines for charting next steps. A valuable resource for both novice and experienced therapists!"

> —**Brian Buzzella, PhD, ABPP**, director of the Family Mental Health
> Program and codirector of the Clinical Psychology Postdoctoral Residency
> Program, VA San Diego Healthcare System

"With a rise in commitment to evidence-based practices comes a flood of psychological treatment manuals. Thankfully, Nguyen Williams and Crandal have contributed a unique addition that answers an unmet and critical need in our field. This must-have protocol offers a flexible approach to real-world cases that often require more than traditional cognitive behavioral therapy (CBT) manuals provide. Packed with practical tools, vignettes, and case examples, *Modular CBT for Children and Adolescents with Depression* is an easy-to-follow, culturally sensitive, one-stop-shop for clinicians treating complex juvenile depression."

> —**Jill A. Stoddard, PhD**, coauthor of *The Big Book of ACT Metaphors*,
> founder and director of The Center for Stress and Anxiety Management,
> and associate professor at Alliant International University, San Diego, CA

"The authors have managed to combine a user-friendly resource that summarizes current cognitive behavioral therapy (CBT) thinking in the treatment of depression, using both relevant and engaging vignettes that put the reader firmly into the therapist's chair. Therapists in the mental health field and beyond will find a range of methods in this book to effectively treat child and adolescent depression."

> —**Kate Shelper, MA, APS**, clinical supervisor and child psychologist at the Child and Youth Mental Health Service, Queensland Health, Australia

"Nguyen Williams and Crandals' book offers a practical and effective approach for treating depression in adolescents. This book is smart, fun, and a great guide for treating depressed adolescents. Therapists will surely find it easy to use and enjoyable."

> —**Alejandra Postlethwaite, MD**, director of behavioral health services at La Maestra Community Health Centers, and clinical professor of health sciences at the University of California, San Diego

"Finally, a cause for celebration in children's and adolescent mental health! Depressive symptoms in this age group are not uncommon, and they are most often treated with a variety of medications, some of which are prescribed off-label and not tested on children, and others which are ineffective or cause unpleasant side effects. Thus, we welcome the arrival of this truly exceptional book for mental health clinicians and psychotherapists who work with children and adolescents with depression. *Modular CBT for Children and Adolescents with Depression* is so fluidly written and engaging that the professional reader feels immediately connected, and it is also eminently readable and seamlessly organized. The book is a brilliant treatise on the common questions both clinicians and clients have about youth depression, with elucidations of the whats, whens, hows, and whys of this profound diagnosis and treatment. The user-friendly therapeutic techniques are clearly described and explained, and are readily applicable in a clinical setting. Furthermore, they are evidence-based—that is, they have been shown to be effective in numerous studies and clinical trials. Katherine Nguyen Williams and Brent Crandal are to be thanked and congratulated on this significant achievement, a seminal step forward in the treatment of depression in our youth."

> —**Saul Levine, MD**, professor of psychiatry and past division chief of child and adolescent psychiatry at the University of California, San Diego, and psychiatrist-in-chief at Rady Children's Hospital

"Nguyen Williams and Crandal have expertly written a user-friendly, well-organized, and practical manual to support clinicians' systematic and flexible use of evidence-based strategies. This book is a must-have resource for both novice and experienced clinicians working in community and private practice settings with children and adolescents experiencing depression."

> —**Lauren Brookman-Frazee, PhD**, associate professor in the department of psychiatry at the University of California, San Diego, and associate director of the Child and Adolescent Services Research Center

"An essential resource for therapists in *real-world* mental health settings working with *real-world* clients for which complex presentations are the norm. [The guide's] applications are straightforward, manageable, and representative of the current state of psychological science."

> —**Andrea Letamendi, PhD**, TEDx Talks speaker, psychological consultant, and director of clinical training at Hathaway-Sycamores Child and Family Services

"There are many therapy books on the market, but many of them range from nebulous to tedious. Nguyen Williams and Crandal have elucidated the best treatments for child and adolescent depression from the field of cognitive behavioral therapy (CBT), and integrated the effective interventions into this important work. This clinician's guide has been long awaited; clinicians finally have a highly readable and tremendously useful therapy manual that will impact the clinical work being done with depressed children and adolescents across the nation and internationally."

> —**Gary Youssef, MFT**, program manager of outpatient psychiatry at Rady Children's Hospital

"Nguyen Williams and Crandal have filled an important gap in treatment manuals for practicing clinicians working with children and adolescents. This guide presents the essential skills to address depression in a succinct and straightforward manner. I not only practice with a modular approach, but also supervise students to think in this way as well. I recommend this book for clinicians who are both new to and familiar with cognitive behavioral therapy (CBT) for depression among children and adolescents."

> —**Hilary Mead, PhD**, supervising clinical psychologist at Seattle Children's Hospital, Psychiatry and Behavioral Medicine

"For therapists working with children and adolescents, *Modular CBT for Children and Adolescents with Depression* is a must-read. The authors have simplified and clarified complex concepts into an easily readable and highly informative book that will appeal to both beginning and more experienced therapists. The often challenging task of implementing cognitive behavioral therapy (CBT) in real-world settings is much more effective utilizing a modular approach, which the authors explain in practical and user-friendly terms. The authors, both of whom are master clinicians, have developed a resource that all therapists should have on their bookshelves. The book is wonderfully organized, easy to read, and written in a conversational style that brings to life the concepts the authors are trying to teach. This is an excellent resource for all mental health professionals!"

—**Sandra Brown, PhD, ABPP**, clinical professor of psychiatry, and
    director of the School of Medicine, UCSD/VA Psychology Internship
    Training Program

"One of the most sweeping changes in health care has been a move away from a 'one size fits all' approach to an era of personalized interventions. In no area of psychiatry is this more essential than for children and adolescents, where a dynamically changing biology and the potential for early treatments to have powerful effects on the life course of illness make individualized approaches an imperative. Nguyen Williams and Crandals' expertly written book provides illuminating, practical, and easy-to-understand guidance for implementing the most effective intervention for conditions affecting over 10 percent of today's youth. It is destined to become a classic in the field."

—**Jay N. Giedd, MD**, professor and chief of child and adolescent psychiatry,
    University of California, San Diego; and past chief of brain imaging, child
    and adolescent psychiatry, National Institute of Mental Health

Modular CBT
for Children
and Adolescents
with Depression

A Clinician's Guide to
Individualized Treatment

Katherine Nguyen Williams, PhD
Brent R. Crandal, PhD

New Harbinger Publications, Inc.

Publisher's Note

This publication is designed to provide accurate and authoritative information in regard to the subject matter covered. It is sold with the understanding that the publisher is not engaged in rendering psychological, financial, legal, or other professional services. If expert assistance or counseling is needed, the services of a competent professional should be sought.

Distributed in Canada by Raincoast Books

Copyright © 2015 by Katherine Nguyen Williams and Brent Crandal
New Harbinger Publications, Inc.
5674 Shattuck Avenue
Oakland, CA 94609
www.newharbinger.com

Cover design by Amy Shoup
Acquired by Melissa Valentine
Edited by Gretel Hakanson
Indexed by James Minkin

Library of Congress Cataloging-in-Publication Data

Nguyen Williams, Katherine, author.
  Modular CBT for children and adolescents with depression : a clinician's guide to individualized treatment / Katherine Nguyen Williams, Brent R. Crandal.
      p. ; cm.
  Modular cognitive behavioral therapy for children and adolescents with depression
  Includes bibliographical references and index.
  ISBN 978-1-62625-117-5 (pbk. : alk. paper) -- ISBN 978-1-62625-118-2 (pdf e-book) -- ISBN 978-1-62625-119-9 (epub)
  I. Crandal, Brent R., author. II. Title. III. Title: Modular cognitive behavioral therapy for children and adolescents with depression.
  [DNLM: 1. Depressive Disorder--therapy. 2. Adolescent. 3. Child. 4. Cognitive Therapy-- methods. 5. Individualized Medicine. WM 171.5]
  RJ506.D4
  616.85'2700835--dc23
                          2015026336

Printed in the United States of America

17   16   15

10   9   8   7   6   5   4   3   2   1   First printing

To my graceful wife, who provides the intrepidity to undertake, and to my darling daughter, who provides the motivation to complete.

—B. R. C.

For my parents, Deacon Peter Can & Yen Nguyen,
who taught me the value of tenacity.
For my energetic young children, Grant, Cole, Kate, & Paul,
who taught me to balance hard work with play.
And for my superhero husband, Paul,
whose awe-inspiring support made this book possible.

—K. N. W.

Contents

Foreword

I am delighted to introduce this terrific new book for psychotherapists, which provides scientifically supported and practical guidance on effective therapeutic strategies for treating children and adolescents struggling with depression. As psychotherapists, we all want to help our clients reduce their suffering and meet their full potential. This is particularly true when children and adolescents are experiencing debilitating and risky depression, and looking to therapists to help ease their pain. With this book, Katherine Nguyen Williams and Brent Crandal give therapists the knowledge and tools to deliver the therapeutic strategies that have been proven to result in the most positive outcomes.

It is rare for one book to meet standards of scientific credibility while also delivering pragmatic, user-friendly resources for therapists, but this book does exactly that. The book achieves an ideal balance by clearly communicating both the rationale and the evidence for specific therapeutic approaches, as well as providing practical guidance and tools therapists can use to implement these approaches. Therapists from all disciplines will learn essential current information supporting the effectiveness of the modular cognitive behavioral therapy approach. The authors have done a great job in distilling decades of research into essential, need-to-know facts, and they communicate these facts very clearly and succinctly. Building on this strong scientific foundation, the authors provide clear, practical guidelines on how to deliver evidence-based therapeutic strategies. They generously share a wealth of adaptable tools and resources to use with a wide variety of clients (such as worksheets and activity suggestions). While the book is focused on treatment strategies for children and adolescents with depression, many of the resources will be useful to therapists with a wider range of clients. For example, there are very useful chapters addressing the challenges of achieving family collaboration, improving therapeutic engagement, making crisis-intervention and safety plans, and preventing relapse.

The modular CBT approach advocated by the authors will appeal to psychotherapists from all disciplines because it respects the need to adapt evidence-based approaches for the unique individual characteristics of clients. With the increased national emphasis on the need to deliver evidence-based treatments, many psychotherapists have expressed frustration, perceiving that such treatments are often inflexible one-size-fits-all models and thus ill-suited to the diverse and unique needs of their clients. In contrast, the modular approach advocated by Williams and Crandal counters this perception and encourages therapists to use the scientifically supported elements of the evidence-based practices in flexible ways to meet clients' unique needs. This modular approach makes intuitive sense, is respectful of therapists' skills, *and* is supported by recent research that has demonstrated superior outcomes of modular approaches to delivering evidence-based practice. Modular approaches to delivering evidence-based practice are at the forefront of the field.

Williams and Crandal are master clinicians and educators themselves, and they have written this book in an accessible, friendly, conversational style that makes it a pleasure to read. They seamlessly weave concise descriptions of groundbreaking research studies with salient clinical vignettes and engaging historical or personal anecdotes. Like all great teachers, Williams and Crandal convey enthusiasm, humor, wisdom, and authoritative expertise. Readers may be surprised how much they've learned after just a chapter or two because it seems so painless!

As a clinical scholar and educator of therapists across multiple mental health disciplines, I am proud to add this terrific book to my recommended must-haves for psychotherapists in training (which, of course, includes all of us; we're "in training" throughout our lifetimes!). Many of us have devoted our careers to finding engaging ways to translate the science of psychotherapy into practice, and I am delighted to have identified a book that achieves this goal so effectively.

—Ann F. Garland, PhD
    Professor and Department Chair
    Department of School, Family, and Mental Health Professions
    School of Leadership and Education Sciences
    University of San Diego

Introduction

Depression Treatment

According to the World Health Organization (WHO; 2012), depression is the leading cause of disability worldwide, with an estimated 350 million individuals of all ages affected. In the United States, depressive disorders affect approximately 11.2 percent of thirteen- to eighteen-year-olds (Merikangas et al., 2010). While there is substantial evidence for the effective treatment of depression with cognitive behavorial therapy (CBT), researchers have demonstrated a high unmet need and poorer outcomes for children and adolescents in community-based settings (Weersing & Weisz, 2002). Some have suggested this has been due to struggles with implementation and treatment fidelity (Asarnow, 2010). Weisz and Chorpita (2012) have suggested that the complexity and comorbidity of youths presenting at community-based clinics may make children and adolescents less ideal candidates for traditional evidence-based treatment protocols. Traditional protocols in clinical research are generally tested with homogenous groups of disorders and have strict exclusionary criteria for their study samples. Therapists have long argued that the participants in these research studies significantly differ from the youths who present in everyday clinical practice at community-based clinics. Because these youths often have complex presenting problems (e.g., trauma history, significant family problems, developmental issues) with comorbid disorders (e.g., generalized anxiety disorder, autism spectrum disorder, ADHD), they may require more individualization and flexibility than is typically offered by the standard, traditional CBT protocol.

Standard Approach to CBT

CBT typically entails a standardized, protocol-based treatment approach. The protocols are disorder-specific and include a step-by-step list of interventions. Generally, the same set of treatment procedures is applied to all children. While many of the well-established and probably efficacious evidence-based treatments for youths with depression are individual and group-based CBT (David-Ferndon & Kaslow, 2008), they are sometimes used without fidelity or applied on an irregular basis in routine usual-care practices. In the only published observational study of usual-care therapy delivered to youths, Garland, Brookman-Frazee, Hurlburt, Accurso, Zoffness, Haine-Schlagel, and Ganger (2010) observed usual care for childhood disruptive behaviors (which included children diagnosed with depressive disorders) in six community-based clinics and found specific discrepancies between usual care and evidence-based care. For example, therapists in community-based clinics used a broad array of treatment techniques, including treatment components that are consistent with evidence-based practice; however, strategies were used with less intensity than typically found in evidence-based practice. Further, while some evidence-based treatment strategies were used frequently (e.g., reinforcement), albeit with low intensity, other key evidence-based strategies were used rarely (e.g., homework assignment). In trying to determine the impact of these elements that were found in usual-care practice, Garland, Accurso, Haine-Schlagel, Brookman-Frazee, Roesch, and Zhang (2014) found that families who received greater intensity on the benchmark practice elements demonstrated greater improvement in the parental discipline outcome.

Why are evidence-based treatments applied inconsistently or with lower intensity in usual-care practice? Therapists in "real-world" settings have cited that a main limitation of evidence-based treatments, such as standard CBT, is the lack of relevance to their client population (Palinkas et al., 2013; Schoenwald & Hoagwood, 2001). They reported concerns about practitioners' lack of control and disruption of the therapeutic process; for instance, applying therapy from a manualized treatment may mean that the therapist has less control over what is covered in treatment and less flexibility with the treatment process. A common view by therapists is that many efficacy trials supporting evidence-based treatments such as standard CBT may not have good external validity; in essence, they believe that the research participants do not adequately represent the complex clients that are typically seen in everyday clinical practice. Thus, therapists in real-world settings may perceive that standard protocols that are applied in empirically supported treatments do not allow sufficient flexibility to be individualized for their complex clients with multiple presenting problems.

Modular Approach to CBT

In recent years, there has been increasing empirical support for a flexible, modular approach to treatment that may serve to address therapists' concerns about the limitations of standard CBT treatment manuals. There had already been evidence in the scientific community that treatments matched with client characteristics result in greater improvement over a shorter period of time (Eisen & Silverman, 1998; Kearney & Silverman, 1990). Among children who did not respond to manualized treatment, one-half to two-thirds showed gains after that treatment was more individually tailored (Ollendick, 2000). In 2004, Chorpita, Taylor, Francis, Moffitt, and Austin evaluated the efficacy of a modular approach to CBT for anxiety disorders in youth. The design allowed for the treatment strategies and techniques to be explicitly matched to the child's individual strengths and needs. The results provided preliminary support for the efficacy of the modularized design. In 2006, a modular approach to depression was developed and compared to psychotropic medication treatment; the investigators found that the combined treatment of modular CBT and SSRI (selective serotonin reuptake inhibitor) medication was superior to pharmacological treatment alone

(March, Silva, Vitiello, & TADS team, 2006). In 2008, Barlow, Gallagher, Carl, and Thompson-Hollands found that individuals with a variety of emotional disorders tended to experience their emotions in similar ways. They also found increased research support for exposure techniques—specifically, that exposing people to emotional experiences, positive or negative, helps them to develop more constructive ways of regulating their emotions. Based on Barlow's work in emotion science, Barlow and colleagues (2011) developed a unified protocol that offered a transdiagnostic set of principles that therapists can apply flexibly to their clients. They combined several core concepts found in all evidence-based treatments for emotional disorders, included key principles for change (research-supported mechanisms for change, such as motivational enhancement to improve treatment engagement), and developed a modular approach that allows clinicians greater flexibility than typical manuals. Barlow and colleagues' *Unified Protocol for Transdiagnostic Treatment of Emotional Disorders* is primarily used with adults with emotional disorders; however, this modular approach has also been developed for children and adolescents, particularly in the areas of how parent-child relational problems and the family unit impact the child's emotional experiences.

Treatment of emotional disorders in children and adolescents has unique challenges that are different from treatment in the adult population. Often, youths are brought into treatment by their caregivers and may present with additional challenges in motivation and resistance level. In children and adolescents, depressive and anxious feelings are often manifested as disruptive behaviors. For instance, depressed teenagers may present with irritable mood. Caregivers may experience or perceive a teenager's irritable mood as purposeful defiance and insolence. In these instances, it is important to address the client's disruptive behaviors and parent-child relational problems when developing the treatment plan for addressing his depression and anxiety. The modular approach is ideally suited to address these kinds of individualized needs that frequently present when working with children and adolescents.

For the remainder of this book, we use the term "parents" as a general term for the caretakers of the child or adolescent, which includes biological, adoptive, and foster parents, as well as individuals acting as parents even though they might not be the client's actual parents. Additionally, we use the term "family" very broadly in this book, to include the diverse definitions of family that many of your clients may use. For some, a family is precisely the nuclear immediate members of the family. For others, it may include a neighbor, pastor, or postal worker.

Empirical Support for Modular CBT

In recent years, researchers have tested the modularized design's capability in treating these youths with multiple presenting problems and complex backgrounds and needs. The modular approach to CBT offers a potential solution to some of the criticisms of standard CBT. Modular CBT allows for the individualization of CBT to address the specific needs of the client while maintaining empirical support. Further, modular

CBT has been developed and empirically supported for the treatment of depression in children and adolescents (Chorpita et al., 2013; March et al., 2006). Modular CBT addresses some of the gaps in the individualization and adaptability of CBT and arms clinicians with the skills necessary to effectively treat child and adolescent depression in community mental health settings (Weisz & Chorpita, 2012).

> Sophia, a licensed clinical social worker, conducts an intake assessment with ten-year-old Gabriela. She identifies that Gabriela has the following presenting problems: irritable mood, difficulty concentrating, social withdrawal, decrease in appetite, difficulty sleeping, and anxiousness about social interactions. Upon further assessment, Sophia discovers that Gabriela engages in maladaptive self-talk, including statements like, "I'm not good enough" and "Everyone will laugh at me if I talk in class." Sophia decides that cognitive behavioral therapy is the treatment of choice for Gabriela; however, she soon finds that a standard CBT model doesn't adequately address her client's specific needs. Gabriela was very responsive to the psychoeducation and mood-monitoring sessions of the standard cognitive behavioral treatment for depression, but her anxiousness in social situations has made it difficult for her to successfully engage in Sophia's CBT behavioral activation assignment of engaging in pleasant activities, such as going to the park after school or participating in an extracurricular activity at school. Because of her client's anxiousness with engaging in social interactions, Sophia decides to stop her use of the CBT for Depression manual midtreatment and change to another treatment manual, CBT for Anxiety, in order to target her client's anxiety symptoms. However, she feels frustrated that the linear, step-by-step approaches in the manuals do not seem to fit the specific needs of her depressed client with social anxiousness.

In 2012, Weisz and colleagues provided a direct comparison between standard and modular designs of CBT in a randomized effectiveness trial with youths presenting with depression, disruptive behaviors, and anxiety. They randomly assigned a total of eighty-four community therapists to usual care, standard manual treatment, and modular treatment. The therapists worked at ten different community-based clinics in Hawaii and Massachusetts and provided individual treatment (with families involved in treatment as needed). Notably, the researchers found that the modular approach outperformed usual care and standard evidence-based treatments on multiple clinical outcome measures. Therefore Weisz and colleagues suggested that the modular approach was a promising avenue to improve on the assets of evidence-based treatments in order to increase treatment effectiveness for practical application in real-world settings.

Evidence-Based Practice and Modular CBT

It is important to consider that using an evidence-based *treatment* does not mean that a therapist is engaging in evidence-based *practice*. In fact, it is quite possible that a therapist's use of an evidence-based treatment is decidedly *not* evidence-based practice. An evidence-based treatment is an intervention or technique that has produced therapeutic change in controlled trials, whereas evidence-based practice is the clinical practice that is informed by evidence about interventions; *clinical expertise*; *patient needs, values,* and *preferences*; and the integration of those needs, values, and preferences in decision making about individual care (Kazdin, 2008). Ultimately, evidence-based practice is about outcomes—being able to clearly link treatment practices with specific positive outcomes for the client and family. Thus, if a therapist is implementing cognitive behavioral therapy with a child who has a significant intellectual disability and severe language delays, then this implementation would not be considered evidence-based practice (given that the client's needs and characteristics should have informed the therapist that cognitive behavioral therapy is not an appropriate treatment).

Using the modular approach to CBT may enhance a therapist's engagement in evidence-based practice. In reviewing the definition, the client's *needs, values,* and *preferences* are taken into consideration and integrated into treatment planning. This is precisely the method of the modular approach: the therapist considers the child's needs and preferences along with other factors, and then selects and sequences the specific modules in a flexible and individualized manner that can be reasonably expected to lead to targeted positive outcomes for the client and family.

Purpose and Structure of This Treatment Manual

This book is designed to address the real-world needs and obstacles encountered by mental health clinicians. We offer practical tools for treating the complex clients that are typically seen in community clinics and many private practices. Guided by innovative research and best practices, therapists will learn practical steps for creating a personalized "client picture" that incorporates safety needs, symptoms presentation, etiology, cultural background, and complex family factors. We include tools to create a pragmatic conceptualization that can be coupled with the specialized treatment interventions of modular CBT and provide therapists with a step-by-step approach to develop effective treatment plans that also meet managed care requirements. This book offers a detailed session-by-session treatment program that includes specific instructions on how to use the modular approach to meet the individualized needs of diverse clients. This manual contains psychoeducation material, in-session treatment exercises, between-session practice ideas, and all the skills-building worksheets necessary for the clinician to conduct an effective modular CBT program with his or her clients. (The worksheets are also available for download at http://www.newharbinger .com/31175.)

This book is intended to be used as a practical guide and useful treatment manual for therapists who are working in real-world practice settings. Therapists who are working in community clinics, private practices, university clinics, and outpatient centers may find this manual to be particularly useful when working with depressed clients who have complex symptom presentations. One of the strengths of this manual, which is in contrast with standard CBT, is the *nonlinear* organization of this modular approach. Each module is its own container, comprised of various practice elements. Practice elements are clinical techniques or strategies, such as relaxation exercises and homework. Many of these practice elements are common core elements of evidence-based practice (Garland, Hawley, Brookman-Frazee, & Hurlburt, 2008). Some practice elements (common to evidence-based practice) are used in usual-care psychotherapy, albeit with variability in intensity and frequency (Brookman-Frazee, Haine, Baker-Ericzen, Zoffness, & Garland, 2010). On the other hand, modules are structured "containers" that contain one or more practice elements (Chorpita, Daleiden, & Weisz, 2005). Modules may take one or more sessions to be completed. Because modules are self-contained, they may be used flexibly and in an individualized manner depending on the specific client and the client's strengths and needs.

In modular CBT, assessment and diagnosis are conducted using an evidence-based approach, which encompasses multimethod assessments and multiple informants. Chapter 1 outlines this evidence-based assessment process, which includes case conceptualization. The therapist develops a case conceptualization of his client, which is an evolving, working hypothesis about the child and helps to tie the client's story into a coherent narrative that continually informs the conceptualization of the child. During the treatment-planning phase (discussed in chapter 2), the therapist uses his case conceptualization to inform his careful selection and sequencing of the modules. The modular approach does not mean that treatment follows a "free-for-all, pick-and-choose-any-CBT-technique" process. But because the modules are stand-alone containers, they may be reordered or even left out completely.

There are core modules, such as the psychoeducation and mood monitoring modules, which are essential to every treatment; however, the order in which the core modules are implemented may be tailored in order to maximize the client's ability to progress through the treatment program. During and after case conceptualization, the therapist considers the supplementary modules that must be included for any particular client. The therapist sequences the selected modules to address the unique characteristics of each client and the client's environment.

Throughout the therapy process, the therapist should periodically reassess the selection and sequence of modules (referring back to case conceptualization). For example, a child who is presenting with parent-child relational problems will likely require the family collaboration module to strengthen the affectionate attachment between youth and parents and to improve contingency management or effective family communication. For an adolescent who is depressed and has social skills deficits, the therapist may organize treatment so the social skills training module occurs early in treatment. For the child who is depressed and has subclinical or secondary anxiety, the therapist may organize treatment so the relaxation training module occurs early in treatment (e.g., before behavioral activation).

Flexible Use of This Treatment Manual

This book may be used in several different ways. First, the book may be read from cover to cover, such as by a student intern learning how to conduct therapy for his or her first practicum. Second, the book may be used as a guide for how to conduct an evidence-based assessment and develop case conceptualization and treatment planning. Lastly, this manual may be used by the experienced therapist who has reviewed the entire book previously but is currently using it with his clinical caseload to conduct individualized, empirically supported treatment. In this scenario, after the therapist has selected and sequenced his chosen modules for each child, he may open the manual to the chosen module on the given session day. Because modules are stand-alone containers of treatment strategies and techniques, the therapist has the ability to use the manual in a flexible, adaptable, and individualized modular approach for children with emotional disorders. Thus, the book has a *nonlinear* organization and may be used by the therapist in a varied manner depending on the characteristics of each child and adolescent in treatment. For more detailed information about how to *select and sequence* the modules to create a well-reasoned and well-thought-out treatment plan, please refer to chapter 2 ("Treatment Planning").

Finally, as delineated earlier in this introduction, there is increasing empirical support for the current trend toward a *transdiagnostic* approach to clinical practice: that is, an approach that focuses on the common psychological processes underlying various symptoms of psychiatric disorders, rather than a symptom-based approach that imposes separate treatment interventions for each disorder (Hayes, Wilson, Gifford, Follette, & Strosahl, 1996). As clinicians in real-world practice ourselves, we have a deep appreciation and understanding of the challenges that clinicians face in treating the challenging clients that often present at community-based practices, where complex conditions are frequently the norm rather than the exception. This book is designed to treat depressed children and adolescents with some symptomology of anxiety, social, behavioral, or parent-child relational problems. In describing the modular approach to CBT in this book, we hope that this clinician's guide will serve as a useful and effective tool for practicing therapists.

Part I

The Foundation

Chapter 1

Evidence-Informed Assessment and Case Conceptualization

An oncologist had a patient show up to his office with a decidedly orange tint to his skin. Concerned about the unusual symptom, the oncologist ordered a barrage of medical tests. He consulted with the manufacturer of the chemotherapy. He reviewed the medical literature. He discussed the atypical clinical case at his treatment team meeting. Bewildered, he finally acknowledged to his patient at their follow-up appointment that he was unable to determine the reason for the patient's orange tint. Upon realizing the level of his doctor's concern, the patient then sheepishly disclosed that his wife had been giving him megadoses of carrot juice and vitamin supplements. How could the doctor have handled this scenario differently? Instead of moving quickly to indirect routes of information, the oncologist could have started with the fundamental step of obtaining a comprehensive history of the patient. Being a good listener is a first important step to understanding your client's needs. This clinical example highlights the importance of good communication in the therapeutic relationship.

On January 4, 2014, the *New York Times* ran an op-ed commentary entitled "Doctor, Shut Up and Listen." In it, Nirmal Joshi, a physician herself, described the failures of doctors in communicating effectively with their patients. Joshi reported that, on average, physicians waited just eighteen seconds before interrupting a patient's narrative of his or her symptoms. The article highlighted a Joint Commission finding that more than 70 percent of serious adverse health outcomes in hospitals were due to communication failures, rather than due to physician technical skills. The provocative thesis of this op-ed article is what many people consider to be commonsense interaction: that the most important aspect of a good assessment is for the doctor to be a good listener. There is an illustrative saying by an anonymous individual: "A doctor who cannot take a good history and a patient who cannot give one are in danger of giving and receiving bad treatment." For any therapist providing mental health treatment, this warning rings true.

Preparing for Assessment

Before embarking on a treatment intervention, comprehensive assessment is essential. And, as illustrated colorfully in the preceding narrative, a comprehensive assessment begins with a thorough history that entails clear communication between the clinician, client, and client's family. Poston and Hanson (2010), in a meta-analysis, found that a high degree of collaboration and personalized feedback was critical in psychological assessment procedures. Building rapport and developing a therapeutic alliance during the assessment process are key to obtaining relevant information. Without the basic building blocks of rapport and alliance, the child or adolescent (and his parents) may not feel comfortable in offering sensitive information about the situation that brought him to the clinic. There are numerous texts and courses that focus on helping the student clinician develop effective interviewing skills. Ackerman and Hilsenroth (2003) described effective clinician interactional style as being genuine, empathic, respectful, and supportive of the client's experiences. This interviewing approach may be facilitated by concrete strategies of accurately identifying the client's emotional experiences, demonstrating reflective listening, and showing a genuine concern and interest in the client's narrative. Without the basic building blocks of rapport and alliance, the clinician will have a difficult time obtaining a comprehensive assessment of the client and his situation and needs.

Clinical Assessment Fundamentals

The primary uses of clinical assessment include the following: describing current functioning (e.g., cognitive abilities, symptom severity); confirming, refuting, or modifying clinicians' impressions derived from less-structured patient interactions; identifying therapeutic needs, recommending interventions, and consulting about prognosis; assisting in differential diagnosis; monitoring treatment over time; managing risk (e.g., minimize potential legal liabilities, identify adverse reactions); and providing skilled, empathic feedback as intervention (Meyer et al., 2001).

When the assessment process is minimized or conducted haphazardly, the clinician may find herself in the situation where the treatment isn't working for the client despite her best efforts. Given that the major purposes of assessment are diagnosis, prognosis, and treatment planning (Klein, Dougherty, & Olino, 2005), it is crucial that the clinician is provided with sufficient time to do a careful and thorough assessment prior to initiating treatment. A study that reviewed data from more than 125 studies indicated that when clinicians rely exclusively on interviews, they are prone to an incomplete understanding of the client's diagnostic picture (Meyer et al., 2001). The authors suggested that a multimethod assessment battery provides a structured way for skilled clinicians to maximize the validity of individualized assessments. In other words, it is recommended that when clinicians are meeting with clients for initial assessment, they should look for a convergence of evidence to support the diagnosis and case conceptualization.

Janelle, a recent graduate, is eager to specialize in depression treatment. She meets her first client, fifteen-year-old Brandon, who endorses multiple symptoms of depression. Janelle diagnoses Brandon with major depressive disorder (MDD), and begins CBT using the modular approach. After eight weeks of treatment, Janelle becomes discouraged as Brandon's score on the Beck Depression Inventory has not decreased significantly. She considers changing the treatment to narrative therapy; however, Brandon discloses that he had witnessed intermittent intimate partner violence between his parents when he was in preschool. Janelle realizes that she does not have the full picture of Brandon's situation and decides to complete a reassessment. This time, she uses a semistructured clinical interview called the K-SADS-PL—which assesses for psychopathology—along with screening measures for a variety of symptoms (including trauma symptoms), and discovers that Brandon has an undiagnosed anxiety disorder along with the diagnosed MDD. Janelle decides to include the CBT module on relaxation and anxiety-management strategies in her treatment plan for Brandon.

An evidence-informed assessment should include a semistructured clinical interview, screening measures, behavioral observations, and case conceptualization. This process can be done within the context of any community-based mental health or private practice setting. For instance, in the mental health system of a large county in a western state, contracted providers are expected to complete an intake document called the behavioral health assessment (BHA). The BHA is a report that contains relevant information such as presenting problems, medical and developmental history, safety concerns, a mental status exam, and diagnosis. In this case, all of the county-mandated documentation to complete the BHA report would be effectively elicited by the evidence-informed assessment outlined in this chapter.

The Clinical Interview

The first step in an evidence-informed assessment is the clinical interview. The most common method of clinical interviewing entails clinical judgment; however, in nearly 100 comparative studies between actuarial judgment and clinical judgment, the actuarial method has equaled or surpassed the clinical method (Hamilton, 2001). The actuarial method obtains objective interpretations that are routinized and derived from empirically demonstrated relationships between data and outcome, whereas the clinical method requires the subjective processing of clinical information in the professional's mind. While there are unique advantages to both methods, the actuarial method has been generally found to be more acccurate (Dawes, Faust, & Meehl, 1989). The biggest limitation to clinical interviewing is that it is prone to clinician biases. Clinicians tend to ignore base rates of disorders, and make multiple cognitive errors in clinical judgment (Grove, Zald, Lebow, Snitz, & Nelson, 2000). For instance, clinicians tend to pay special attention to, or actively seek, information that confirms their expectations, a tendency known as confirmation bias. In clinical assessment, this may lead to the clinician missing important data about the client's presenting problems. Although there is data supporting the actuarial method, this method can be difficult to implement in traditional clinical practice. Another way to reduce clinician biases and improve accuracy in clinical interviewing is to use a semistructured clinical interview (McDermott & Hale, 1982).

Semistructured clinical interviews consist of a formal interview guide. This guide is a list of questions and topics that need to be covered during the intake conversation, usually in a particular order. The interviewer follows the written guide but is able to follow topical trajectories in the conversation that may stray from the guide when he or she feels it is appropriate. Unlike structured clinical interviews, the semistructured clinical interview allows for more open-ended questions, and the clinician is able to use optional probes and generate unstructured questions to clarify information. Because of this optimal balance between structured and unstructured clinical interviews, semistructured clinical interviews are recommended for use in evidence-informed assessments when possible. The most commonly used semistructured clinical interviews for children and adolescents are the Kiddie-Schedule for Affective Disorders and Schizophrenia-Present and Lifetime Version (K-SADS-PL), Child and Adolescent Psychiatric Assessment (CAPA), and Diagnostic Interview for Children and Adolescents (DICA). The K-SADS-PL is a cost-effective measure as it is in the public domain and is a freely available semistructured clinical interview that is also used commonly in clinical research.

Screening Measures and Questionnaires

Because a multimethod approach to assessment is more likely to elicit a comprehensive clinical picture, the clinical interview is usually insufficient in arriving at diagnosis, prognosis, and treatment planning. In addition to the clinical interview, clinicians are recommended to routinely incorporate screening measures in their comprehensive assessments. Measures can be costly and can cause response fatigue in the respondent; thus, it is inadvisable to administer numerous screening measures to each and every client without first carefully considering the need for the information. Rather, based on the initial presenting problems, the clinician may administer a broad-based measure (such as the Achenbach System; e.g., Child Behavior Checklist, Youth Self Report), which measures a variety of potential symptoms that cut across disorders. The initial use of a broad-based measure is recommended, given the significant rates of comorbidity (e.g., anxiety, trauma) and the complex presentations of symptoms with childhood depression. Clinicians are recommended to administer screening measures to multiple collateral parties who are knowledgeable about the client's behaviors. These parties often include the parents, but may also include grandparents, teachers, stepparents, and anyone else who is knowledgeable of the child's behaviors and functioning. Obtaining screening measures or questionnaires from multiple parties can also help the clinician determine the client's functioning in multiple domains (e.g., school versus home behaviors). These comparisons of the client's behaviors and symptoms across multiple areas of functioning can greatly inform his diagnostic profile.

In addition to broad-based measures, disorder-specific measures targeting a previously designated list of presenting problems are required to augment the assessment. For instance, the Child Depression Inventory (CDI) and Beck Depression Inventory (BDI) are two highly used, reliable, and valid measures assessing depression. The Child Depression Inventory has both self- and parent-report versions. The Center for Epidemiological Studies Depression Scale for Children (CES-DC) is a twenty-item self-report depression scale that was developed by the National Institute of Mental Health (NIMH). This measure is in the public domain, so it is freely available at no cost. While the concurrent validity is poor for younger children, it is validated for use with adolescents (Faulstich, Carey, Ruggiero, Enyart, & Gresham, 1986).

Limitations of Measures

As with any single data point in an assessment, the reliability and validity of the screening measures are paramount. In the above section, we have described screening measures that we recommend based on their reliability and validity; however, the validity of a measure is also highly contingent upon the willingness of the respondent to answer openly and honestly. Given that youths are often brought in by their parents, there may be instances when the clinician is confronted with a reluctant participant in the assessment. Other times, due to the child's developmental level, he may have poor insight into his own symptoms and situation. Likewise, parents may also overreport or underreport their child's behaviors and symptoms on the questionnaires. The clinician should be mindful of the face validity of certain questionnaires; face validity refers to whether the questionnaire looks like it is measuring what it is intending to measure. When a questionnaire has face validity, the respondent can easily access the purpose of the measure, which may then impact the response style of the respondent. Administering the measures to multiple informants (e.g., school personnel, parents, grandparents) and comparing the results can help paint a clearer picture of the child's functioning across domains or can serve as additional data points in the likelihood that a respondent is over- or underreporting the child's symptom or behavioral profile. In addition, using multiple methods of assessment (e.g., school behavioral observations in conjunction with questionnaires) allows for converging evidence.

> Gary, a seasoned clinician, greets a new client who presents with depressed mood, difficulty concentrating, changes in appetite, sleep disturbance, and hypervigilance. Using a semistructured clinical interview, Gary identifies and rates the severity of various symptoms. He also discovers that his client has had nine foster placements and was initially taken into protective custody due to physical and sexual abuse. In addition to the clinical interview, Gary

administers the Child Depression Inventory (both self-report and parent-report versions), as well as the Trauma Symptom Checklist for Children (TSCC). The data from the questionnaires allow Gary to develop an accurate case conceptualization for the client, and subsequently, plan for an effective and more individualized treatment for him.

Behavioral Observations

Behavioral observations may be conducted in both unstructured and structured formats. Within the clinical interview format, you will conduct a mental status exam, as well as obtain general observations about the client's behaviors, hygiene, interpersonal style, and nonverbal cues (e.g., eye contact, directed facial gaze). If clinically warranted, you may also use a structured behavioral observational tool, such as the Dyadic Parent-Child Interaction Coding System (DPICS). Behavioral aspects that may be measured are frequency, latency, intensity, and duration. There are advantages to using structured behavioral observations. Some populations may have a limited ability to report on their own behaviors and feelings (e.g., children, developmentally delayed clients). There are also behaviors that may be hard for a person to report on accurately. Further, rating scales essentially ask another person to summarize unsystematic behavioral observations that he or she has made over a period of time. As such, rating scales are vulnerable to differences in how raters define and perceive a particular behavior, to errors in recall (e.g., overly influenced by recent and salient events), to response biases, and to parental psychopathology or mood, and may be less sensitive to changes in behavior. Also, parents may at times lack a developmental context for understanding a child's behavior.

Case Conceptualization

Case conceptualization is the result of integrating all the information you have obtained from the assessment process. In this instance, the therapist is like a detective. You have gathered as many data points as possible, and now you are ready to use the data to paint a clinical picture. Once you have gathered your comprehensive data using multiple sources of information (clinical interview, measures, and behavioral observations), you will put that information together in a coherent story and timeline in order to develop a case conceptualization. In short, the case conceptualization is a "mental picture" of your client, along with the salient contextual factors that play a role in this mental picture. A major purpose for the case conceptualization is to identify treatment goals and develop an effective treatment plan for your client. Additionally, if treatment is not progressing along, you may reexamine the case conceptualization to aid in identifying barriers to treatment.

Once you arrive at the case conceptualization, it is not complete. It is important to remember that your case conceptualization for your client is *always* evolving; it is a working hypothesis that is continually reassessed and reworked, as needed, throughout treatment (Stoddard & Williams, 2012). Stoddard points out that conceptualization is an individualized formulation based on a general theory, wherein general theory refers to negative thoughts about life events that produce symptoms, and formulation refers to specific thoughts in a situation that produce symptoms in this particular client. Prior to collaborating with the client and family regarding the development of the treatment plan, you will provide feedback to them regarding the client picture that you are working from and elicit their feedback. This feedback should be obtained on an ongoing basis throughout treatment as your case formulation is a *working* hypothesis that may require revisions.

Developing the Case Conceptualization

Once you have completed your multimethod assessment using multiple informants (when possible), you are ready to develop your formulation of the case. In the CBT framework, case conceptualization entails identifying the antecedent behaviors and cognitions that trigger the client's maladaptive thoughts and behaviors. The clinician generates written hypotheses regarding the client's situation and contingencies for his behaviors through answering the following question: how do the client's depressive symptoms relate to his cognitions? The clinician identifies how the maladaptive cognitions have led to problematic behaviors. For instance, the clinician might write down that the client's automatic thought that he is unattractive may have led to the core belief that he is unworthy of love, which has, in turn, led to his behavior of social withdrawal and feelings of hopelessness. In the CBT case conceptualization, the antecedent behaviors and cognitions that precede the client's maladaptive behaviors should be clearly described by the clinician. Precipitants, triggers, cultural identity (e.g., acculturation), behaviors, consequences, treatment interventions, and barriers to treatment should be incorporated in an effective case conceptualization. For student clinicians, the case conceptualization is an excellent tool to be used in supervision and should arise in discussions about the client on a routine basis. For instance, case conceptualization is discussed when identifying goals for treatment, barriers to treatment, and roadblocks in treatment progress.

There are numerous models for case conceptualization, including a transtheoretical approach to case formulation and a computerized case conceptualization model (e.g., Jose & Goldfried, 2008; Meichenbaum, 2009), and excellent books dedicated entirely to developing a solid case conceptualization (Sperry & Sperry, 2012). For a more in-depth look at these case conceptualization models, we recommend these resources to clinicians. For the purpose of this treatment manual, we will provide an example of a case conceptualization using a CBT-focused technique developed by Jacqueline Persons (2012). We recommend therapists read Persons's guide for a particularly comprehensive explanation of how to develop case formulation.

Case Conceptualization Example

Kate is a ten-year-old Vietnamese American (cultural identity) girl who was born in San Diego, California, to immigrant parents (cultural acculturation). She has tested into the gifted and talented education program (cognitive ability) and comes from a family of high-achieving siblings (family context). Her three older sisters have graduated with honors from prestigious universities. Her mother reported that Kate tends to be perfectionistic (origin, antecedent), and that she recently withdrew from social activities (behavior) following a poor performance on a test (precipitant). Despite a significant family history of depression and anxiety (origin), those family members have not received psychopharmacological treatment or therapy (barriers). Kate has begun exhibiting crying spells (behavior), social withdrawal (behavior), and refusal to attend school (behavior). Her father has verbally and openly compared her poor school performance to her older sisters' academic achievements (origin, antecedent), which is likely to have contributed to her core beliefs that she is unworthy and doesn't belong in the family (mechanism, beliefs). Treatment will focus on challenging the client's cognitive distortions, eliciting behavioral activation, and teaching relaxation skills, with an understanding of the client's cultural identity and family context. Barriers to treatment include the client's social withdrawal (potential therapy attendance issue) and the family's reluctance to seek treatment for depression and anxiety (potential refusal to accept psychopharmacological treatment).

In the case conceptualization example of ten-year-old Kate, what additional information would be helpful? Questions for the clinician to address include the following: What is Kate's perspective on seeking therapy? What core beliefs does she hold? What are her current coping mechanisms? What is her cultural identity or level of acculturation? As the clinician learns more about Kate during the progression of treatment, she is able to add information to the case conceptualization on an ongoing basis. In turn, the treatment goals and plan are reconsidered as major additions shape the case conceptualization.

Summary

A comprehensive assessment begins with a thorough history that encompasses clear communication between the clinician, child, and child's family. A multimethod assessment battery, which includes a semistructured clinical interview and standardized, reliable, and valid measures, provides a structured means for skilled clinicians to maximize the validity of individualized assessments. Clinicians can then use the data to consider the convergence of evidence in supporting the diagnosis and case conceptualization. In the next chapter, we will discuss treatment planning based on a solid case conceptualization.

Chapter 2

Treatment Planning for the Modular Approach

On the first day of summer in 2005 in New York City, Snapple was determined to break the Guinness World Record for largest popsicle. Just eight summers earlier, a team from Holland mounted a twenty-one-foot, ten-ton popsicle colossus and earned the title of world record champions. Snapple hoped to outshine this feat and commandeer the world record. The twenty-five-foot Guinness World Record hopeful was prepared in Edison, New Jersey, and transported at subzero temperatures to Union Square in New York City. Upon arrival, a towering crane attempted to hoist the oversized pink summer treat into its record-qualifying upright and freestanding position. It was at this peak of suspense that the more than seventeen-ton slushy behemoth was found to be no match for the noon sun on an eighty-degree day. A sugary pink deluge soaked the Guinness judge's shoes on its way through the streets of downtown Manhattan. The Dutch record remained intact, and firefighters were left to hose away the sweet kiwi-strawberry residue. You can imagine the media headlines: "Disaster on a Stick," "Snapple Popsicle is Flopsicle," and "Giant Popsicle melts, floods New York park" (Associated Press, 2005; Schwarz, 2005; Gayle, 2005).

Treatment Plan Fundamentals

What happened on that sticky summer day that can help us think about treatment planning for modular CBT? Even though the Snapple team had a reasonable vision, a reasonable goal, and good intentions, their hopes of a world record dissolved along with the popsicle. What else would they have needed? Perhaps they would have benefited from better information about the conditions they would be facing. This is similar to the *conceptualization* therapists create for each client. There were a lot of contextual factors at play in making the popsicle, like the heat, the time needed to prepare the crane and hoist the giant popsicle, the rate of melting, and the time before the popsicle became unstable, as well as the internal temperature of the popsicle. The world-record hopefuls might also have benefited from a more complete conceptualization of the goal and the context for that goal in order to have a good chance of beating the Dutch team. Third, it would probably be important that all team members agreed to the plan (the way they prepared, froze, transported, and hoisted the popsicle), ensured the plan was appropriate given the context, and carried it out well. Finally, the team might have needed more room for *flexibility* in their plan. As soon as problems surfaced, the team seemed ill-prepared to adjust and adapt. Constructing the world's largest freestanding popsicle in New York City might seem like a bit of a stretch for therapy comparisons; however, any momentous goal requires a thoughtful, appropriate, and responsive plan that is well executed. Helping children, adolescents, and families change patterns of thinking, feeling, and acting to lessen a child's depression and increase well-being is nothing less than momentous. Both goals highlight the crucial role of a thoughtful plan.

Before we discuss the specific steps of creating a treatment plan, we offer a background of three crucial components to equip you with a clear approach to treatment planning: a solid conceptualization; treatment plan acceptability, appropriateness, and fidelity; and flexibility when executing the plan.

Built from a Solid Conceptualization

In the previous chapter, you read about how to take advantage of evidence-informed assessment strategies and other sources of information to create a comprehensive case conceptualization. The case conceptualization provides a framework on which to build a sturdy treatment plan, but the two steps are inescapably connected. The treatment plan will help strengthen your client conceptualization. Both evolve and adapt over the course of treatment as you learn more about the client, her symptoms and strengths, and the contextual factors that may contribute to her recovery.

After the clinical assessment is completed, the therapist synthesizes the assessment, collateral, observational, and interview data to form a case conceptualization and develop a treatment plan. The conceptualization informs the plan, and the plan directs the interventions. Therefore, treatment planning is the keystone for effective modular CBT.

To illustrate, consider a fourteen-year-old client who comes to treatment stating the loss of his uncle when he was twelve years old as the source of his negative mood, which seems to be the primary treatment concern. The client and his father may agree that this is the only identified cause of his isolation and mood lability. The treatment plan for this teenager would emphasize grief and bereavement themes and interventions focused on the negative cognitions related to the teenager's loss of his uncle. Upon further evaluation, however, the therapist discovers a pervasive pattern of negativity and discord in the client's family interactions and the home. These constant negative interactions might be the underlying triggers for distorted thoughts related to the uncle's death as well as numerous other negative thoughts, inappropriate behaviors, and the deepening of the teenager's depressed mood. A treatment plan informed by this updated conceptualization would look very different. Instead of an emphasis on grief and bereavement, the plan and interventions would focus on family patterns as current triggers in the teenager's life. While the teenager's distorted beliefs about his uncle passing away would eventually be restructured, they would be secondary to other interventions.

With this example in mind, there is a need for therapists to continuously gather information about their clients. The client conceptualization is a fluid process that occurs throughout treatment. Fortunately, clients constantly provide feedback to therapists by way of their responses to different interventions. If treatment is not working, a good first step is to reevaluate the conceptualization and plan. A therapist needs the mental flexibility to reevaluate his assumptions, periodically check the way he understands his client, and approach treatment barriers in a nondefensive, solution-focused manner.

The example also illustrates that as the conceptualization becomes more clearly defined, the treatment plan should reflect these changes. Although the interconnectedness of the conceptualization and treatment plan makes logical sense to most therapists, the actual practice is sometimes challenging in clinical settings. Therapists are often pressured (and sometimes overwhelmed) by challenging caseloads, which can result in a misaligned conceptualization and treatment plan. Treatment teams, clinical supervision, consultations, and periodic treatment plan updates are used to help avoid disparate conceptualizations and treatment plans. Consistently keeping attention on the case conceptualization and how it aligns with the treatment plan will help ensure effective treatment.

Treatment Plan Acceptability, Appropriateness, and Fidelity

Treatment plan *acceptability* is demonstrated when the client, family, and therapist have expectations that the plan will address the targeted needs and that it can be successful. Treatment plan *appropriateness* refers to using the right plan for the targeted problems, short-term objectives, and overarching goals. Treatment plan *fidelity* refers to implementing the treatment process and interventions in a way that is consistent with the plan.

TREATMENT PLAN ACCEPTABILITY

Treatment planning is the process of the client and therapist agreeing on how to use time in treatment, where to focus attention, and how to define treatment success. The broad conversation of goals, treatment steps, and outcomes usually requires cooperation among the client, family, and therapist. It is important that the therapist understands the client and family's goals for attending therapy and helps them understand how treatment will help them reach their goals. At the same time, the appropriate interventions and processes required to reach the overarching goals are part of the therapist's expertise. The therapist is the specialist on how therapy promotes positive change, and the client is the expert on her life, her struggles, and her reason for attending therapy. Therein lies the cooperative agreement between therapist and client. By acknowledging and respecting the client's expertise while also demonstrating knowledge, credibility, and positive expectations for treatment success, the therapist is starting a collaborative treatment-planning process.

Collaborative treatment planning cannot be completed without client and family participation. If the family or client is unwilling to participate in the treatment-planning process due to problems with engagement or low motivation, the therapist should (a) continue to assess and attend to client safety, while (b) focusing on treatment engagement and identifying motivation for participating in therapy. More in-depth treatment cannot proceed successfully without this collaboration and mutual commitment. Chapter 12 provides instruction on client engagement in treatment and guidance to overcome motivational barriers to treatment. It can be easy to charge ahead in treatment without a purposeful consideration of treatment plan acceptability, but client engagement in all steps of treatment (assessments, treatment plans and goals, and interventions) greatly contributes to the success of those steps. Through collaboration, a focus on engagement, and shared responsibility for treatment steps, a therapist can maximize treatment plan acceptability.

TREATMENT PLAN APPROPRIATENESS

A collaborative framework will support acceptability of the plan from the client's point of view. However, the therapist will identify the most urgent and salient objectives and will match these with appropriate modules and interventions, as well as additional services that may be needed, such as a psychiatric evaluation or case management services. A CBT conceptualization emphasizes a focus on immediate needs for the client and use of targeted, action-oriented interventions. However, an appropriate treatment plan must also be informed by the existing contextual and ecological factors that contribute to the problems and solutions. This includes current parent, caregiver, sibling, extended family, community, cultural, school, and social factors. Researchers have demonstrated that CBT intervention effectiveness is often improved through integration of ecological and contextual factors (Mash & Barkley, 2006). The CBT view acknowledges that in addition to the child, key individuals and family members should also be actively involved in the treatment process and treatment plan. Therefore, an appropriate treatment plan will lay out how family members and other individuals contribute to specific objectives and the overarching goals of treatment.

The subsequent chapters provide a background and rationale within each module and clearly describe the purpose for each individual module. The remaining sections in this chapter provide information about sequencing the core and supporting modules to promote positive treatment outcomes given the unique case conceptualization for each client. Taken together, implementation of interventions and modules that align with the targeted problems will contribute to treatment plan appropriateness. This means the therapist follows the treatment steps in a way that is consistent with the case conceptualization and theory behind modular CBT.

TREATMENT PLAN FIDELITY

The therapist also ensures that interventions are implemented in a way that matches the plan. The therapist's fidelity to the treatment plan can be tested by changes in the symptom presentation, unexpected reactions to interventions, new client or family problems, or transitory problems that distract clients from the focus and goals of treatment (sometimes called "crisis of the week"). It is the therapist's role to sort through these obstacles to identify genuine problems that require further attention and possible plan revision versus the less pressing but more common treatment distractions. Ideally, the treatment plan is adjusted based on changes in the conceptualization, which is based on new evidence that helps the therapist reconsider symptom presentation and etiology. Therapists should be careful about getting drawn into transient problems that would make them adjust the treatment plan too easily. Treatment would be less effective if the treatment plan is restructured based on current passing dilemmas, brief periods of a client not responding to interventions, or temporary relapses. To maintain treatment fidelity, the therapist implements an appropriate treatment plan thoughtfully, purposefully, and consistently. The following section provides guidance for sorting through new information to know when and how to adjust the treatment plan.

Treatment Plan Flexibility

One of the primary strengths of a modular approach is the potential for treatment individualization; however, this strength can also be a hurdle. The capacity for flexibility should not be interpreted as the emphasis on flexibility. Adjusting a treatment plan should be driven by changes in the case conceptualization and based on information from multiple sources (including behavioral observations, case consultations, and results from standardized assessment tools). In other words, therapists should avoid treatment plan changes based on assumptions or stressful clinical situations. Instead, the framework of modular CBT encourages therapists to strengthen their clinical judgments with an objective point of view.

In the past, therapy was often guided exclusively by clinical judgment. Therapists relied on their perceptions and reasoning to gauge key treatment elements such as severity, treatment type, dosage, progress, and outcomes. Although therapists undergo rigorous training to develop the skills to make the best judgments possible, research has repeatedly shown the need for objective feedback to enhance clinical decision making. Time and time again, research has illustrated that we are frequently and unknowingly influenced by biases and assumptions (Dawes, Faust, & Meehl, 1989; Kahneman & Tversky, 1972, 1982; Meehl, 1954; Tversky & Kahneman, 1973, 1974). Sometimes we rely on these assumptions to our benefit and sometimes to our detriment, but we have a very difficult time discerning which is which.

Traditionally, clients were also expected to gauge treatment progress in the same way, leaving them disproportionately susceptible to their own assumptions and beliefs. This is particularly problematic for depressed clients who are often influenced by misattributions and misinterpretations. With both the client and therapist relying on their own perceptions throughout treatment, determining treatment progress was, for the most part, subjective.

More recently, however, researchers and treatment developers have found ways to utilize an empirical approach to gauge the treatment process. For example, rather than relying solely on his perceptions or asking a client to describe her depressive symptoms, a therapist using modular CBT can ask the client, a caregiver or family member, and a teacher; can collect standardized data from several sources of information; and can conduct a behavioral observation in the child's school. In most evidence-based treatments, collecting ongoing information from more than one source has been adopted. A therapist using modular CBT will seek the "Goldilocks" balance of minimizing the influence of mistaken assumptions while maximizing the responsiveness and flexibility of the treatment plan to the client's needs.

Use of Assessment Tools

If you were to regularly visit your physician for treatment of a heart condition, you would expect your doctor to routinely check your blood pressure. You might be alarmed if she just relied on her judgment without evaluation. Should depression be treated differently? Brief, empirically supported depression assessment tools like the Beck Depression Inventory or the Child Depression Inventory can help therapists accurately gauge symptom severity and treatment progress while also taking extra steps to evaluate safety risks.

To be meaningful, therapists should follow the instrument administration by reviewing the client's responses. This will let the client know that you are focused on helping with depression and informing her of her therapy progress. The results from these measures may also serve as valuable feedback to the child as she tracks her own progress in treatment. A depressed client may have difficulty identifying her own improvement in therapy, especially if she feels hopeless or negative about herself. A small but observable symptom reduction, as indicated on the brief assessment tool, may serve as client feedback that can help with her motivation in continuing treatment. Ultimately, using assessment tools can help focus the direction of the sessions and can provide the therapist with a clear picture of the client's dynamic needs. By tracking results over time, ineffective treatment interventions can be identified and modified accordingly.

Treatment Planning

After the assessment is complete and the conceptualization begins to take shape, one or two sessions should be used to collaboratively develop the treatment plan. Prior to this session, the therapist will make a draft and have a good sense of his proposed treatment plan. Through the treatment-planning session(s), the therapist should have a finalized and collaborative plan. Therapists may encounter blurred lines between treatment-planning themes and the psychoeducation module since a large part of the therapist's role when planning the treatment is to educate the family about what the plan is, how it works, and what expectations and responsibilities accompany the participating individuals who are involved in the plan.

Treatment Plan Modules

When treating depressed children or teens, there will be consistent markers of depression across clients. Certain general indications will be noted in depressed youth. These include sad affect, depressed mood, flat affect, isolation, social disinterest, anger outbursts or mood lability, suicidal thoughts or behaviors, decline of interest in previously enjoyed activities, low energy, low self-esteem, hopelessness, or a negative outlook on self, world, or future. Based on the consistent problems associated with the general markers of depression, a core group of modules and interventions have been developed as essential components for modular CBT treatment of depression in youth.

Core Modules
Psychoeducation
Mood Monitoring
Behavioral Activation
Addressing Maladaptive Cognitions
Relapse Prevention

These core modules include psychoeducation, mood monitoring, behavioral activation, addressing maladaptive cognitions, and relapse prevention. Psychoeducation includes increasing awareness of depression and the ways thoughts, feelings, and behaviors can contribute to improving mood. Mood monitoring emphasizes increased awareness of changes in mood and improved articulation related to feelings. Behavioral activation focuses on developing active and effective engagement in pleasant or social activities. Addressing maladaptive cognitions helps with identifying and replacing persistent negative thinking with accurate thinking. Finally, relapse prevention supports strengthening and extending newly developed skills to additional settings. The table "Treatment Planning with the Core Modules," which can be found at the end of this chapter (and online at http://www.newharbinger.com/31175), was created to help therapists closely align the case conceptualization with core modules and targeted treatment goals.

Supporting Modules
Safety Plan and Crisis Management
Relaxation Training
Social Skills Training
Affect Regulation
Family Collaboration
Problem-Solving Skills
Treatment Engagement

While there are similarities across all youth struggling with depression, the unique expression of depression can differ from child to child. Some children will have disruptive home environments that contribute to the depression, while others will not. Some children will have co-occurring challenges related to anxiety, and other children will struggle with social skills. For this reason, modular CBT includes supporting modules to expand the utility and individualization of treatment beyond fundamental depression treatment. With the supporting modules of safety plan and crisis management, relaxation training, social skills training, affect regulation, family collaboration, problem-solving skills, and treatment engagement, therapists are able to create a treatment plan that closely and clearly ties the child's presentation and primary concerns with appropriate interventions. The safety plan and crisis management module is used to enhance client safety by addressing crisis risks. A main objective of relaxation training is to develop capacity to increase relaxation to reduce or avoid excessive anxiousness or anger. Social skills training emphasizes the development of active and effective engagement in social interactions. Affect regulation focuses on developing capacity to respond to triggers and regulate emotions to improve mood stability. The family collaboration module is focused on improving family capacity to consistently increase positive interactions, and reduce negative ones. Through the problem-solving skills module, clients and families will be better equipped to identify solutions and overcome barriers, eventually without the therapist's help. Lastly, treatment engagement focuses on boosting family and client engagement and motivation in the treatment process. The table "Treatment Planning with the Supporting Modules," which can be found at the end of this chapter (and online at http://www .newharbinger.com/31175), was created to help therapists closely align the case conceptualization with supporting modules and targeted treatment goals.

Treatment Plan Organization

Treatment plan organization includes careful sequencing of the specific modules—usually a combination of core and supporting modules. The core modules are ordered in the typical treatment sequence. Psychoeducation is a common first step in treatment as it frames the remaining modules and establishes a shared understanding and vocabulary. Mood monitoring is ordered next because it involves straightforward themes and is typically necessary prior to addressing maladaptive cognitions. While behavioral activation is particularly effective for individuals with severe depression and may aid in getting relief, it can require a moderate amount of buy-in from the client and can be challenging early in treatment if the client doesn't understand the purpose. On the other hand, highly engaged clients get a lot of "bang for their buck" with this module, and it is sometimes shuffled into a different "batting order" in the treatment plan based on the case conceptualization. Addressing maladaptive cognitions is perhaps the most essential module in the overall treatment for most clients and often requires several sessions. The addressing maladaptive cognitions module also requires a strong foundation to be effective. For this reason, it is usually included midway to later in treatment. Relapse prevention inherently fits at the end of treatment, with very rare deviation from this placement in the plan organization. Despite these typical sequencing considerations, core modules can be shuffled and rearranged to align with the case conceptualization.

The supporting modules are not ordered in particular sequences and are intended to be organized based on the case conceptualization. Safety plan and crisis management will be a useful module when there are safety concerns such as suicidal ideation or self-harming behaviors. Relaxation training is a module that quickly provides applied skills that most children learn easily, which supports client engagement. Therefore, this module is often provided early in treatment. Social skills training can be more complicated depending on the level of the child's social skills deficits, so it may require multiple sessions. It is usually ordered later in the treatment course if the skills deficit is mild, but may be ordered earlier in the course if the social skills deficit plays a prominent role in the child's maladaptive cognitions or depressed mood. Affect regulation can be a challenging module that typically builds on psychoeducation and relaxation training, so this module tends to be provided later in treatment. The family collaboration module is one of the more flexible modules. Based on the needs of the child and family, this module can be used early in treatment to promote solidarity or later in treatment to allow the child to focus in treatment individually. This module is strongly connected to the conceptualization and the role of familial factors on the client's symptoms or safety. Problem-solving skills might be embedded in the treatment plan but may also be added, as needed, if it becomes apparent during the treatment course that the child has poor problem solving skills. Finally, treatment engagement is also intended to be flexible, with the module added as needed or with themes from the module integrated at different points during treatment. Once you have a general plan of selected modules, you should start a therapy binder (electronic or paper, depending on the adolescent's preference) in which all worksheets and psychoeducation materials are routinely organized. The goal of the therapy binder is for the child to have helpful and individualized materials to refer to, as part of relapse prevention, after the therapy course has concluded.

Components of a Treatment Plan

The treatment plan includes identification of the presenting problem, an overall (long-term) goal, several short-term objectives, accompanying interventions, and expected outcomes. The "Modular CBT Treatment Plan," which you'll find at the end of this chapter and in downloadable format at http://www.newharbinger .com/31175, provides an example of how this plan can be created. The overarching goal is a description of what the therapist, child, and family (if applicable) strive to gain by the end of treatment. It should be written in jargon-free language that is easy for the client and family to understand and should have a high level of acceptability for everyone involved in treatment. When using language in the treatment plan, picture the plan as something that could go on your client's refrigerator or be easily explained to the client's teacher. The objectives are focused and emphasize the changes that should occur as a result of a given intervention. The objectives are connected to specific modules. The interventions are more specific components within the module. For example, the mood monitoring module may include tracking mood as an intervention but may also include activities that help the client practice describing feelings to another person. Objectives often have more than one intervention connected to them. Finally, the expected outcomes are measurable, observable changes that will demonstrate the client or family has developed the appropriate skill or objective that was being targeted. Expected outcomes should be objective and should be illustrated to both the client and therapist that new behaviors and skills have been acquired.

Strengthening the Treatment Plan

Treatment planning does not occur solely at the beginning of treatment—it is a fluid, ongoing process that includes safety and risk considerations as well as client and family cultural characteristics.

Ongoing Treatment Considerations
Presenting Needs
Acuity, Crisis, and Safety
Therapeutic Alliance
Family Involvement
Changes in Ecology
Response to Treatment
Client and Family Strengths

Clients and families are continuously progressing and adjusting to treatment, and several factors can contribute to treatment progress or barriers. Some include changes in the presenting problems and needs (e.g., increased isolation, decreased anxiety); acuity, crisis, or safety risks; therapeutic alliance; family involvement in treatment; changes in the client's ecology (e.g., changes in school, change of caregivers, divorce, change in psychiatrist); expected variations in the client's or family's response to treatment; and changes in the client's or family's strengths. These considerations continue to inform the case conceptualization and promote a continuously improved treatment plan. Earlier in this chapter, we discussed the flexibility and responsiveness of the treatment plan to the needs of the client. With the focus on developing a rich conceptualization of your client, these factors can help clarify the difference between normal or superficial client and symptom changes during treatment so you will know when adjustment of the treatment plan is needed. As you attend to these factors throughout the treatment process, you will deepen and refine your conceptualization and adjust the treatment plan in alignment with your conceptualization.

Safety and Risk Considerations

With depressed youth, there are several safety and risk factors that must be recurrently evaluated. These specific safety- and risk-related presenting problems include suicidal ideation, suicidal behaviors, homicidal ideation, homicidal behaviors, history of hospitalizations, history of emergency treatment, history of crisis intervention, availability of emergent or crisis care, and history of inpatient treatment. When clients show no indication of traumatic stress but have a history of exposure to traumatic events, therapists should be careful to continuously assess for trauma-related symptoms and maintain a heightened awareness to potential trauma-related triggers and potential need for trauma-focused treatment, such as trauma-focused cognitive behavioral therapy (TF-CBT; see http://tfcbt.musc.edu for more information).

In addition to carefully and consistently assessing for risk and safety for clients with these presenting needs, the treatment plan must be responsive to these unique needs. Safety- and risk-reduction needs always take priority in treatment when there is need for such care. As these needs arise, the therapist switches from a modular CBT model to a crisis-and-safety-focused approach. When safety and risk needs arise, short-term crisis-prevention models will offer more appropriate interventions, and a transfer to a higher level of care may be necessary. Once the client returns to an appropriate level of stability for outpatient mental health treatment, the therapist may proceed with modular CBT. Clients with complex presentations will benefit from specific sequencing of the treatment modules. For example, some clients may be especially triggered by isolation, so behavioral activation may precede mood monitoring since behavioral activation will be more immediately connected to reduced risk for suicidal behaviors for that client. Ongoing screening and assessment of safety and risk factors is recommended for clients with problems related to suicidality or homicidality. Additional supportive individuals in the client's life should also be enlisted to support the client's safety and reduce risk as much as possible.

Cultural Considerations

Given the current understanding and evidence about culturally sensitive treatments, it is important to use a culturally informed lens to consider each unique case and to form the case conceptualization in particular. We also recognize that significant culturally based modifications to the overall treatment plan may not be necessary given the flexibility of the modular approach and research of culturally adapted, evidence-based treatment. Some researchers have suggested that significant treatment modifications only need to be applied when problem areas arise or when there is a clear, foreseeable mismatch with a particular client (Lau, 2006). Others have found evidence that there are few differences between ethnically and culturally diverse groups in the way they respond to evidence-based practices (Huey, Tilley, Jones, & Smith, 2014). As stated by Huey et al. (2014), "[There is] increasing evidence that EBTs"—meaning evidence-based treatments—"can be successful with ethnic minorities when used by practicing therapists in real-world clinical settings" (p. 328). The collaborative treatment-planning process allows for open discussion about the fit of the proposed treatment plan within the family and client cultural context. We encourage therapists to utilize a culturally sensitive lens for their conceptualization of the case and as they develop the treatment and organize the key modules and interventions.

Summary

Treatment planning for modular CBT is a collaborative and ongoing process, inherently tied to the case conceptualization, enhanced with ongoing assessment, and responsive to changes during the course of treatment. By integrating core and supporting modules, an individualized treatment plan can be developed to enhance the fit of treatment to the client's and family's needs. Successful treatment planning is at the center of successful modular CBT treatment for depression in children and teenagers. The following chapters provide detailed information about each module. When used in the context of a thoughtful treatment plan, this information will strengthen the efficacy of these modules to mitigate or eliminate the impact of depression in your clients' lives.

Treatment Planning with the Core Modules

Targeted Problem	Objective	Core Module	Example Interventions from Module	Expected Outcome / Example of Skill Development
Limited Understanding/ Insight About Depressed Mood	Increase awareness of depression and the ways thoughts, feelings, and behaviors can contribute to improving mood.	Psychoeducation	Develop understanding of the cognitive triangle and the ways thoughts, feelings, and behaviors impact mood.	Improve understanding of how thoughts, feelings, and behaviors contribute to particular negative affect, demonstrated by teaching someone about the cognitive triangle.
Limited Awareness and Low Articulation About Feelings and Mood	Increase awareness of changes in mood and improve articulation related to feelings.	Mood Monitoring	Improve mood awareness and articulation through mood monitoring/tracking.	Demonstrate increased "affect expression" behaviors (articulating feelings three times per day or more) across two or more settings.
Inactive or Ineffective Engagement in Pleasant or Social Activities	Develop active and effective engagement in pleasant or social activities.	Behavioral Activation	Practice engaging in pleasant or social activities and identify impact of experiences on thoughts and feelings.	Initiate engagement in one pleasant or social activity daily without prompting, and identify one or more associated positive thoughts and feelings for each activity.
Persistent Negative Thinking that Leads to Negative Affect and Mood	Identify and replace persistent negative thinking with adaptive thinking.	Addressing Maladaptive Cognitions	Identify use of cognitive distortions and practice replacing distortions with accurate thoughts.	Recognize five examples of cognitive distortions across two or more settings in a week and autonomously replace distortions with accurate thoughts (track and describe on worksheet or discuss with supportive adult or peer).
Newly Developed Skills with Tentative Generalizability	Strengthen and extend newly developed skills to additional settings.	Relapse Prevention	Identify new responses to triggers or identify opportunities to use newly developed skills.	Demonstrate mastery of new skills when confronted with triggers or challenging situations on three or more occasions and across two or more settings (role-play mastery may be substituted if necessary).

Downloadable copies of this table are available online at http://www.newharbinger.com/31175. (See the very back of this book for more details.)

Treatment Planning with the Supporting Modules

Targeted Problem	Objective	Supporting Module	Example Interventions from Module	Expected Outcome / Example of Skill Development
Safety Risks (e.g., suicidal ideation or self-injurious behaviors)	Enhance safety and stability and reduce risk of crisis.	Safety Plan and Crisis Management	Develop crisis-management plan that includes support from multiple individuals.	Eliminate suicidal ideation or intent to harm self.
Intrusive Anxiety or Anger Problems Contributing to Depressive Presentation	Develop capacity to increase relaxation to reduce or avoid excessive anxiousness or anger.	Relaxation Training	Develop capacity to use deep breathing, progressive muscle relaxation, and vivid imagery skills to manage anxiety or anger.	Demonstrate autonomous use of relaxation skills to effectively reduce anxiety or anger three or more times in one week across two or more settings.
Loneliness, Limited Social Support, or Low Confidence in Social Interactions	Develop active and effective engagement in social interactions.	Social Skills Training	Strengthen comfort with assertiveness, communication, and social interaction skills in social settings and among peers.	Use assertiveness training autonomously to respond to teasing in one or more social situations; use communication skills to strengthen one or more friendships and increase time engaged in social activities.
Intrusive Anger or Mood Instability Problems Contributing to Depressive Presentation	Develop capacity to respond to triggers and regulate emotions to improve mood stability.	Affect Regulation	Demonstrate use of affect regulation skills to promote stable mood when confronted by usual triggers.	Effectively and autonomously utilize reappraisal strategies three or more times in two or more settings to correct cognitive distortions and enhance mood stability.
Unbalanced Expression of Positive and Negative Experiences Within Family Context	Improve family capacity to consistently increase positive interactions and reduce negative interactions.	Family Collaboration	Improve quality and increase frequency of supportive communication among family members in the home.	Participate as a family in shared activity each week during a month for one hour in which family members engage in constructive communication 90 percent of the time or more.

Difficulty Overcoming Challenges and Limited Coping Ability	Strengthen client's ability to identify and execute solutions when confronting obstacles.	Problem-Solving Skills	Develop a goal and strategy followed by taking action.	Utilize effective coping skills in novel settings or when confronted by triggering events.
Low Motivation or Participation in Treatment Steps	Boost family and client engagement and motivation in treatment.	Treatment Engagement	Improve awareness of reasons for participation in session.	Consistently attend treatment and participate actively in between-session practice activities.

Downloadable copies of this table are available online at http://www.newharbinger.com/31175. (See the very back of this book for more details.)

33

Modular CBT Treatment Plan

Client Name: _____   Date: _____

Family Member _____   Family Member _____
Name: Role:

Therapist Name: _____   Client Age: _____

Supervisor Name: _____   Client Grade: _____
(if applicable)

Treatment Goal (long-term):

Strengths/Skills to Help Reach the Goal:

Targeted Problem (observable):	Targeted Problem (observable):
Treatment Objective (short-term):	Treatment Objective (short-term):
Module:	Module:
Intervention(s):	Intervention(s):
Expected Outcome (observable):	Expected Outcome (observable):

Download a full-scale copy of this form online at http://www.newharbinger.com/31175. (See the very back of this book for more details.)

Part II

The Treatment Modules

Chapter 3

Safety Plan and
Crisis Management

Anjelica, a seasoned therapist, completed a comprehensive assessment for a new client, twelve-year-old Mattias. In collaboration with Mattias and his parents, Anjelica identified goals for treatment and developed a treatment plan. Mattias appeared to have opened up to his therapist and was comfortable discussing his thoughts and feelings within the context of the therapy sessions. A good therapeutic alliance had developed in the course of treatment thus far. Last week, treatment focused on developing coping skills, and Mattias appeared responsive, attentive, and active in the skills-building treatment session. Mattias seemed to be making good progress overall, but this week his mother asked to speak with Anjelica separately at the beginning of the session. She informed Anjelica that she had discovered Mattias looking at a website with stories about suicide. Anjelica met with Mattias afterward, and he acknowledged that he has had passive thoughts about the world being a better place without him. Anjelica conducted a thorough suicide risk assessment and eventually concluded that Mattias did not meet criteria for psychiatric hospitalization; however, she was concerned that he remained at elevated risk for suicide.

While the terms "suicidal adolescent" and "crisis management" conjure up the image of an extremely high-risk situation whereby a client requires involuntary psychiatric hospitalization due to a suicidal plan, strong intent, and high lethality, the above scenario with Mattias tends to be more common in the typical treatment course for depressed children and adolescents. When working with this population, you need to continuously monitor for potential risk for suicide and self-injurious behaviors, even when the client appears to be progressing along well in treatment.

Preparing the Module

According to the Centers for Disease Control and Prevention (CDC, n.d.), suicide is the third leading cause of death for young people between the ages of ten and twenty-four years old. A US survey of adolescents in grades nine through twelve in public and private schools found that 16 percent of students reported seriously considering suicide, 13 percent reported creating a plan, and 8 percent reported trying to take their own life in the twelve months preceding the survey (CDC, n.d). Furthermore, the risk of self-injurious behavior or suicide is even greater among depressed youth (Davies, Raveis, & Kandel, 1991). This sobering reminder draws attention to therapists' responsibilities when working with depressed youth. Safety planning and crisis management are critical components of a therapist's skill set and can sometimes even be lifesaving. In this chapter, we discuss the role of crisis management for self-injurious behaviors and suicidal thoughts within the context of modular CBT. After this brief background, we offer specific approaches to enhance the client's safety and develop a crisis-management plan.

Background

Self-injurious behaviors are intentional behaviors with the purpose of harming oneself and may include purposefully cutting or scratching one's arms, burning one's skin, and hitting oneself. Although these behaviors are frightening to parents and can pose significant harm to the child's health, they are usually not considered suicidal behaviors; rather, they are considered to be the child's attempt to relieve some emotional distress that is perceived to be unbearable to the child. In order to be considered a suicide attempt, the behavior must be coupled with a conscious thought of ending one's life. To be sure, pediatric depression is associated with higher risk of suicide; 38 percent of depressed youth had made a suicide attempt by age seventeen (Kovacs, Goldston, & Gatsonis, 1993). One of the most significant predictors of suicide attempt is a previous suicide attempt. In a long-term follow-up study of first-time suicide attempters, 38 percent completed suicide within five years (Brådvik, 2003). Thus, a prior suicide attempt (including lethality, plan, and intent) must be considered when developing a crisis-management plan or considering treatment options for the child or adolescent.

Clinical Rationale for Module

Studies on depression and suicide risk have highlighted the role of the hopelessness construct in increasing a youth's risk of suicidal intent (Kazdin, French, Esveldt-Dawson, & Sherick, 1983). In Kazdin and colleagues' study, a high level of hopelessness was associated with significantly more severe depression and lower self-esteem than a low level of hopelessness. Negative expectations toward oneself and the future were also related both to depression and suicidal intent. Moreover, children who experienced high levels of acculturative stress were found to be at risk of experiencing critical levels of depression and suicidal ideation (Hovey & King, 1996). This particular study looked at immigrant and second-generation Latino Americans and demonstrated the importance of considering the child's cultural context when assessing for risk factors.

Because studies indicate that the child's perceived family environment plays a role in alleviating suicide risk (Asarnow, Carlson, & Guthrie, 1987; O'Donnell,

O'Donnell, Wardlaw, & Stueve, 2004), clinicians must assess both the child and his family system. Perceived family conflict and family-environment instability are risk factors for suicide among children and adolescents (Asarnow, Carlson, & Guthrie, 1987). In order for the risk assessment to be thorough, the clinician should interview the child individually and document his risk and protective factors. The family should also be interviewed, and their role as support people is critical during the crisis-management phase.

Using the Module

In conducting a risk assessment, many mental health treatment clinics have safety-planning and crisis-management procedures in place. For example, a hospital-based clinician may have access to established evidence-based protocols that are part of her agency's procedures. However, if there are no safety-planning procedures readily available, the clinician may avail herself to the following resources: Suicide Prevention Resource Center (http://www.sprc.org), Joan Asarnow's presentation Assessment of Depression & Suicide Risk: Strategies for Matching Youths to Optimal Interventions, and Donald Meichenbaum's presentation on Child and Adolescent Depression and Suicide: Promising Hope and Facilitating Change (both presentations are available at http://www.melissainstitute.org). In particular, Meichenbaum's presentation includes information related to suicide and risk assessment, including Assessment and Treatment: A Checklist of Clinical Activities for Working with Depressed and Suicidal Youth, Assessment of Suicidal Potential, and Suicide Assessment Strategies: Useful Mnemonics. This resource contains useful worksheets and checklists that therapists may find easily applicable when working with depressed youth.

An integral and essential component of every risk assessment or crisis management is consultation. Regardless of the clinician's level of experience, clinicians are strongly recommended to incorporate consultation in their risk assessments and crisis managements. The consultation should be with a licensed, experienced clinician when possible, and should be documented immediately.

Crisis Management

When an intake interview or clinical assessment results in the identification of safety risk factors or moderate risk for crisis, you should discuss these concerns with the client and family and develop a safety plan immediately. Sometimes safety risks aren't identified during the intake and treatment planning process. For example, a client may reveal that he experiences suicidal ideation as trust is developed in the course of treatment, or a safety risk may be discovered at a later date by a family member (as in the case example of Mattias earlier in this chapter). At any point that these safety concerns come to light, they immediately become the priority until the risk or crisis is stabilized and the client's safety is established. There are a number of ways therapists may respond to safety risks. Crisis management includes use of a risk assessment, consideration of protective factors, a thorough consultation with colleagues or other relevant professionals affiliated with the care of the child (e.g., psychiatrist), and a thoughtful prioritization of subsequent steps. Contingent upon the severity and level of risk for the client, the next steps for treatment options are wide-ranging. If the risk for self-harm is imminent, then involuntary psychiatric hospitalization may be prudent. If the client's level of self-harm risk is considered to be minimal, then a crisis-management plan may be developed before continuing with modular CBT treatment. If the client has significant difficulties with suicidal ideations but does not meet criteria for involuntary psychiatric hospitalization, then cessation of modular CBT and a referral to a crisis program, partial-day hospitalization, or a specific suicide intervention program may be warranted. An example of an evidence-based suicide intervention program is the cognitive behavioral therapy for suicide prevention (CBT-SP; Stanley et al., 2009).

When you are working with a child or adolescent who is at minimal or low risk for suicide, then a safety plan may be developed as a precaution; however, this should *not* be used as a "no-suicide contract." Rather, clinicians should be keenly aware that there are no reliable data supporting the effectiveness of no-suicide contracts in preventing suicide (Drew, 2001; Kelly & Knudson, 2000) or of shielding clinicians from malpractice liability (Pfaff, Acres, & Wilson, 1999). When a client presents with possible suicide or self-harm risk, the clinician should actively and thoroughly assess for potential harm (e.g., lethality, plan, intent, access to means, prior history, protective factors) and respond to the risk with an appropriate level of action (e.g., involuntary hospitalization, removal of dangerous items from child's home). This active assessment is an ongoing process (to be addressed at every session, rather than as a one-time response). Ongoing, proactive risk assessment, along with the appropriate actions commensurate with level of risk, is likely to be more effective than a no-suicide contract in supporting the clinician against malpractice liability.

How does a clinician demonstrate that she is engaging in an ongoing, active risk assessment? The safety plan (also known as a crisis-management plan, crisis-prevention plan, or risk-assessment plan) is a collaborative effort between the clinician, the child, and the child's support people (e.g., parents, grandparents, teachers) that focuses on the identification of the risk, ways to mitigate that risk, and action steps for parties to take if the risk becomes increasingly elevated. This effort must be documented, reviewed, and revised on an ongoing basis at the beginning of each session for the remainder of the treatment course. There are many examples of crisis-management plans and safety plans available on the Internet, and many employers at mental health institutions and clinics provide their clinicians with a recommended plan. At the end of this chapter (and available online at http://www.newharbinger.com/31175) is an example of a plan that may be used.

The crisis-management plan should always comprise of identification of potential risk behaviors and triggers for those behaviors, a description of coping or alternative strategies that the child may employ (ideally, these are coping strategies that the child has previously demonstrated his ability to use), steps or actions that the child's support people (e.g., family members, teachers, friends) can take to help the child in using his coping strategies and to maintain risk reduction, and a list of specific crisis-oriented resources (including names, telephone numbers, and addresses) that the child or support people can use in a crisis situation. This plan should be developed in collaboration with the child and support people, and the agreement to follow the crisis-management plan may be formalized with each party's signature on the plan. It is important to note that signatures do not release the therapist from any liability, nor do they reflect an increase in the likelihood that the child or family will follow through with the steps in the plan. In this case, the signatures merely serve to indicate that all parties were involved in the development of the plan. Copies of this plan should be disseminated to the child, his family, and the clinician's chart record for the child. There should be clear instructions to place the plan in easily accessible locations (e.g., on the refrigerator at home, in a wallet or purse, on the child's smartphone) for ease of use when indicated. And as mentioned above, this plan should be reviewed and revised as needed throughout the entire treatment duration. Again, it is important to highlight that the crisis-management plan should not take the place of involuntary psychiatric hospitalization when there is imminent risk, but rather should be employed when the risk appears to be minimal and the child and family members appear willing to follow the steps in the plan.

Between-Session Practice

How can the clinician increase the likelihood that the child and parents will follow the crisis-management plan? The crisis-management plan should be posted in visible locations that are easily accessible to the child and family (e.g., electronic version on a smartphone, handwritten plan on the refrigerator). The client and family members are encouraged to review the crisis-management plan so the steps are familiar and so the coping strategies listed in the plan are practiced on an ongoing basis. For instance, if the adolescent and his parent identified that the parent would encourage the adolescent to use his coping strategy of listening to calming music, then the parent should ensure that the appropriate electronic device (e.g., smartphone) is available for the adolescent and remember to verbally encourage the adolescent to listen to calming music on a nightly basis. When necessary, parents sometimes help promote the client's safety by "sanitizing the home environment," which entails modifying the home environment to remove accessible high-risk items that may be used for suicide or self-harm (e.g., putting knives in locked containers, removing bleach from the laundry cabinet, removing or locking up guns). If an adolescent is having active suicidal ideations with intent and a plan, then sanitizing the home environment is usually an insufficient response whereas involuntary psychiatric hospitalization may be appropriate. On the other hand, if the client is not having active suicidal ideations, but has a history of some impulsivity with intermittent passive suicidal ideations, then removing or locking up potentially dangerous items from the household environment may be beneficial.

Summary, Feedback, and Next Steps

At the close of the initial crisis-management plan session, you should summarize the overall plan and review the action items for each member of the family, the between-session practice assignments, and the purposes for the between-session assignments (practice). There should be a clear understanding of the child's level of self-harm risk and protective factors. The crisis-management plan should be viewed as a working document that is modified as often as needed in order to ensure that it is easy to use, easy to understand, and useful when the child is having difficulty with self-harm thoughts.

Common Hurdles and Solutions for Therapists

The most common barrier in crisis-management planning is ensuring that the suicide risk assessment is thorough and addresses all areas of imminent risk. Because of the sensitive nature of suicidal ideations, sometimes the child or adolescent does not disclose or acknowledge his true cognitions or feelings. This may result in a less-than-optimal crisis response. Because of the recognition of limitations associated with using only the child's report, a thorough suicide risk assessment incorporates interviewing family members and reviewing the client's observed behaviors (e.g., as observed by the therapist, as well as reported by others in his day-to-day life). Contacting his teachers or school counselor to elicit his school behaviors (with consent and authorization for release of information obtained in written documentation) may be prudent. In addition to the traditional clinical interview, administering a depression questionnaire (such as the Child Depression Inventory or Beck Depression Inventory) may offer additional information as some youths may feel more comfortable disclosing self-harm thoughts or actions via written versus oral format.

Summary

While this module on crisis-management planning may never be used for treatment of youths who don't have any self-harm thoughts or behaviors (thus, it is generally considered a supplementary module), the research literature suggests that many depressed children and adolescents will engage in passive or active suicidal ideations. For these youth, incorporating this module in treatment is considered essential. Depending on how and when the child's suicidal or self-harm risk presents during the course of treatment, the need to use this module may occur on an unexpected basis. Thus, it is recommended that clinicians review this module before initiating modular CBT and be able to flexibly apply it when the need arises during the course of modular CBT treatment.

Safety Plan Instructions for Therapists

This page is for the therapist's reference only.

1. Review the full instructions for the safety plan, which can be found in chapter 4.

2. Complete the following pages with your client and your client's family.

3. Make copies of the completed plan for the client, the client's support people, and the therapist's file (or client's chart). Do not give this instructions page to your client.

4. Have the client place the plan in an easily accessible location (e.g., on the refrigerator, bedroom wall). If the client wishes to use a smartphone, have him or her take a picture of the plan using the phone's camera function.

5. Document the safety-planning process in the client's record.

6. Some important cautions: This safety plan should not be used as a no-suicide contract. Also, the signatures here do not actually mean that the client will follow the plan. Finally, the safety plan is an evolving document. Be sure to review it regularly.

Safety Plan

1. Client's Risk Behaviors, including triggers ("What suicidal thoughts do I have? What triggers those thoughts?"): _____

_____

2. Client's Coping Strategies ("What can I do to make myself feel better when I am triggered to have the above risk behaviors?"): _____

_____

_____

3. Client's Family and Support People's Actions to Support the Child ("What can I, as the support person, do to help the child use his or her coping strategies and stay safe?"):

_____

_____

_____

4. In the case of an emergency or high-risk situation (list some examples)

_____

_____ ,

I will contact the following resources*:

   911 / Police Department (telephone number): _____

   County Mental Health Crisis Hotline: _____

   Suicide Prevention Hotline or Crisis Chatline: _____

   On-Call Hospital Psychiatrist: _____

* These telephone numbers should be saved on my smartphone when possible.

Child's Signature: _____
                              "I agree to follow this plan."

Family or Support Person's Signature: _____
                              "I agree to support the child by following this plan."

Downloadable copies of this form are available online at http://www.newharbinger .com/31175. (See the very back of this book for more details.)

Chapter 4

Psychoeducation

Five bandmates grouped at the Okeh Records recording studio on a snowy February day in the Windy City. As the center of the jazz universe in 1926, Chicago had drawn many talented musicians, including a young, gifted Louis Armstrong from New Orleans. On this chilly day, Armstrong and his Hot Five recorded several songs that would become benchmarks in jazz history, although one song in particular helped establish Armstrong's legendary status. As the story goes, Armstrong accidentally dropped the sheet of lyrics while recording "Heebie Jeebies," leaving him unprepared for the chorus.

The group was recording at a rapid pace; that day alone, Armstrong and his Hot Five recorded six songs. When the lyrics dropped to the floor, rather than stop the recording and waste the tape, Armstrong later explained, "I immediately turned back into the horn and started to scatting, just as nothing had happened." Scat singing is an improvisational form of singing, with the voice making wordless syllables or hornlike noises. "When I finished the record, I just knew the recording people would throw it out. And to my surprise they all came running out of the controlling booth and said, 'Leave that in.' My, my…I gave a big sigh of relief" (Armstrong, 2001, p. 132).

If you were standing in front of that microphone with the tape rolling, the band playing, and the lyrics on the floor, what might you have done? Armstrong turned what would have been a moment of hesitation for most people into a moment of brilliance. While it has been claimed and later refuted that Armstrong invented scat singing at this moment (Edwards, 2002), it is unquestionable that his uncanny reputation for improvising is perfectly personified in this instance. This recording of "Heebie Jeebies" would go on to become a jazz hit, and Armstrong's musical success would continue for decades.

This urban legend of improvisation offers a parallel for children and youth struggling in mental health treatment. The CBT treatment process relies on preparing the child or teen and family in the session with learning and practicing, followed by applying the skills out of the session at home, at school, or even while alone. It can be easy to forget that children, teens, and families will need to integrate and incorporate the new thinking and skills into their lives. Ultimately, the success of treatment relies on their ability to improvise and use those skills flexibly in different settings. Just as Armstrong's lyrics dropped to the floor, your clients will not have your immediate guidance when new challenges come up.

Brent and Poling (1997) pointed out that eventually, CBT clients must use their strengths outside of therapy to confront challenges and grow. This means that whey they're without your guidance, they will have to improvise to make it work. The reason

Armstrong was able to improvise in that moment was because of his clever and flexible understanding of melody. Similarly, your preparation of your clients will help them develop the knowledge and dexterity they need to take themes and skills out of your sessions and into their lives. Starting with the psychoeducation provided in this module, you are developing a base that will propel your clients past obstacles in real-world settings toward skill mastery.

Preparing the Module

Psychoeducation is teaching psychological topics with the goal of strengthening self-awareness and capacity for change. During this module, therapists share a lot of information in order to set the stage for clients and families to progress toward treatment success. This means you will take time to prepare before each psychoeducation session to design an outline of key topics you plan to cover. In the following sections, we provide information about the key topics that can be covered in this module.

Background

One of the unexpected roles you assume in the course of therapy is the role of a teacher. It can be an overlooked role—and not many therapists decided to be therapists because of a desire to teach—but without doubt, as a therapist you are also a teacher. Although you also have several other roles, a very important portion of your role as a therapist is to teach new information in a manner that is motivational to the child. Fortunately, therapists tend to be good at attending to others' internal processes, which is an important part of effective teaching. Therapists tend to notice and adjust when they pick up on cues that someone is confused or bored.

The topics covered in modular CBT psychoeducation for depressed children and adolescents are directly important to clients. In fact, when deciding to come to therapy, one of the main things many of your clients and their families envision, hope, and expect is to talk with someone who can help them understand why and how the problem is happening and to hear there is a solution. This module occurs very early in treatment because that is exactly what therapists provide through psychoeducation.

Clinical Rationale for the Module

Since each module includes a psychoeducation component to introduce specific important topics, this module is designed to provide the overarching framework—the introduction to depression, modular CBT, mechanisms for change, and expected outcomes. The themes in this module can also help the client see the forest from the trees. In other words, these themes may be used throughout treatment to help orient clients and families to the overall direction of treatment. Like any of the other modules, you will revisit these themes throughout the treatment process, zooming out from the individual modules and reminding the client about the overall rationale, expectations, and treatment process.

Preparing for this module involves knowing the material you plan to teach, similar to a teacher developing a lesson plan. With that in mind, we provide several examples and scripts to help guide you as you accommodate this information. As preparing the module and using the module are strongly connected, most of this chapter is focused on the "Using the Module" section. The best way to prepare for this module is to be familiar with the key topics you want to cover and to have a clear outline in your mind, possibly written down in front of you. As you teach, you are shining the spotlight in the session on the topics that will receive attention and help you move toward reaching treatment goals. The remaining sections of this chapter cover the different components you will want to provide. After you become familiar with each of the components, you will be able to organize, expand, narrow, adapt, and tailor these components to best fit your clients and their families. This chapter provides a suggested blueprint, but not the perfect blueprint for every client and family. Be thoughtful about how these topics connect to your specific client and about different teaching styles or activities that can help your client internalize these lessons and acknowledge your role as a teacher. You are instrumental in guiding and supporting your clients and their families toward mastery of these topics so they can draw connections, improvise, and incorporate them in their lives.

Individually Tailoring the Module

This module will usually be the first module following assessment. Psychoeducation may also be revisited as needed; for instance, it may be helpful to provide additional psychoeducation following treatment planning. It sets the stage for subsequent modules and helps establish a foundation of knowledge that clients and families will use in later modules.

The Role of Parents and Families

Particularly in this module, it is beneficial that parents or caregivers are involved in the session. First, this sets the tone for their involvement and feelings of responsibility for working toward a solution throughout treatment. Second, if a parent ends up not continuing in treatment, she or he will at least have a framework and basic understanding of what you will be helping her or his child achieve. Third, psychoeducation skills are accessible for most people. Any parents who are hesitant about being able to support the therapeutic process will see that these skills are not overly challenging and are easily adopted into the home environment. They will be more likely to feel engaged instead of hesitant early in the process.

The way the therapist frames parental involvement strongly guides if and how the client and family feel connected to the treatment process. If the therapist's attitude is that parents are key figures of support and strength to build new skills and help clients become stronger than depression, families are more likely to be involved in the process. This session should initiate a discussion between the client, family members, and therapist to collaboratively understand the interconnected environmental contributors and solutions for depression. As they understand these themes, they will also understand the importance of their role in treatment.

Additionally, it may be helpful for parents and caregivers to know that when families are engaged in CBT treatment of depression, there is greater likelihood for success (Lewinsohn, Clarke, Hops, & Andrews, 1990). Some researchers have even suggested it may be near impossible to achieve successful treatment outcomes without active participation from parents (Birmaher et al., 2007), perhaps because parents can provide additional information about symptoms—depressed youth can sometimes be unreliable informants—as well as additional support and scaffolding outside of treatment, and help ensure the client's safety. Additionally, parents will often change their own behaviors that may have worsened their mood or their child's mood. The client will feel less isolated on her path of skill mastery if she is accompanied by parents or caregivers. Children or teenagers and parents can remind each other about between-session practicing and mastery of skills. Finally, parents may find unique ways to modify new skills to be more consistent with the family's cultural background and can help therapists teach things in ways that will make more sense for clients. For these reasons, we strongly encourage you to engage parents and caregivers and ensure they are involved in this module.

Using the Module

First Steps

The first steps for this module are perhaps more straightforward than other modules. The check-in is brief since there is no between-session practice or previous skills to review. If self-harm or suicidality are concerns for your client, you will evaluate changes and progress with the safety plan and crisis-management strategies since the previous session. Setting the agenda includes writing a general outline of the key topics you plan to discuss followed by a discussion about between-session practice. You can briefly review the previous session and treatment-planning results. Outside of these key themes, you are ready to begin the psychoeducation dialogue with your clients and their families.

Skills Training

Generally, there are five primary topics you will cover during this module. These are first providing a treatment overview, then psychoeducation about depression for children and youth, followed by a description of modular CBT for depression, an introduction of the cognitive triangle, and a description of the CBT theory of change including expected treatment outcomes. The following sections describe each component in detail. It is not essential that each specific aspect of these topics is covered, as different clients and families will have individual needs. Therapists should use their clinical judgment to determine the level of detail they would like to provide and the information that will contribute to the client's and family's clarity, understanding, and engagement in the treatment process.

Treatment Overview

First, you will provide a broad overview of treatment at this point, including how this session fits with overall treatment and a summary of the treatment-planning session. Briefly, you will review the key topics that emerged during the treatment-planning session and how those results lead to the current module. You will also briefly explain the key topics that will be covered in the session and help the client and family understand how this module connects to the assessment, treatment plan, and the goals they have for therapy. There are a number of ways to tie this information together, but the following example gives one illustration of how the different discussion points can be synthesized.

Orienting a Teenager to Modular CBT Treatment

Therapist: Since starting therapy, a lot of what we've done is get to know each other and figure out together what we can do to address the concerns that brought you to therapy. You told me that you feel sad a lot of the time and that even when you hang out with friends, you feel down, so you prefer to stay alone in your room most days (you said you are alone pretty much every weekday afternoon for about five hours and most of the day on Saturday). We also learned that sometimes you worry you will never be really happy and the thought to hurt yourself comes into your mind a few times most weeks (you guessed about two to five times per week). Last week, we made a plan that included modular CBT to help with depression. I talked a little about the different modules we would use. These modules are like stepping stones to get across a river. As you learn new skills during each module, you'll be getting closer and closer to the goal of being in better control of your mood and feeling better. (*Describe the elimination or reduction of specific symptoms the client has shared with you at this point and the specific treatment plan objectives or goals.*) Each module builds on the last one, so as you become really good at one module, we'll move to the next.

Today, we start the first module. That means instead of talking about some of the difficult things you've been dealing with, we get to talk about how to start building your "muscles" for overcoming those difficult things. Today, I'll be teaching you about how depression affects other teenagers; how common it is; how people get more control over their feelings, thoughts, and behaviors; and how these things can help you feel happier and stronger than depression.

Depression for Children and Youth

What is depression? What does it mean if someone is depressed? How does someone become depressed? What does depression feel like? Who can get depressed? Is it permanent, or can it be fixed? Some of these questions may have already come up during the assessment, and you may have already started this conversation. It is beneficial to start discussing these questions as early as possible. Many of your clients and most of your clients' parents or caregivers will have these questions. Alternatively, many clients and families may just be orienting and beginning to understand mental health treatment. They might not have enough information yet to ask these questions. By introducing this topic, you are orienting *and* teaching. When you begin the process of orienting the family and client to this module, you are guiding them and helping them understand that instead of talking about deficits or the challenges that occurred that week, you will first be talking about the big picture and then getting into the ways that big picture fits or doesn't fit for your client.

If you are treating a young person who struggles with depression, there are common, probable experiences your client and her family are experiencing. By talking accurately about how depression affects young people, your clients and their families will trust you more. They are more likely to trust your credibility, and their expectations for treatment will improve as your comments resonate for them or as you help them talk through their main concerns. Sometimes therapists feel apprehensive about "jumping in" with such emotionally heavy topics. The best remedy for that hesitation is to test the water. Through practice, you will learn that families and clients know you are there to discuss serious things. Most of your clients have seen therapists in the media or have heard about therapy from friends, and they expect you to be open about mental health. Your comfort with these topics will give them a positive example of how to talk about feelings and emotions. The more comfortable you feel talking to them, the more likely your clients and their families will feel at ease in the discussion.

One way in which psychoeducation is an intervention is families and clients learn (often for the first time) how to talk about the problem. They learn the vocabulary, they learn how to act with each other, and they learn it is no longer a taboo. Internalizing, avoiding, and ignoring depression leads to misunderstanding and misinterpreting the issue and to many other secondary reactions, such as anger, guilt, and resentment. Often, you are breaking the status quo of avoiding or ignoring, misunderstanding, or misinterpreting the issue. If used effectively, families will often go home after the sessions from this module feeling empowered to continue the discussion about depression. If that happens, you have been successful with psychoeducation.

Since depression is a very common mental illness, therapists tend to receive training and education about the disorder. The "Common Questions and Answers for Children, Teens, and Families About Depression" section discusses specific topics about depression for children and adolescents that may be useful to bolster your existing knowledge of depression and to help you answer typical questions and dispel common misconceptions.

Common Questions and Answers for Children, Teens, and Families About Depression

What is depression?

Everyone feels sad sometimes, but these feelings usually pass after a few days. When someone has depression, that person will have trouble with daily life because of extreme sadness that lasts for two weeks or longer. Depression can interfere with school, friends, family relationships, and even sleeping and eating. Depression is a serious illness that affects the brain, but it is treatable, usually with therapy and often with medications, depending on the severity of the depression. For children and adolescents, depression can appear as irritable mood. Instead of appearing sad or down, depressed children and adolescents can appear irritable and easily frustrated.

What are the signs and symptoms of depression?

Different people have different symptoms. Common symptoms of depression include some combination of the following:

- Feeling sad or "empty"
- Feeling hopeless, irritable, anxious, or guilty
- Feeling easily frustrated or having frequent tantrums
- Loss of interest in favorite activities or social activities
- Not being able to concentrate or remember details
- Not being able to sleep, or sleeping too much
- Overeating, or not wanting to eat at all
- Thoughts of suicide, or suicide attempts
- Aches or pains, headaches, cramps, or digestive problems

What causes depression?

When something challenging happens, it can be tempting to want to blame someone; however, depression is an illness and is not anyone's fault. Depression is caused by a combination of genetic and environmental factors.

Genetics and Brain Chemistry: Depression is more of a risk for people with a family history of depression. The brain involves a complex interaction of systems and regions, and there are chemicals in the brain that contribute to mood. Depression can be caused by a number of systems within the brain, but sometimes there are parts of the brain that have too much or too little of important chemicals, which can make it difficult to receive the signals that help the person feel happy or can cause the person to get too many of the signals related to feeling sad. (Some families, children, and youth will benefit from a basic explanation of how genes are shared within families and how genes may contribute to an illness.)

Environment and Stress: Some of the things that cause depression include behaviors and ways of looking at the world. These behaviors and thinking patterns can sometimes be learned (and changed) in the home. Loss of a loved one, changes or conflicts in important relationships, and other stressful situations may trigger depression.

Is depression common for children and teens?

About 5 percent of children and adolescents suffer from depression in the United States. The children and teens at the highest risk for depression often have problems with anxiety, acting-out behaviors, attention, or learning, or have experienced serious stress, trauma, or grief.

Does depression look the same in everyone?

No. Depression affects different people in different ways. Some children with depression may pretend to be sick, have stomachaches, refuse to go to school, cling to a parent, or worry that a parent may die. Older children and teens may get into trouble at school and be irritable. A serious depression risk is when young people talk about suicide or hurting themselves.

What can I do to help keep my depressed son or daughter safe?

- Offer support, understanding, patience, and encouragement.

- Talk to him or her, and listen carefully.

- Take comments about suicide seriously, and report them to your loved one's therapist or doctor.

- Invite him or her out for walks, outings, and other activities.

- Remind him or her that with time and treatment, the depression will lift.

What can I do if I feel really depressed?

You will learn a lot more about how to answer this question through therapy. A few important things to know when you are feeling depressed are it's easy to believe that you are alone, that no one could understand, or that you are unimportant. This leads to keeping feelings and thoughts private and inside. Even though it can be difficult, it is important to remind yourself there are actually many people who care and want to help. You might work with your therapist to make a list of who those people could be. One of the important things to do when you are feeling depressed is to talk to those people. Let them know how you're feeling, especially if you think about doing something that isn't safe. Let your therapist, teacher, parent, or other adult know when you're feeling especially depressed. Remind yourself that those feelings are temporary and they will pass.

Adapted from National Institutes of Health (NIH Publication No. 11-3561; Revised 2011).

Clearly the topic of depression is broad, and you will only need to cover the parts that are useful to your client and her family. During the assessment and treatment planning, keep an open ear to any "blind spots" or misconceptions you hear about depression or the client's symptoms. You can also make sure to continuously check in with the client and her family about their questions as you cover this topic. New questions can come up as your client and her family learns more.

If a client or family member is asking specific questions about depression and you aren't sure of the answers, it is appropriate to be transparent and let the client or family member know you aren't sure. It's not reasonable to expect yourself to answer every question that a child, teen, or caregiver might bring to you. However, it's usually a good sign when your clients and their families have questions and are curious to learn more. Many therapists will research those questions immediately in the session, taking time to show the family member how and where to research on the Internet if additional questions arise. This is a good way to model how to effectively search for accurate and evidence-based information on the Internet (e.g., academic medical center websites, National Institute of Mental Health, Centers for Disease Control and Prevention, American Psychological Association, PracticeWise) and how to avoid misinformation.

Fortunately, there are numerous resources to help you, your clients, and their families understand depression and how it impacts young people. (A list of online resources for therapists, caregivers, and young people appears at the end of this chapter and is available online at http://www.newharbinger.com/31175.) If clients or families bring questions that are particularly important to the psychoeducation process for the family, you can recommend a between-session assignment. For example, you can ask the client's foster mother to look up three resources on depression and bring them to the next session, or you can ask your client to teach his father three new things he learned about depression (especially if his father was not able to attend the session; a family member could help your client complete this type of assignment).

Modular CBT for Depression

In addition to generally discussing depression, you will also provide basic information about modular CBT and how it connects to the treatment of depression. The goal with this portion of the discussion is to let your client and client's family know why you have selected modular CBT as the treatment and what they can expect from treatment. By transparently involving your client and client's family in your decision-making process, you are increasing their ownership of the treatment process (Birmaher et al., 2007). It will help your client and her family know that (a) there are treatments that are known to be effective for reducing the impact of depression and (b) the treatment you have decided to use and have been discussing with them during the treatment-planning process is one of these treatments, and it has good scientific support for helping children and teens impacted by depression.

Depression is caused by a combination of environmental and genetic factors. With that in mind, modular CBT has been developed to provide skills to address the environmental factors that contribute to depression. For mild, moderate, or brief depression, modular CBT alone can be expected to be effective. For severe, chronic, or treatment-resistant forms of depression, a combination of modular CBT and psychotropic interventions is suggested by researchers (Birmaher et al., 2007).

Psychotropic treatment is sometimes controversial or intimidating for clients and families (understandably so). Parents and caregivers will come to treatment with a range of attitudes. It can be alarming to parents if a professional suggests their child or teenager takes daily mood medications. On the other hand, some parents will expect psychotropic treatment immediately or instead of modular CBT. Because this topic can be sensitive and require additional conversation, it is a good fit for the psychoeducation module. Take time to listen, understand, and discuss concerns with clients and caregivers. With sensitivity and respect toward your client's values, provide information consistent with your level of training and expertise on psychotropic interventions. Emphasize that the first step, if the caregivers decide to use that intervention, is a psychiatric consultation, which means they get to ask a psychiatrist their questions and learn about the decision from a medical professional. Similarly, as a therapist, it is important to recognize that you are making a referral for a psychiatric consultation—not for the child or teen to start medication—that decision will ultimately be left to the caregivers, in consultation with a medical professional. As a therapist, it is important to know (and it is important to let your clients know) that psychotropic interventions are part of the evidence-based treatment approach for severe, chronic, or treatment-resistant forms of depression. If there are not psychiatric services available to clients in your area, seek out medical professionals who are familiar with, and sensitive to, mental health treatment. Become familiar and develop professional relationships with the medical professionals in your area who are trained and skilled at helping children and adolescents with mental health problems.

In terms of psychotherapy, it will be helpful for your clients to know that you have selected modular CBT so you can individualize the treatment process while still emphasizing the core, empirically supported skills that have been shown to reduce depressive symptoms. However, the effectiveness of any intervention is largely dependent on client and family engagement in the treatment.

Therapist: One thing I've seen in the past, with the families who are working in modular CBT, is that the kids and families who really put their effort into learning these new skills and who attend therapy regularly have more success. When families miss sessions or forget to practice between sessions, they lose their momentum and forget the things they are trying to learn. It makes therapy less helpful, and treatment progress moves a lot slower or stops. Modular CBT is a lot about learning and practicing things with me, but the best practice happens afterward when you try the things you're learning in your day-to-day life. When families and kids really work on these skills, especially at home or school, they see real progress. Nobody's perfect, and it can be hard to learn new things. I understand that, and I'll help when the going gets tough, but when you're trying, I know things will go much better, and I believe you'll see the changes and progress you're hoping for.

Cognitive Triangle

The cognitive triangle is a central theme for describing the modular CBT treatment process. The concept was first introduced by Clarke, Lewinsohn, and Hops (1990) and has become a standard building block in CBT treatments for children, youth, and families (J. A. Cohen & Mannarino, 2008; Curry et al., 2000). To start, draw a triangle on a board or piece of paper in the session. As you write "thoughts," "feelings," and "actions" at each corner of the triangle, take time to discuss each concept, making sure clients understand the difference between a thought and a feeling, a feeling and an action, and an action and a thought. Then, take a moment to illustrate how these concepts work together.

The Cognitive Triangle

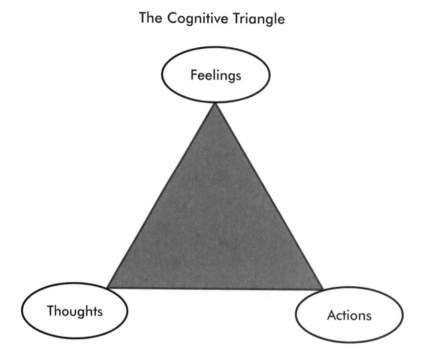

Therapist: Let's practice something. Go ahead and close your eyes for a moment. I'm just going to ask you to imagine that I'm holding a bag of lemons. Imagine that I just took one of the lemons out of the bag—one of the biggest lemons you've ever seen. You can imagine the bright yellow skin of the lemon and all the bumps and smooth parts. Imagine me taking that lemon and cutting it into big slices and putting those slices onto a plate. You can hear the knife cutting through the lemon skin. You can see a little mist spraying out as I cut. As I place the juicy lemon slices on the plate, you can see all the yellow lemon juice collecting on the plate. I mean, these lemon slices are super juicy. You can probably smell it. Now imagine that I pass you the plate. You can see all the slices and the lemon juice moving around. I ask you to choose one slice. You choose one slice. Then, you put it in your mouth and start drinking the lemon juice. *(Pause.)* Go ahead and open your eyes. What was that like?

Client's: Father	*(smiles)* That was sour!
Client:	*(smiling)* My mouth is watering.
Therapist:	Do you see any lemons now? Are there any lemons in this room?
Client:	*(shakes head)*
Therapist:	There probably aren't even any lemons in this building. We were just imagining. So what just happened? It seemed like you were eating something really sour. Why did your mouth water? Why did it feel like you put a lemon slice in your mouth? Well, it turns out that if you think about something and really imagine it, it seems real. Parts of your brain act the same when you imagine something and when it's actually happening. Do you know what that means? You thought about something, your mouth started to water, and your body thought it was real. It means your thoughts are powerful! If you think something enough, you believe it and it can become kind of real. In fact, you can change your feelings, your actions, and even your mood by being in charge of your thoughts. That's how powerful you are. For example, if I wake up in the morning and think to myself, *Today is going to be a bad day*, what's going to happen?
Father:	It will be a bad day.
Therapist:	That's right! It probably *will* be a bad day. When I spill breakfast on my shirt, I might say to myself, *I knew today would be bad!* But if I wake up and think, *I'm going to make today awesome! I'm going to make today super awesome!*—what then?
Client:	You'll have a good day?
Therapist:	That's exactly right—if you think, *Today will be fun* or *I'm going to do my best to have a good day*, you have a much better shot at having a fun day, especially if you have a good habit of thinking that way most days. There are really three things that work together in your life and make the biggest impact on what happens for you every day—three things that you can control. Those are thoughts, feelings, and actions. Let me show you how this works…

The next step in discussing the cognitive triangle is to help your client understand how thoughts, feelings, and actions are interrelated. Using the example of the bad day, talk through how thoughts lead to feelings and feelings lead to actions. Many therapists draw two-way arrows on a cognitive triangle image that connect thoughts to feelings, feelings to actions, and actions to thoughts as they discuss how each can influence each other. An example will help clarify how thoughts, feelings, and actions are interconnected and how they all contribute to creating habits (sometimes referred to as upward and downward spirals). One example is to describe how the thought *Today will be horrible* contributes to feeling pessimistic or grouchy. With this example, you can show how a minor setback could be amplified or positive experiences discarded if someone is thinking *Today will be horrible* and feeling grouchy. When possible, use examples that are relevant for your client. The following script builds from the previous discussion about the cognitive triangle and provides some guidance on how these themes can be woven together.

Therapist: So I woke up and told myself, *Today will be horrible*, and I felt grouchy. It made me notice the things that were horrible, so my actions were to act grouchy to others as I noticed the bad parts of my day and to ignore the good parts. I might have talked about how bad the day was with other people and been kind of angry. What happens when we're grouchy? Do people want to be friendly to you when you're grouchy?

Client: (shakes head)

Therapist: Nope. You're right. People usually don't want to be around someone who's grouchy. So, I'm grouchy, noticing the bad things, and not noticing the good things, *and* people don't really want to spend a lot of time with me. What will I tell myself at the end of the day? Probably, *I knew it was going to be a horrible day. I was right!* Was I right?

Client: Not really, because you made it worse.

Therapist: That's right! You're really smart. I'm impressed with how well you're learning this idea. So what will I think when I wake up tomorrow? Will I be looking forward to a good day? No. I'll probably be thinking it will be horrible again, and I'll probably be right again. My friends are learning that I'm grumpy a lot of days, that I say grouchy things, and that I notice the negative stuff. So if I do that over and over, it becomes a pattern. I'm starting to make a negative habit, and the habit gets stronger and stronger. It's called a downward spiral. I have good news though. Really good news...and this is the key. This is the center of some of the new things I'll teach you: the spiral works the opposite direction.

Describe in detail how the same pattern happens in a positive direction, using examples that mirror the previous discussion. Once you describe the upward spiral, introduce the skills that will help the client learn to start making an upward spiral with her mood, including changing thoughts and noticing feelings, and remind the client how powerful her thoughts can be and that she can be in control of her thoughts (based on the lemon example) with practice.

Note that this section is focused on the cognitive triangle. This concept is commonly mislabeled the "cognitive triad." The cognitive triad was developed by Aaron T. Beck (1976) in his work with depressed adults and refers to the negative thoughts depressed individuals often have about themselves, the world, and the future. It can be a helpful framework when exploring cognitions with caregivers and clients, but it is a separate concept from the cognitive triangle.

CBT Theory of Change

Now that you have provided a treatment overview, information about depression for children and youth, and a brief description of modular CBT for depression, and have introduced the cognitive triangle, the final topic to discuss with clients and families is how the CBT framework is expected to help alleviate symptoms of depression, and the outcomes you, your client, and her family might anticipate. This is a synthesis of all the information previously given. At this point, your client and her family are now familiar with depression and are beginning to understand the fundamental framework for modular CBT. Discussing the theory of change and expected outcomes will help them also understand how the framework of modular CBT contributes to the elimination or significant reduction of the depressive symptoms.

The way depression treatments affect an individual child or teen varies widely (Birmaher, Arbelaez, & Brent, 2002; Costello et al., 2002; Lewinsohn, Rohde, Seeley, Klein, & Gotlib, 2000). While some youth will respond quickly to treatment, others may experience symptoms of depression throughout their lifetime in spite of treatment. Therapists aren't able to consistently predict which clients will develop persistent depression from those who will respond to treatment. Researchers have encountered poorer outcomes when the depressive presentation includes multiple depressive episodes, comorbidity, persistent subclinical symptoms (including hopelessness or pessimistic cognitions), low socioeconomic status, and persistent exposure to adverse events (Birmaher et al., 2007).

We provide this information to prepare therapists to identify potential treatment obstacles; however, any individual client is able to succeed in treatment. It is important for therapists to recognize risk factors that suggest a combination of modular CBT and additional interventions (i.e., psychotropic interventions, case management, parent training, or in-home support) might be more effective than modular CBT alone. You can expect to see clients with seemingly unsurpassable barriers overcome depression; however, these types of treatment successes rarely occur without a clear connection to an appropriate intervention plan.

Children, youth, and families who are successful in treatment have experienced change. The types of changes you will encourage through modular CBT focus on increasing awareness; changing patterns of thoughts, feelings, and behaviors (with new skills); reaching mastery of new skills; and moving on to developing other new skills. There should be gradual improvement from one module to the next. New skills emerge, replacing old behaviors and resulting in small improvements in mood if the old behaviors actually contributed to depression and the new skills are actually used across settings. Improvement for some clients will be dynamic and drastic while others will experience more obstacles or smaller successes. As a therapist, you are gauging this change throughout treatment to identify and remedy treatment barriers. Clients may benefit from understanding how the following topics are connected to their changes in depression and their progress in treatment.

INCREASED AWARENESS

In 1749, Benjamin Franklin invented the lightning rod. Many people in the mid-eighteenth century still believed lightning was a punishment of mystical origins. Franklin, however, was able to demystify the lightning bolt, understand its origins and characteristics, and subsequently invent a way to control it. Many things seem out of our control when we fail to understand them. Depression is often misinterpreted by clients and families. By increasing awareness of the dynamics that contribute to depression, clients and families begin to realize they are in control. It is not a nebulous (and therefore uncontrollable) dysphoria. Instead, there are patterns (thoughts, feelings, and behaviors) that can be changed, adjusted, or controlled to reduce the power of depression. Increased awareness provides empowerment and is the key mechanism behind psychoeducation.

LEARN NEW THOUGHTS AND SKILLS

As understanding increases, you will encourage your clients to experiment with alternative thoughts and behaviors. When they begin to notice and understand thinking patterns, they can conduct small tests in their lives: "I'm going to try thinking, *I can study and get a good grade*," or "This time I'll think, *I can take a break to try and notice things that make me feel happy*." Testing new thoughts and behaviors can start showing your clients and families how to take more control over depression and will strengthen their empowerment. When successful, these tests of new changes will reinforce new thoughts (and allow old thoughts to be extinguished). Over time, the seeds for new habits can start to grow, starting your clients on the path of an upward spiral.

You can refer to the cognitive triangle and let clients know that you will continue to talk to them about thoughts, feelings, and actions, and how they will start to change some of the thoughts that lead to depression and replace them with thoughts that are more accurate. There are also social skills, activities, and other behaviors that will be part of the treatment to help change some of the actions that influence depressive thoughts and feelings.

SET GOALS

Goals are included in treatment in several ways. From the treatment plan, the agenda, and the between-session practices to progressing from one module to the next, goals are an integral part of modular CBT. Between-session practices are written down because goals that are written down are more likely to be met. Between-session practices are reviewed in each session because therapists need to know how clients are progressing on targeted goals to ensure overarching stepwise development of skills. It can be helpful to let clients and families know that with your help, they will continue to make and reach goals with each module to progress toward the larger goals of the treatment plan.

MODEL NEW SKILLS

One way of teaching new skills will also include modeling—therapists and other family members providing examples through their actions. By seeing the behavior, it will be easier for clients to learn. This is a good topic to cover with the client in front of her parents to help the parents know one of the ways they can take responsibility for helping their child learn new ways of acting and thinking. Modeling can include doing and also talking to show different ways of thinking about challenging situations.

PRACTICE

Finally, let your client know you will ask her to "practice, practice, practice." Young people often appreciate analogies about the value of practicing. You can draw from sports heroes, musicians, artists, or inventors to drive this point home. Let clients and families know how important practicing is in modular CBT treatment to help explain the role of between-session practices. It can help to point out that one hour of therapy is actually less than 1 percent of their week and that practicing outside of therapy is *essential* if they are going to learn new skills, which is why you will offer support to help them reach the goal of practicing often.

Reach Mastery of New Skills

Each of the modules represents a set of skills that, once strengthened, will reduce the role of depression in the client's life. We refer to this skill-acquisition process as "reaching skill mastery." When explaining this concept, you can explain that once the client and family demonstrate a sturdy understanding or utilization of the skills outside of therapy sessions, it will be time to move on to the next module. Some children will respond to the term "superhero" or "superheroine," or to the phrase, "become a pro." The decision about reaching mastery can be determined collaboratively. The individuals involved in treatment can decide which indicators are needed to reach mastery. When the therapist, client, and any other family members or supportive individuals involved in treatment agree that the specific skills have been appropriately developed, the client can move on to the next module.

There may be times when not everyone agrees or the skill is partially developed, but for the sake of continuing progress and moving forward, the client and family may move forward with partial skill acquisition. This decision will include an understanding that the therapist, client, and family will continue to discuss and check in on these skills in the following modules. Therapists should be cautious of depressive thinking, behavioral patterns, or family dynamics that can intimidate or frustrate clients as they try to reach mastery. Reaching mastery should continuously be framed as an achievable goal of general skill acquisition. This idea of mastery is intended to motivate, encourage, and empower individuals to become their own therapists (Brent & Poling, 1997). Because depressed children often feel like they are different and alone, it is beneficial to let them know that you have helped other children who have felt the same way. Further, it may be helpful to assure your client that many other children and adolescents have successfully graduated from the treatment program.

Long-Term Treatment Outcomes

Through developing a set of skills and reducing depressive symptoms, the ultimate goal of modular CBT for depression is to empower clients and families to experience greater happiness in their lives. Youth and families who overcome depression will be more aware of positive aspects in their lives. They will better understand and have more control of the things that bring pleasure. Those experiences will be more accessible to them and experienced in greater fullness and with more frequency. Of course, ups and downs are part of life and any treatment process. Some of the negative thinking or sad mood symptoms are common for most people and will persist after treatment. Depression can be a chronic and persistent disorder for some, and it is good for clients and families to know the recovery process can take time and that depression can impact the client for an extended period.

Also, after the conclusion of therapy, stressors can contribute to relapse for many clients. This is a normal process; however, with the skills acquired during modular CBT, these relapses can be brief and will provide opportunities for clients and families to deepen their capacity for confronting the symptoms of depression. Progress takes effort, and you are there to help them on this path. The goal is not perfection but instead to learn skills and ways of approaching obstacles to keep moving forward even if there are challenges along the way.

Between-Session Practice

Between-session practices are very useful and can be exciting for your clients during this module. The typical practice associated with this session is for your client to teach someone else about these themes. If you have time in the session, you can ask your client to teach you about the cognitive triangle. Use this experience to gauge her understanding and readiness to teach someone else without your help. It can be fun to switch seats in session during the practice to let your client try on the role of being her own therapist. You can ask probing questions to guide her teaching. If your client decides to teach a parent for her between-session practice, this in-session practice can also model to the parent how to be a "good student" for the client. You can provide coaching to both the client and the parent to ensure a successful practice.

Typically, between-session practices of teaching three or four times (to the same or different people) will help solidify the themes. When your client returns, you can ask her to teach you again to make sure the information has not drifted and to remind her of specific pieces she may have missed. Variations on this assignment include having parents teach the client or taking turns; making a family activity of drawing and explaining the cognitive triangle and conspicuously posting it in the home; and having the client teach friends, write a paragraph about the triangle, or draw it out on her own. An alternative between-session activity, instead of teaching, could include your client noticing and jotting down any thoughts, feelings, or actions that may be related to depression or feeling happy. This "noticing journal" can have a few examples from the week or one to two from each day of times when the client noticed elements of the cognitive triangle in her life. A variation of the noticing journal would be to notice an example of the downward spiral or upward spiral. You might suggest an example or two of each spiral (upward and downward) so your client doesn't follow a potential inclination of exclusively noticing the negative.

In either approach to between-session practice, find ways to involve the parents and ask them to complete the same practice the client chose. One example of mastery for this module is that the client is able to present and teach the key psychoeducation topics with minimal or no prompting.

As a last step for this session, you will provide feedback on the strengths you saw from your client and other participants, summarize what was covered, and discuss next steps for mastering the topics presented in this module or for moving to the next module.

Summary, Feedback, and Next Steps

At the close of the session, take time to find out which parts stood out to your client and her family. Find out which parts were most interesting, might be most helpful, or were most confusing. With the client's help, create a summary of the session. The summary, while a brief step, helps your client translate what you discussed into small, meaningful chunks. It helps to organize all of this new information into a mental outline. Young people in particular benefit from this step because they are able to remember themes and topics after they leave the session. See if your client can tell you what she understands about her next steps, about the family's next steps, or the goals of therapy. This is a great opportunity to solidify between-session-practice plans while assessing your client's comprehension at this point.

Common Hurdles and Solutions for Therapists

Some children have difficulty teaching any topic. Based on the client's capacity for understanding and teaching these themes, find ways for her to experience success with these topics, maybe teaching just to you and then broadening her teaching potential with other individuals in her life. Be open to different ways of teaching (i.e., drawing pictures, writing). You can ask your client to rate her comfort, understanding, and confidence with these themes on a scale of one to ten and ask her how confident she would need to be to reach mastery, then help her achieve that goal. It can be fun for young clients to take the therapist's chair and a dry-erase marker and begin to teach others. When there are significant learning disabilities, encourage your client to rely on her parents for help, offer reminders, allow her to use notes, and take other steps that provide support in a way that will still allow her to take ownership of the material.

Summary

The psychoeducation module can be a fun and unassuming introduction into the skill development of modular CBT. The themes are often intuitive for clients and families and often feel familiar. This gives families and clients the opportunity to reach mastery relatively quickly and get a first treatment step behind them. Teaching these themes in fun, collaborative, and dynamic ways creates an atmosphere that is supportive, interesting, and accessible for clients and their families. Clients have the opportunity to learn about themselves and get answers that take the confusion out of depression. Taken together, the psychoeducation module is often a strong way to encourage engagement in treatment and to initiate a strong treatment process.

Psychoeducation: Depression Resources

American Academy of Child and Adolescent Psychiatry

Depression Resource Center
http://www.aacap.org/AACAP/Families_and_Youth/Resource_Centers/Depression
_Resource_Center/Home.aspx

Facts for Families: The Depressed Child
http://www.aacap.org/App_Themes/AACAP/docs/facts_for_families/04_the
_depressed_child.pdf

American Psychological Association

Understanding Depression and Effective Treatment
http://www.apa.org/helpcenter/understanding-depression.aspx

Helpguide.org

Parent's Guide to Teen Depression
http://www.helpguide.org/articles/depression/teen-depression-signs-help.htm

Harvard Health Publications

What Causes Depression?
http://www.health.harvard.edu/mind-and-mood/what-causes-depression

MedlinePlus

Helping Your Teen with Depression
http://www.nlm.nih.gov/medlineplus/ency/patientinstructions/000646.htm

National Alliance on Mental Illness

Depression: In Children and Teens
http://www.nami.org/Template.cfm?Section=By_Illness&template=/ContentManage
ment/ContentDisplay.cfm&ContentID=88551

National Institute of Mental Health

Depression in Children and Adolescents
http://www.nimh.nih.gov/health/topics/depression/depression-in-children-and
-adolescents.shtml

Depression and High School Students
http://www.nimh.nih.gov/health/publications/depression-and-high-school-students
/depression-high-school-students_141730.pdf

Downloadable copies of this informational sheet are available online at http://www
.newharbinger.com/31175. (See the very back of this book for more details.)

Chapter 5

Mood Monitoring

Think of a bank account. Each day you have hundreds of deposits and withdrawals in this account. These transactions are automatic, of course. After all, it would be unrealistic to keep your eye on every transaction throughout the day. On good days, your deposits outweigh your withdrawals. On other days, withdrawals may leave you overdrawn. By and large, your balance keeps increasing, and you feel like a pretty conscientious investor.

Now consider a second bank account, similar to the first but with serious accounting errors. Unnecessary automatic withdrawals are scheduled several times each day. To make matters worse, it is difficult to distinguish the correct withdrawals from the errors. Although small, these withdrawals are frequent, and they add up, making it near impossible to break even by the end of the day. Good days are few and far between. More often than not, days end with the ledger in the red. With the balance decreasing overall, the owner of this account might consider himself a poor investor. How would you think about repairing this second bank account? If you decided to fix the mistaken withdrawals and increase deposits each day, you'd probably start by monitoring the transactions.

Now consider mood in terms of these two bank accounts. All of us have hundreds of interactions each day that lead to thoughts, feelings, and actions. We might think of a positive experience as a deposit, a negative experience as a withdrawal. Many of us will have more positive experiences on typical days and will feel generally good about ourselves, the world, and the future. A depressed child or adolescent will have errors in his thinking throughout the day, most of which are automatic. Even ambiguous cues, like a rushed tone of voice, can be transformed into a negative interaction. Although most daily interactions only impact us slightly, the mistaken or mislabeled negative experiences comprise a steady flow in a depressed person's life. With automatic negative interpretations of these interactions, slowly and gradually they can become a stream of damaging thoughts, feelings, and emotions. Positive interactions can be overshadowed by the steady undercurrent of perceived negativity. Over time, the child might start to internalize these negative messages as he develops his core beliefs about himself, the world, and the future.

With the bank account, in order to reduce mistaken withdrawals and increase deposits, the solution lies in understanding the transactions; with depression, the first step to intervening with this problem is to assess and understand it. It is important that a therapist accurately understands the salient daily emotions of the client and how these affect the client's mood. It is even more important that the client understands which experiences affect him throughout the day and how he reacts to the experiences. By introducing the mood monitoring module, the therapist is teaching the client how to recognize, consider, and be aware of broad feeling types and varying intensities throughout the day. The therapist is also developing and refining her own conceptualization of this unique client. This basic skill of mood monitoring lays groundwork for other modules but is also a powerful intervention of its own.

Preparing the Module

Easily skimmed or underutilized, mood monitoring is at the core of modular CBT for depression. This chapter highlights a framework for the concept of mood monitoring. We discuss the background and clinical rationale for mood monitoring. This background is intended to help therapists form a textured and flexible understanding of mood monitoring in preparation of using this module. After framing the concept of mood monitoring, we describe how to use the mood monitoring module. Implementing the module includes planning the agenda, using interventions and teaching techniques, and finding ways to involve parents or caregivers. This chapter will help support effective use of mood-monitoring skills in the successful treatment of depressed children and adolescents in the context of modular CBT.

Background

One first distinction you can make that will help with your understanding of mood monitoring comes from the *Diagnostic and Statistical Manual of Mental Disorders, Fifth Edition (DSM-5)* definition of mood:

> A pervasive and sustained emotion that colors the perception of the world. Common examples of mood include depression, elation, anger, and anxiety. In contrast to affect, which refers to more fluctuating changes in emotional *"weather,"* mood refers to a pervasive and sustained emotional *"climate"* (American Psychiatric Association, 2013, p. 824).

It is important to note the distinction between *mood* and *affect*. While *mood* is pervasive and sustained, *affect* is our experience of emotion, which changes much more often. To put it in terms of the bank account metaphor used at the beginning of this chapter, affect is based on bank transactions (deposits and withdrawals) while mood comes from the overall balance of the account over time.

For therapists, it is important to clarify that mood is made up of an ongoing stream of emotional interactions and the ways a person reacts to those interactions. When we talk about mood monitoring for treatment of depression, it means we look at the general pattern of emotions the child or adolescent experiences throughout his week and between sessions, since we know these have contributed to his overarching depressed mood.

Developmental Considerations: Depressed Mood for Children and Youth

Depressed mood in children and adolescents can often be experienced in ways that are similar to adults. Depressed children and adolescents are prone to see themselves as worthless, inferior, or inadequate (Blankstein & Segal, 2001), with pervasive negative expectations (A. T. Beck, 1976). Negative misperceptions contribute to frustration, sadness, and anhedonia (loss of interest in pleasurable activities). For young people, however, the expression of depression can also be very different from adults. While teenagers are more likely to describe negative views about themselves, the world, and the future, young children are unlikely to report feeling hopeless or depressed (Hammen & Rudolph, 2003).

Based on age and development, affect can be expressed and experienced in different ways. Most children and many teenagers are not able to understand or explain when they experience distress. Instead, young people will be irritable or angry, uncooperative, or disinterested (Ryan et al., 1987) and generally have greater difficulty communicating their emotions or mood with others (Hammen & Rudolph, 2003). Age and developmental differences are part of why the key diagnostic criterion in children and adolescents includes not just depressive mood but also irritable mood (American Psychiatric Association, 2013). Additional nonverbal indicators of depression can include poor school performance, refusal to attend school, somatic complaints, hypersomnia, clinginess, or preoccupation with death or dying. While just one of these symptoms alone would not characterize a depressive disorder, they can indicate underlying concerns related to depression.

Clinical Rationale for the Module

Being aware of emotion is the ability to acknowledge and examine one's own feelings and mood. Articulating emotions involves decoding the internal experience and expressing it in some way. To wholly articulate an emotion, we need the ability to label (accurately identify from a range of emotions) and scale the feeling (describe the intensity). These two elements are important in the overall course of treatment since the ability for emotional awareness and articulation has been strongly connected to positive overarching mental health (Garber, Braafladt, & Weiss, 1995; Eisenberg & Fabes, 1992; Hubbard & Coie, 1994).

Children who are seen for treatment of depression will be more likely to have affective difficulties. Researchers have found that poor mood awareness and articulation can predict experiences of negative affect, intense affective reactions, and greater rumination on negative mood. Better mood labeling, on the other hand, can predict the individual's experiences of positive affect, extraversion, high self-esteem, and greater satisfaction with social support (Swinkels & Giuliano, 1995; see Southam-Gerow & Kendall, 2000, for a review). Children and youth who are depressed are more likely to have difficulties recognizing and expressing emotion.

Emotional awareness can be thought of as the doorway to emotional change, and emotional articulation as the vehicle. With limited awareness of emotions, it is certainly difficult to articulate emotions. Without articulation, depressed young people lose the benefit of other people's opinions and points of view. Internalizing detaches them from the essential process of scaffolding and shaping that helps each of us prune or refine our interpretations and cognitions. Without this socialization, negative and incorrect interpretations take root and are strengthened through continued use.

During this module, therapists help clients become better aware of the experience of emotions (including the normal physiological reactions to emotions), and articulate these emotions. This process will include identifying and labeling emotions, distinguishing emotions from thoughts, and describing both the range of effect and its intensity. The mood monitoring module starts the process of understanding emotions; the client will begin to learn that emotions are adjustable, and that when it comes to emotions, each of us is in our own driver's seat. This basic truth can be completely new information for young people and can have a meaningful and lasting impact on the rest of their lives.

Negative Affect

A goal of modular CBT for treating depression is to reduce inaccurate thinking. Effective therapists focus on feelings resulting from mislabeled and misinterpreted situations (J. S. Beck, 2011). It is important for therapists to avoid "cheerleading" or trying to analyze all sad feelings. In this module, therapists focus on becoming aware of the emotions that are artificially inflating the client's negative perception. These misperceptions are then directly confronted with the addressing maladaptive cognitions module (chapter 7). By helping your client monitor the mislabeled or misinterpreted emotions early in treatment, you are helping him begin to realize these emotions can be changed and that thoughts impact his mood, and you are preparing the client to be successful with later modules.

Case Example: Mood Awareness and Articulation

With a former depressed thirteen-year-old client, John, it became clear through the course of the intake assessment that his father's military deployments triggered a depressive pattern and contributed to John's behavioral and emotional problems. Every deployment cycle seemed to exacerbate his depression and behavioral problems. At first, when I introduced the mood monitoring module and asked about his feelings, he offered very basic descriptions or just shrugged his shoulders. "Bored" seemed to be his favorite emotion.

With some youth, being bored is a defensive response, and it suggests they might not trust you yet and are unwilling to discuss or consider their emotions at that moment. In other cases, being bored is a very honest response and provides a great deal of information. "Bored" sometimes means

"I don't want to think about it because it's too hard," or "I don't know what I'm feeling, and I don't know how to figure that out, so I'm not open to thinking about it." These are pretty complicated ideas, and children or teens may genuinely not understand emotions well enough to respond with more information.

For John, being bored offered a glimpse into an undeveloped, rudimentary understanding of his own feelings. He felt bored because that was how he understood his feelings. His feelings were confusing to him and probably overwhelming, so disengaging from emotional themes (or being bored) was the most complete response he could give at that time. Emotions weren't often discussed in his family. As he progressed in the module, he developed his feelings vocabulary and his understanding of different emotions, and practiced his awareness of these emotions. Instead of ignoring or compartmentalizing his feelings, he started to describe his fears about his father's safety during the deployments and his sadness based on his mistaken assumption that his father didn't care about the family very much. This change in monitoring mood was the most challenging hurdle in John's treatment but also pivotal to his progress.

Fit of Topic with Overall Treatment

Mood monitoring is one of the most fundamental modules of modular CBT. In the course of this module and treatment, you and your client will be developing a shared language so you can move forward with other mood-focused skills and modules. Subsequent modules, such as addressing maladaptive cognitions and affect regulation, build on the client's ability to (a) recognize and understand his emotions and (b) monitor his mood. When therapists successfully implement this module, clients gradually become skilled at noticing and accurately communicating their emotions. Over the course of treatment, you will be talking about feelings with your client, identifying trends and habits related to your client's feelings, and continually checking in and refining mood-monitoring skills. Simultaneously, your client will be developing a deeper, applied understanding of the "when, what, how, and why" of his own feelings. For these reasons, mood monitoring is core to modular CBT.

Using the Module

Equipped with the information from the preceding sections, the various pieces of this module should be purposeful and feel cohesive with the other modules for your client. The following sections are designed to introduce and teach these skills effectively. We present some of the key pieces needed for a mood-monitoring session, including structuring the session, approaches for psychoeducation, using the agenda, and strategies for building the skills. Ultimately, your goals with this module are to help your client understand why and how to monitor his mood, build his capacity to develop these skills, and strengthen his ability to progress toward the overarching treatment goals.

When to Include the Module

Even clients with limited emotional range will have a basic understanding of emotions and mood. This is one of the advantages of this module: mood monitoring is familiar. When taught effectively, therapists are shaping and expanding familiar ideas. Most young people will recognize the themes you introduce and teach. Mood monitoring, however, further builds on these existing skills by helping young people keep track of and understand their moods in a broader context.

With that in mind, this module is useful for building trust and getting familiar with the client's current emotional skills, and is helpful early in treatment. We suggest implementing mood monitoring early in treatment, perhaps following the psychoeducation module. In this way, it can be used to build rapport, to evaluate further modules, and to set a familiar framework for the remaining modules. With all modules, crisis prevention and safety are prioritized above skill building. As a core module, this module serves as a building block for subsequent steps.

Cultural Considerations

Mood is a concept that can be very culturally influenced. If you ask three people with different backgrounds to describe mood, you are likely to get three very different answers. From the Spanish phrase *ataque de nervios* ("attack of nerves") to the condition of neurasthenia (defined in China as "physical and mental fatigue; physical pains such as headaches; and other sleep, memory, and sexual ailments"), it is clear that mood is not uniformly defined across the globe (Guarnaccia & Pincay, 2007). These cultural differences also include various religious and spiritual explanations for mood problems.

Language matching and incorporating culturally syntonic content are relevant cultural considerations for this module. Whenever possible, treatment should be provided in the language of origin for the person participating in treatment, and language should always be considered in culturally informed treatment. Language matching can include identifying interpreters, making sure there are bilingual staff available, finding or creating worksheets in different languages, and adapting the therapist's language to use phrases that are commonly used in the client's family. Finding ways to match language, whenever possible, will contribute to engagement in treatment as well as treatment progress and outcomes.

Even when the language comprehension is high, concept comprehension can be limited when therapists talk about emotions and the rationale for this module in terms that the client's family does not understand. It can be a valuable use of time to open the module with conversation or activities that will help you understand the orientation of your client and his family toward emotions and mood.

Involving Parents and Caregivers

Given the importance of mood monitoring in the remaining modules, therapists should strongly consider involving parents and caregivers in this module. Since therapists are attempting to help children and teens develop new communication skills regarding their emotions and mood, parents and caregivers can extend the lessons of the therapy session at home and reinforce these new mood-articulation skills. You can include parents and caregivers in every step described in this session. By including them in the conversation, they will also understand the purpose of encouraging emotional communication and mood monitoring.

One topic that would be important to emphasize with parents or caregivers is that when depressed children are confronted with negative emotions, their emotional processing capacity is reduced (Greenberg, 2007). In other words, young people who feel down will have greater difficulty dealing with emotions. Parents and caregivers may be more helpful if they support their children's practice of communicating emotions when they are relatively happy or at times of the day that are less challenging. During homework time or right after school may be when depression is triggered and children will have more trouble discussing their emotions. Teach parents to set their children up for successful practicing at home.

It will also be important to emphasize that parents use appropriate parenting-communication skills when they check in with their children about their feelings. This will include briefly teaching parents about carefully listening for feeling words, reflecting back feelings, and using descriptive or labeled praise. You may decide to introduce these communication topics now during this module. A brief introduction and a quick practice may promote parents' ability to support learning these skills. Therapists can also enlist parents as partners by asking them to model the emotional-awareness and emotional-articulation skills. This will provide support to your clients to further generalize these new skills.

Structuring the Session

Like other modules, the general structure of the first mood-monitoring session is to start with a check-in, a review of homework (from previous modules), setting the agenda, a brief introduction to put the module in context of the broader course of treatment, psychoeducation, skills training with feedback, and discussing next steps. For many therapists, one of the challenges with manualized or structured treatment approaches is being able to effectively structure the session with the essential elements for that session. What if the family is in crisis? What if symptoms have worsened in the past week? Certainly, there are numerous obstacles that could "hijack" the session, and the needs of your client should take a primary role in guiding the session. Providing structure and leadership is an important preliminary step to help clients succeed. Since this module is implemented early in the course of treatment, setting the tone is particularly important in this module. The way you conduct the review (discussing changes since the previous session) and create an agenda will help overcome most barriers to implementing the module effectively. Before the session, the therapist might write the session structure on a dry-erase board or poster.

Example:

- *Check-In and Agenda Setting (5–10 minutes)*

- *Homework Review: Psychoeducation (5 minutes)*

- *Skills Training: Mood Monitoring (20 minutes)*

- *Current Concerns (5–10 minutes)*

- *Assigning Between-Session Practice (5 minutes)*

- *Summary, Feedback, and Next Steps (5 minutes)*

FIRST STEPS

Check-In. Since this module is implemented early in treatment, make sure you are evaluating any crisis or safety risks during check-in. As the therapist, you can guide the session by shining a spotlight on the topics that are important while scaling back emphasis on less relevant topics. Open-ended questions and reflections will help open the conversation while close-ended questions will focus the conversation on specific topics. Alternate between these types of questions to gently steer the check-in toward targeted topics. The key things you might specifically evaluate during the mood-monitoring check-in will include the following:

- Changes in safety or crisis-related needs

- Changes in symptoms since the previous session

- Progress with collateral services

    - Initiating a psychiatric consultation

    - Collaboration with case management

    - Additional services related to the client's treatment

- Changes in medication compliance or dosage

- Engagement in treatment (when needed)

Once you've gathered the essential information, offer a focused summary as a transition to the next topic. You can work on creating the agenda as you move through the check-in by writing key topics on a dry-erase board or asking the client to write the agenda and key topics on a piece of paper.

Agenda Setting. After going through the check-in, you may have already identified key topics that could be discussed. You will also add "learn about mood monitoring," "practice with feedback," and "choice time." Collaboratively, you, the client, and family members will triage the key topics for the session. When therapists transparently discuss the value and rationale for each piece of the agenda, this collaborative process of developing the agenda becomes easier over time.

Any safety risks (i.e., suicidal ideations or attempts) will be triaged to the top of the agenda and should be addressed prior to skills training. Most other topics can be integrated into the session and current module or prioritized after the key elements of the session. Modular CBT is helpful to clients because new skills are developed in a cohesive and thoughtful framework that promotes new learning and behavior change. Postponing key modules and replacing these with ad hoc skills training is like building a roof before you build the walls. The skills may be good skills to learn, but without context they will quickly dissipate and will slow progress in treatment.

Therapist: So we have three things for the agenda: learn about mood monitoring, practice with feedback, and choice time. Alexia, you also mentioned that you wanted to talk about your fight with your friend this week, and Alexia's mom, you would like to talk about Alexia refusing to play with her friends after school. We have forty minutes left in the session. I think talking about getting along with friends and making sure Alexia gets out to play with friends is important. It also seems like both of those might be connected to Alexia feeling sad a lot of the time. We could talk about mood-monitoring skills, but while we learn these new skills, we can figure out how being a friend affects Alexia's feelings. Or we can save the friend topics for the end and decide how much time we have, and Alexia can choose to talk about that for choice time. What do you think works better for each of you?

With this scenario, the therapist can use examples during the skills training to incorporate Alexia's friends or her mother's concerns about Alexia staying at home, which will help them feel that the therapist is responsive to their needs although she will also be helping them progress in treatment. In this way, the therapist is maximizing their time in treatment through skills building.

Homework Review. Reviewing between-session practice or homework from the previous session will let the family know that homework is important for treatment progress. (Conversely, ignoring homework will send an unintended message to the client that homework is not important for treatment.) This is also an important step for reminding and priming the client and her family about topics from the previous week. Whether homework is completed or not completed, it is still worthwhile to review the main themes from the past week and help the client develop a summary about the previous session. If the homework was not completed, take time to investigate and problem solve in the interest of promoting success with homework in the future (not in a punitive way but using a collaborative treatment-success-enhancing tone). It may be important to revisit and practice the skills from the previous session prior to moving on with new themes. If you decide to help the client complete the homework in session before moving forward, let the client and family know you're doing this and why. You'll also be teaching your client that practicing matters and that the assignments really help her crystallize fundamental knowledge or skills prior to progressing further in treatment. You can remind the client of homework success steps (i.e., writing the homework assignment down, asking for help from a family member, receiving a reminder call from the therapist) at the end of this session when you discuss his next homework assignment.

Skills Training

To build a client's capacity for mood monitoring, the following topics are presented in this section: identifying and labeling emotions, distinguishing emotions from thoughts, recognizing the range of emotions, and recognizing emotional intensity. Different children and adolescents will benefit from different interventions. Prior to implementing these interventions, therapists will need to know which topics of awareness and interpretations need most attention.

Providing information regarding mood and emotions is the starting point for mood monitoring. Based on the skills-training activity you choose, the psychoeducation piece can be brief. For example, if you plan to play Emotion Bingo, your client will primarily learn by doing. Also, you may have introduced some of the themes related to emotions and mood in the previous psychoeducation module when discussing the cognitive triangle. The main topics that you want to get across will be based on the client's developmental level, his current understanding, and the information provided in "Preparing the Module." An example script is provided here, tying the information to the cognitive triangle.

Therapist: So, we talked about the cognitive triangle when we were reviewing last week's session. Do you remember? Thoughts lead to what?

Client: Feelings?

Therapist: That's right! Great memory! I can tell you've really learned about the triangle. And who's in charge of thoughts?

Client: Me?

Therapist: Exactly right! What about emotions?

Client: Me?

Therapist: Right again, but it's harder to change emotions than thoughts. If you wanted to think of a pink elephant in a polka-dot bikini right now, you could do it right away. Did you imagine a pink elephant in a polka-dot bikini?

Client: (nods and smiles)

Therapist: So you're really in charge of your thoughts. But if you wanted to feel really happy, that would be a little harder. Our feelings have to do with what we're thinking about the things going on around us and with our actions. Remember, thoughts lead to feelings on the triangle. If you thought about the happiest day you ever had, you'd probably feel pretty happy, relaxed, or supported. If you thought about when your teacher got upset with you, you might feel embarrassed, sad, or frustrated. Today, we're going to learn how to understand emotions and feelings, and then we'll learn how to become a "feelings Jedi," someone who can be in charge of his feelings better. But to become a Jedi, we have to know what we're feeling. The first steps are noticing and talking about feelings. Today, we're going to do an activity to start learning about lots of new feelings and how to keep track of them.

IDENTIFYING AND LABELING EMOTIONS

Interventions for identifying and labeling emotions are focused on developing the client's feelings vocabulary. These interventions are also helpful to develop a trusting relationship. These activities tend to be general and not focused on the client so that he feels comfortable exploring the topics without any pressure. As he becomes comfortable, the therapist can personalize the information more and more.

Feelings Word Race. The Feelings Word Race is a fun way to start talking about emotions and is useful for children and teenagers. The therapist invites the client and family members to write down as many feeling words as they can in two or three minutes. Then, each person takes turns naming one feeling on his or her list and describing what it means to him or her. During the process, the therapist is learning about the client's and family's emotional awareness. You can award points for each word and extra points for listing feelings that other people didn't list.

Emotions Bingo. This game is played just like regular bingo, except an emotion is called out each round (instead of a number or letter), and the therapist can take time to discuss the feeling and its meaning after each feeling is called. This game is better suited for young children. You can add thoughts to the bingo cards, as well as an extra level of complexity by asking players to distinguish feelings from thoughts before they place a marker on their card.

Emotion List. The "Feelings Word List" table, located at the end of this chapter and online at http://www.newharbinger.com/31175, offers a list of emotions that you can use for this intervention. To keep this intervention exciting, you can add dice (the person scoring the highest number gets to pick the next emotion), points for correct answers, extra points for describing situations when the client has felt that way, or a variation of hot potato so that the person left holding the "potato" gets to choose an emotion from the list and describe it. There are countless other ways to make this activity exciting and engaging for children, adolescents, and families. Be sure the emotions listed are appropriate given the developmental level of the child or youth.

DISTINGUISHING EMOTIONS FROM THOUGHTS

Many young people need help understanding the difference between their automatic thoughts and their feelings. This can be a fun opportunity to practice noticing the difference and for clients to show off to family members once they have the difference clear. It is also an opportunity to introduce the idea of automatic thoughts. Eventually, asking your client to teach you or a family member the difference between thoughts and feelings will give you a good sense of his comprehension. The following activities can help a young person clarify the difference if he is struggling with this concept.

Feelings Tower. Using wooden blocks with feelings and thoughts written on them, the therapist can organize the blocks into a tower. With the blocks stacked up, each person can take turns pulling a block from the bottom of the tower and stacking it on top. If the block has a feeling listed on it, the player describes when someone might feel that way. If a thought is on the block, the player describes the accompanying feeling. You can add points for each correct answer and name the winner with the most points when the tower topples over.

Coloring Feelings. The main focus of the coloring-feelings activity is to ask the child to pair colors with feelings. The child or adolescent can then color inside the outline of a face or a body with different feelings based on where he feels those emotions. To make this exercise helpful for distinguishing emotions from thoughts, you can ask the client to describe one to two thoughts that accompany those emotions. One benefit of this type of activity is that many children and teens enjoy using art, especially when they struggle with language skills (J. A. Cohen, Mannarino, & Deblinger, 2006).

RECOGNIZING THE RANGE OF EMOTIONS

Recognizing the range of emotions is an aspect of mood monitoring that is often necessary across ages. It is likely that young people with depression will benefit from learning to expand their emotional range. In addition to using the list of emotions provided in the "Feelings Word List" table, the following activities can help a child or adolescent consider emotions more broadly.

Matching Game. On note cards or sticky notes, write nine emotions that may be commonly experienced but uncommonly acknowledged by your client. On three to nine separate note cards or sticky notes, write brief situations that may trigger the emotions. Describe the emotions to your client. The matching occurs when the client remembers what the emotions mean and matches them with the appropriate situations. You may also leave some situation cards blank and ask your client to put his own situations on the cards. Take turns if you feel your client needs additional help learning the emotions and model the thinking process while you describe it out loud.

Emotionation. Let your client know that he will be practicing using his emotion imagination to make up stories about different kids. Teach your client about one emotion he may commonly experience but uncommonly acknowledge. Once you have described the emotion, ask your client to create a story about a kid who would feel that way. Take turns for as many new emotion words as you would like your client to understand.

RECOGNIZING EMOTIONAL INTENSITY

The main idea for this section is to teach that we experience different levels of a feeling at different times, also known as scaling. Scaling is an essential part of mood monitoring, and we recommend teaching some form of this in your module. This way of communication is easy to learn and easy to implement in the context of a family and will help you communicate with your client in the future. It is a crucial step in treatment and should lead your client and his family to start communicating about emotions by labeling and scaling.

Feeling Thermometer. The feeling thermometer is the most well-known tool therapists use for helping kids recognize, understand, and communicate their feelings. Part of the reason it is so well known is that it is also a lot of fun and easy to understand. Show your client a visual thermometer (see the "Feeling Thermometer" figure at the end of this chapter, as well as the full-color version available online at http://www .newharbinger.com/31175) or help your client draw one that he can take home, and describe how the thermometer can be used. (The same activity can be done with an emotion ladder, which will be discussed in greater depth in the affect regulation module in chapter 10; a worksheet for this is also available at http://www.newharbin ger.com/31175.)

Therapist:	How did you feel when your mom said you couldn't visit your dad last night?
Client:	Mad.
Therapist:	Great job telling me a feeling word about how you felt! Now, I have one piece of the picture, but I need one more piece to really understand you. I want to really know how mad you were feeling. Using the one-to-ten scale on the thermometer [or "green-and-red," if using the full-color version available online], how mad were you when you found out you couldn't visit your dad?
Client:	Nine, I think.
Therapist:	Wow. A nine? That's almost the most mad you've ever been. Is that right—almost the maddest you've ever been?

Client: (nods)

Therapist: I really like how you're sharing your emotions right now. I'd bet you're not quite as mad as you were last night, but you're still probably upset now that we're remembering it. How mad are you right now talking about it?

Client: Like a seven.

Therapist: Wow. You've gone down two points. You're still more than halfway but not as mad as last night. What do you think would make you feel a two or three…or even a one? How mad were you before we started talking about it (when you weren't thinking about it)?

When using the thermometer, we suggest keeping it simple and sticking to a one-to-ten scale. Teenagers may use half points or decimals and young children may prefer using colors (green, yellow, orange, red), but in either case you are using the same core message.

Some children and youth will have trouble using the full one-to-ten scale. They will only use extreme numbers (one and ten, or one, ten, and five). Keep alert for this and make sure you give examples that encourage use of the middle sections of the thermometer. You can help some children and teens grasp the idea with anchoring (i.e., What would a ten or a one look like?) or drawing out examples for lesser used parts (i.e., When might you feel happy at a three? How about angry at a seven?), or you can create a thermometer with personal experiences for the child's life filled in for each level so your client is clear on the varying degrees in different situations.

There are alternative metaphors to communicate the concept of a range or scale, and these may work better than a thermometer. For example, a therapist might find that using a speedometer with a child who is fascinated with cars gets the message across just as well if not better. We encourage you to use your creativity if you choose to use a different way of teaching about scaling. If clients or families understand and grasp the idea, you've introduced it successfully. If they don't, try to identify some adjustments to help make the message clearer.

Between-Session Practice

After practicing affect awareness and articulation in the session, therapists should have had an opportunity to gauge their client's progress with the new skills. We suggest practicing several times, starting with less emotionally charged topics and working up to more challenging emotional themes. After twenty to thirty minutes of practice with your feedback, most young people will be ready to practice further without your guidance. To master this new skill, your client will need to be able to demonstrate self-directed affect awareness and articulation, and be able to monitor his mood. Between-session practices will start your client on a path of practicing these skills without reminders, guidance, or immediate feedback. That is a lot to tackle, and it might take more than one session (maybe even several sessions depending on the child's level of attunement with emotions). Recognize your client's efforts and strengths, and set your client up for success in the upcoming weeks. Find out what he thinks is doable, develop strategies to help him remember, and identify support people who can offer guidance. Remind your client that in order to really learn the skill, it takes practice, practice, practice. In general, find solutions and help your client plan so he takes advantage of the time between sessions. Some therapists like to use metaphors to drive the point home.

Therapist: If I go to the gym and lift weights one time, am I going to be buff? No way, José! How many times do I have to go to the gym?

The standard homework assignment for the mood monitoring module is to complete a mood log for the week (see the "Mood-Monitoring Tracking Sheet" at the end of this chapter or in downloadable form at http://www.newharbinger.com/31175). The mood-monitoring log asks the client to describe the affect he notices once to several times during the day and to use the feeling thermometer to articulate the degree that he experienced the affect. Some therapists also ask about hours of sleep, time of day for the emotion, and how long the emotion lasted to help understand their clients better and to prime clients to look for cues for their emotions in the environment. This can help clients understand that their mood is modifiable and potentially in their control based on their existing skills and insight.

At first, you might just get a baseline and let your client notice whatever emotions he notices. After he shows the ability to do that, start to guide him toward acknowledging and articulating negative and positive affects accurately. It is important to eventually focus on affects that the client tends to misinterpret or misattribute. Part of mood monitoring for your client is experiencing positive emotions accurately as well.

While discussing homework or between-session practice with your client, you can also assign a task for your client's parents or caregivers. This can include playing one of the games you used in the session during the week, or practicing using the feeling thermometer with the child three to five times during the week or one to two times each day. You can ask them to support or help their child complete the mood-monitoring log on a regular basis (either by helping complete it or by having a periodic discussion about what their child has completed). Another joint homework assignment is to have caregivers or parents to ask your client to teach them or the family about the feeling thermometer and provide praise for the pieces he remembers.

Using Tools to Help Build Skills

There are several mobile apps and online resources to help with mood monitoring. Mood-tracking apps in particular are helpful for teenagers because of their quick access, reminders, and interactive interface. If your client or the client's parent has a smartphone, you can suggest he uses reminders or operating system assistants to remind him to "talk about emotions for five minutes on Wednesday when we get home from school." Social media can also be helpful in planning for between-session practices. Your client can take advantage of video or instant chat to articulate emotions to a family member or can send a photo of his mood-tracking chart to a peer or family member. This is an opportunity for therapists to think creatively about using technology to support skill building in a way that overlaps with a client's typical day-to-day activities.

Summary, Feedback, and Next Steps

At the conclusion of the session, take a moment to ask your client about his goals for the week, how he would like to feel in terms of emotions or mood, what he would like to accomplish with his between-session practice, and what his expectations are for practicing and mastering the new skills. You can ask the parents or caregiver similar questions if you've assigned homework to practice. Also, ask about what topics stood out to your client, what was new information, and what he already knew. It can be very useful to ask what he liked about the session and what he would change for the next session.

Before moving forward to another module, help your client know that he will need to master the skill of mood monitoring so the other skills can be helpful. Encourage your client to take ownership of mastering mood monitoring and of progressing in treatment. Help link the topics and skills from this module to the overall goals he has for being in therapy and the things he would like to see changed in his life in terms of his mood.

Common Hurdles and Solutions for Therapists

Commonly, clients underestimate the value of mood monitoring while overestimating their existing mood-monitoring abilities. Because of this combination, a hurdle therapists may encounter during this module is getting clients to "buy in" to mood monitoring. Nonetheless, superficial mastery of the skills presented in this module will likely lead to problems later in treatment. An important step that will help therapist and client overcome this potential hurdle is the therapist's approach to the module. Therapists can view this module as an essential step along the pathway to successful treatment. Many clients will have significant limitations in their capacity for monitoring their moods; all clients will benefit from improving their ability to monitor their moods.

Therapists should anticipate the familiarity of the themes presented in this module but simultaneously communicate to the client and his family that there is a real need for improved ability to monitor his mood. With an open and instructive approach, the therapist can let the client know that she expects to help the client experience meaningful changes during this module. Sometimes clients will briefly stall in this module by skipping homework. Even if clients demonstrate limited commitment, the therapist should maintain an attitude that mastery of mood monitoring is essential for moving forward. "Go slow early to go fast later" can be your motto. Take time to show your client that only a genuine approach to developing mood-monitoring skills will lead to change and help him move forward. As the therapist, you are setting the tone for how much these skills matter. You can draw from the engagement strategies in chapter 12 if clients continue to appear resistant during this module.

Summary

Your client's ability to understand and communicate his mood builds on the psycho-education module and lays a foundation for the remaining modules. The mood-monitoring link in the modular CBT chain serves several important purposes—including helping you know whether your client feels his mood is changing during the remainder of treatment. As you help your client make progress through treatment, help him monitor this change and notice the positive deposits he's making into his mood bank account. Help him exercise this new skill by understanding and noticing his mood with each step of treatment.

Feelings Word List

Positive Feelings

friendly	understood	patient	warm
at ease	enchanted	strong	amused
relaxed	capable	inspired	cozy
comfortable	happy	peaceful	interested
content	sympathetic	appealing	liked
keen	optimistic	determined	cared for
alert	hopeful	pleased	esteemed
sure	brave	relieved	affectionate
approved	loved	glad	fond
untroubled	empathic	calm	excited

Challenging Feelings

moody	envious	resentful	unloved
gloomy	unhappy	bitter	angry
dismal	bored	fed up	hurt
grouchy	disappointed	frustrated	lonely
tired	inadequate	sad	cynical
indifferent	helpless	depressed	worthless
unsure	resigned	sick	abandoned
impatient	shy	fatigued	degraded
dependent	uncomfortable	worn-out	humiliated
unimportant	baffled	useless	panicky
regretful	confused	weak	trapped
bashful	nervous	hopeless	horrified
puzzled	tense	rejected	afraid
self-conscious	worried	guilty	scared
edgy	perplexed	embarrassed	exhausted

Downloadable copies of this resource are available online at http://www.newharbin ger.com/31175. (See the very back of this book for more details.)

Feeling Thermometer

A full-color version of this image can be downloaded online at http://www.newhar binger.com/31175. (See the very back of this book for more details.)

Mood Monitoring

Mood-Monitoring Tracking Sheet

	Monday	Tuesday	Wednesday	Thursday	Friday	Saturday	Sunday
What was the feeling?							
How strong was the feeling? (Intensity rating)							
What time of day (morning, lunchtime, afternoon, night)?							
How long did you feel that way?							

Downloadable copies of this form are available online at http://www.newharbinger.com/31175. (See the very back of this book for more details.)

85

Chapter 6

Behavioral Activation

For many physical health conditions, one of the oft prescribed treatments is physical activity, such as walking. If you wander into any given maternity ward, you will no doubt find laboring women walking up and down the hallways in an effort to progress the labor to delivery mode. On the postsurgery hospital floor, colorectomy patients are encouraged to walk the hallways in order to reactivate their digestive system. Overweight individuals are advised by their medical doctors to take active walks daily. In schools, some administrators have set up morning running clubs because of the data supporting that physical activity helps students to concentrate better in the classroom.

With depression, it is no different. Common manifestations of depression are lethargy, fatigue, and a low level of energy, and one of the most effective ways to target those symptoms is to elicit behavioral activation from the child or adolescent. While walking is a popular form of behavioral activation, there are a plethora of options that can be individualized to the client (e.g., playing basketball, going swimming, meeting friends at the park). The role of behavioral activation should not be understated; some researchers propose that it is an active ingredient for change in cognitive behavioral therapy. A study analyzing components of cognitive behavioral therapy found that the behavioral-activation component of cognitive behavioral therapy resulted in significant improvement in alleviating depressive symptoms and reduced relapse rates over a two-week follow-up (Gortner, Gollan, Dobson, & Jacobson, 1998; Jacobson et al., 1996). A follow-up randomized trial study compared behavioral activation, cognitive therapy, and antidepressant medication to a pill placebo in treating depression and found that behavioral activation was comparable to antidepressant medication in reducing initial acute distress (Dimidjian et al., 2006). Importantly, behavioral activation was found to be particularly effective with individuals with severe depression. Given this compelling support for the impact of behavioral activation on depressive symptoms, this module offers powerful tools for children and adolescents struggling with depression.

Behavioral activation has its roots in operant conditioning. When individuals avoid and escape certain activities (e.g., social activities), they are less likely to be rewarded throughout the day for engaging in productive activities (Ferster, 1973). According to this behavioral model, individuals may develop depression because they do not experience response-contingent positive reinforcement throughout their daily lives (Lewinsohn, 1974). For instance, a teenager attends dance class but is rarely given praise or encouragement (response-contingent positive reinforcement) by the teacher. Over time, lack of reinforcement may result in behavioral deactivation: the teenager stops attending the dance class due to the lack of positive reinforcement. The behavioral deactivation may generalize and could result in the teenager avoiding other activities as well. With the continued behavioral deactivation and lessened reinforcement, the individual may eventually experience depression due to the absence of reinforcers. In the behavioral activation model, when individuals avoid distressful situations (e.g., classes, tests, social events), the avoidance may allow the child to escape distress in the short term, but then it also inadvertently results in the child not experiencing mood-lifting environment reinforcers (e.g., praise from a teacher, good grade on a test, laughing with a peer). As the child continues to avoid school and social activities, she may experience new problems such as increased conflict at home, problems with completing schoolwork, and feeling isolated. The behavioral activation model attempts to break this cycle by assigning activities that directly target the function of the avoidance behaviors (Dimidjian et al., 2006). In cognitive behavioral therapy, behavioral activation is mainly achieved by monitoring weekly activities and scheduling pleasant ones (Lewinsohn, 1974). The primary goal of behavioral activation is to enable the individual to act in ways that are reinforcing, in order to increase the likelihood that she will continue to engage in those rewarding activities.

Preparing the Module

Clinical Rationale for Module

Depressed children and adolescents tend to avoid school and social activities and become isolated at home. Because these behaviors tend to contribute to continued depression, this module prepares you to help your client become more behaviorally activated. The clinical purpose of this module is to immediately change this status quo by assigning pleasant activities that help youth become less isolated and more active. This allows the depressed child to experience positive reinforcement and, ultimately, interrupt the cycle of inactivity and depression. Eventually, the reinforcing cycle may be self-perpetuated: By participating in activities with reinforcement that are meaningful to the child (e.g., encouragement, praise, intrinsic reward), the child becomes more willing to engage in the behavior. Thus, these positive behaviors are likely to gain traction and continue without therapist guidance.

Clinical Snapshot: Chiara

Chiara is a twelve-year-old African-American female who presents with depressive symptoms. She used to enjoy participating in drama camp, dance classes, and after-school activities at the Boys and Girls Club. For the past several months, Chiara has gradually withdrawn from these extracurricular activities.

Chiara's parents have become increasingly concerned that Chiara spends much of her time at home in her room. Although she continues to do a minimal amount of chores, Chiara no longer dances or engages in any physical activity. She endorses feeling tired and listless much of the time. She reports, "Drama camp and dance classes just aren't fun anymore. I used to like to do those things, but now I'd rather just stay home watching TV."

In therapy, Chiara acknowledged that she has stayed at home and avoided drama camp and dance classes for so many months that she is now anxious about returning to the activities. She stated, "It's just easier to sit on the couch and check out. I don't have to get dressed to go anywhere. But now I have thoughts that if I did go back to drama camp, I'd be terrible at it and everyone would laugh. Then I feel even worse about myself."

Individually Tailoring the Module

In cognitive behavioral therapy, behavioral activation is mainly achieved by scheduling pleasant activities and monitoring weekly activities. Because children develop and become increasingly independent from their parents, peer relationships and school-related interactions take on a more prominent role in their lives. For adolescents, the quality of peer interactions (and lack thereof) often significantly impact their general mood. Thus, in working with adolescents, the clinician should emphasize socially oriented activities when scheduling pleasant activities for behavioral activation. Special care should be taken to obtain parent input as some activities may not be logistically or financially possible for the family. For instance, a child may identify riding a bicycle to the park as a pleasant activity, but the parents may not be able to afford a bike or the family may live in an unsafe, high-crime neighborhood. Furthermore, it may be helpful to consider strength-based activities for the child or adolescent when identifying pleasant activities. For instance, assigning sports activities for an athletic child may be strength-based and a good fit for her, but not for a clumsy child who is inexperienced in sports. Therefore, behavioral activation requires identifying activities that are feasible and likely to actually reinforce the child or adolescent.

Using the Module

Equipped with the information from the "Preparing the Module" section, the various pieces of this module should be purposeful and feel cohesive with the other modules for your client. Ultimately, your goals with this module are to help your client develop active and effective engagement in pleasant or social activities, as well as identify the impact of experiences on thoughts and feelings.

When to Use the Module

Based on the clinical research literature, behavioral activation should occur early in treatment and before cognitive-restructuring work. This module may be particularly helpful for children and adolescents who are moderately or severely depressed. Unless clinically indicated otherwise, it is recommended that the psychoeducation and mood monitoring modules are delivered prior to the behavioral activation module.

Cultural Considerations

Clinicians should also take into consideration culturally specific issues, which can be done by checking in with the parents. It is important to assess their cultural expectations of the child's behaviors. For instance, the family may value or prefer the adolescent to spend time at home reading books. They may be reluctant to schedule outdoor activities because it's not commonly done in their family or culture. These familial or cultural expectations should be addressed early during the first session of this module; it may be necessary to adapt and individualize the behavioral activation based on these cultural expectations. For instance, in the above example, the adolescent may be encouraged to join a book club rather than a sports team.

Involving Parents and Caregivers

In order to maximize your success in helping the child develop an effective list of pleasant activities, it is essential to talk with the parent separately before meeting with the client. The clinician should collaborate with the parents on their preferred activities for their child, as well as any limitations or barriers that they may have with regard to specific activities. Armed with this information, you will be in a well-informed position to guide the child or adolescent in identifying pleasant activities. Because behavioral activation often requires active support or action from parents, it is particularly important in this module to take special consideration in explaining the rationale for behavioral activation. Oftentimes, depressed children and adolescents exhibit their depression with irritable mood, which may frequently lead to conflict with their parents and other family members. Thus, parents may have initiated restrictions on their child in response to her misbehaviors. For instance, depressed twelve-year-old Joe is very irritable and spends much of his free time in his room watching television. Because he doesn't do his chores or finish all of his homework, his parents have placed privilege restrictions on him (e.g., he is not allowed to go out with friends). Unless the clinician takes the necessary time and effort to explain the rationale for behavioral activation and collaborate actively with the parents, the parents may view the clinician's assignment of pleasant activities to the child as contrary to their disciplinary attempts. In other situations, the child may be seen as a problem child or scapegoated for a variety of reasons.

Without the parents' engagement and collaboration, the child may not be able to follow through on the assigned pleasant activities or the parents may have trouble supporting their child. Thus, it is critical that the clinician makes a special effort to meet with the parents separately, fully explain the rationale for behavioral activation, address any of their concerns about the activities, and collaborate in identifying appropriate activities that they can support the child engaging in as part of behavioral activation.

The discussion with the parents may be completed via telephone before your scheduled therapy session or in person immediately before your session with the child. Your case conceptualization will help guide the manner in which you collaborate with the parents. For instance, if you have an adolescent with a conflictual relationship with her parents, she may resent that you are meeting with them first before meeting with her. This may result in a negative impact on your therapeutic alliance with the adolescent. Thus, in this scenario, it may be preferable to speak with the parents on the phone before the day of the therapy session in order to obtain the needed information. Use your clinical judgment and the information you gathered through the intake assessment to develop a plan that will effectively include the parents to support the success of this module.

In addition to the identification of pleasant activities, parents, caregivers, and other important individuals (e.g., teachers, peers, siblings) may also serve to help the adolescent successfully engage in the behavioral activation. Because a depressed adolescent's motivation tends to be very low, it is often helpful to have a parent or close peer "scaffold" the adolescent's behavioral activation efforts. For instance, a parent may pick up the adolescent from home to drive her to the beach for a sunset walk. A close peer may drop by the adolescent's home to work on an after-school project together. A sibling may look up movie times and accompany the adolescent to a Saturday night movie viewing. Although the adolescent's motivation may have been very low at the beginning, as she participates in these activities that were initiated by others, she may find herself enjoying the activities, which then serves as a reinforcer for the activities.

Structuring the Session

Before each session, the clinician should write the session structure on a dry-erase board or poster. For some children, it may be helpful to have a timer for each section.

Example:

- *Check-In and Agenda Setting (5–10 minutes)*

- *Homework Review: Mood Monitoring (5 minutes)*

- *Skills Training: Pleasant Activities (20 minutes)*

- *Current Concerns (5–10 minutes)*

- *Assigning Between-Session Practice (5 minutes)*

- *Summary, Feedback, and Next Steps (5 minutes)*

First Steps

Check-In. The first few minutes of the session may be spent checking in with the child. Refer to the dry-erase board and prime the client for the session structure.

Therapist: As you can see on the dry-erase board, we will be checking in on how you've been doing, reviewing how the mood charting has been going for you, and then talking about how to schedule pleasant activities. Now, how are things going for you this week? Are there certain things that you'd like to make sure that we talk about today?

Agenda Setting. Any concerns or situations that were brought up during the check-in process may be placed on the agenda for later discussion. These may be issues or situations that may have arisen over the past week (sometimes known as the "crisis of the week"). The problem of discussing these issues and situations at the beginning of the session is that these concerns may then end up taking much of the therapy session time; thereby, the child or adolescent may then lose out on the skills-training component of the session. These issues should be tabled to the current concerns section of the session. The exception is if the current concern may be used as part of an example in the skills-training portion of the therapy session.

Therapist: You may remember from last week that we will be setting the agenda at the beginning of every session. You mentioned that you got into a fight with your mother—would you like to put that on the agenda for discussion?

Homework Review. The next few minutes should be spent reviewing the client's homework assignment from the previous session. It's important to hold the child or adolescent accountable by checking in with her regarding whether she has completed her therapy homework. One of the best predictors of whether a client will follow through with her therapy homework assignments is if the therapist follows up with her about them and holds her accountable. If the adolescent did not complete her homework assignment, then it is recommended that you spend a little time at this point in the session to help the client complete her homework assignment. You may also engage the client in problem solving to overcome her barriers to completing future homework assignments. For instance, if the client did not complete her mood-monitoring charts because she lost the worksheet, you and the adolescent may problem solve and agree to have her input her mood ratings on her smartphone instead. You may even help her to choose an app that is appealing to her.

Provide Children and Teens with a Behavioral Activation Rationale

One clear method to describe the patterns and consequences that emerge from behavioral withdrawal and depression is with the cognitive triangle. Start by reminding the client of the CBT principles introduced in the psychoeducation module. Explain, or ask the child to help explain, the definitions of thoughts, feelings, and actions. Provide examples along the way or use examples from previous modules or successes in therapy. Follow the definitions by describing the relationship between thoughts, feelings, and actions (sometimes drawing arrows between the points of the triangle helps at this point). Be sure to explain how when people feel sad, they tend to withdraw from activities that they normally enjoy. A consequence of this behavioral withdrawal is a worsening of their depressed mood as they spend their days avoiding enjoyable activities and socially isolating. And one of the most effective ways to boost their mood is to engage in a pleasant and enjoyable activity in order to break the cycle.

With this introduction or review complete, choose an example or issue that was discovered during the assessment or that the client previously brought up. The more important and individualized this issue is to the client, the more engaged she will be in the intervention. Take time to encourage your client to describe why the issue is a problem or how she would like the issue to be different. Prior to completing the rationale portion of the session, switch seats with the client and ask her to teach you about the triangle with an example. Use lots of descriptive praise, enthusiasm, and support; help her if she gets stuck.

This approach has several benefits:

- The child has an opportunity to gain mastery over the core material (in cognitive triangle) that will contribute to all modules.

- The therapist has an opportunity to further assess automatic thoughts by drawing examples from the client.

- If you use the cognitive triangle for further cognitive restructuring, you've already completed the first step.

Skills Training

Didactic. Using your case conceptualization and the information provided in this chapter, explain the individualized rationale for behavioral activation with your client. The following example is for a child who has already developed mood-monitoring skills and is moving on to behavioral activation.

Therapist: You have already been practicing how to rate your moods and record them using the feeling thermometer. Today, we'll be learning how to do something that is just as important. When people feel depressed, what do they tend to do?

Client: They cry. They want to be left alone.

Therapist: Yes, they tend to stay at home and do very little. Sometimes they stay in their room alone and feel even more down because they're not talking to any friends. They feel lonely. One of the best ways to not feel lonely is to go out and do something, like talk with friends, go to the movies, or play at the park. When you force yourself to go out and do something, you are likely to feel less lonely. You may even find yourself enjoying the activity and that it lifts your mood. Now, let's think about activities that you might enjoy doing. What are some things you used to do before you felt depressed?

Modeling. When the child is moderately or severely depressed, she may have a particularly difficult time thinking of any enjoyable activity. One effective tool the clinician may use—frequently throughout all of the modules, but especially in this one—is modeling. In the behavioral activation module, you may use modeling by identifying potential pleasant activities for yourself. It is helpful to be explicit in your thought process.

Therapist: In trying to think of pleasant activities that I could do, I want to think of something that doesn't cost a lot of money. You know, I used to play tennis a long time ago. I haven't done it in a while, but I think it might be fun to try again. There's a tennis court in my neighborhood, and it's free to play there. Another idea is taking an art class again. There's a free art class at the school, and I can check online to see if there's any availability at this time. What about you? Let's come up with a list of possible activities that you might be able to do for your pleasant activity schedule. What did you used to do for fun? Let's see if we can brainstorm different ideas together.

Given that you've already spoken with the child's parents before this session, you may already have some well-informed ideas of activities that the child may enjoy. If the child has difficulty identifying activities because of her depression, you may provide prompts by suggesting the activities that were previously identified by her parents.

In collaborating with the child or adolescent on developing a list of activities, keep in mind that there are three types of activities that should be represented on the list. First, there are routine activities, such as grooming, bathing, getting dressed, checking e-mail, cooking meals, and making the bed. Second, there are goal-oriented activities, such as doing homework, reading a book, working on a project, and hiking a trail. Finally, the third type of activity that should be highlighted is socially oriented tasks, such as going to the movies with a friend, texting a friend, going out to dinner with the family, and playing a sports game with friends. See the "Brainstorming List of Pleasant Activities" worksheet at the end of this chapter and online at http://www .newharbinger.com/31175.

Therapist: I noticed that all the activities on your list are routine daily activities. These are great activities to include on your weekly schedule! Let's also think about other types of activities. For example, social activities like going to the movies, instagramming, or playing ball with a friend may help you feel less lonely. And goal-oriented activities, like finishing a project or walking a mile, may help you feel good about yourself. Can you think of any social or goal-oriented activities to add to your list?

Role-Play with Feedback. After identifying a list of at least ten potential pleasant activities, review the list together and discuss potential barriers for the different activities. Rank the activities in order of ease and motivation. Select one of the highly ranked activities to role-play with the child. For instance, a child may have identified talking with a friend as a potential activity, but also identified being shy as a barrier. Role-plays should always begin with the therapist modeling the behavior; then the roles are switched and the child practices the behavior. The clinician should always provide praise as well as any needed corrective feedback. Role-playing will also give the client an opportunity to begin thinking through how she will actually make this behavior happen. Your client can start to envision doing this behavior (similar to imaginal exposure) as she develops a plan for how this behavior could happen and how to overcome possible roadblocks.

Therapist: Okay, let's role-play the activity of talking to a friend on the phone. I'll go first, and then we'll switch and you can practice calling me… That was an excellent job of practicing a phone call with a friend! Another way of starting the call is to ask your friend if this is a good time to talk. You can then ask her if she did anything fun over the weekend.

Between-Session Practice

Weekly Schedule. Guide the adolescent in choosing a variety of routine, goal-oriented, and social activities. Once you have a substantial, agreed-upon list of activities, collaborate with the client in scheduling the activities into a weekly planner. A blank "Weekly Schedule: Scheduling Pleasant Activities" worksheet is available at the end of the chapter and for download at http://www.newharbinger.com/31175. If the adolescent has a smartphone or tablet where she can schedule her pleasant activities, encourage her to do so; many children in this technology-driven environment may prefer to use electronic methods. For some children, you may need to type up a schedule to print and have them hang up in their room. Other children may prefer the weekly schedule worksheet, which they can put in their backpack. The medium of the method is flexible and should be based on the client's preference. The primary point here is to have the client follow through on the assigned activities and record the information somewhere. The following is an example of one type of weekly schedule.

	Monday	Tuesday	Wednesday	Thursday	Friday	Saturday	Sunday
Morning	Shower	Walk to school	Talk to Jill	Text a friend	Morning walk	Call or text a friend	Cook breakfast
Afternoon	Go to park	Text a friend	Walk the dog	Sit with friend at lunch	Work on school project	Write in journal	Hiking with Mom
Evening	Walking	Play basketball	Finish science project	Walking	Play basketball	Go to movies with a friend	Watch show with family

Summary, Feedback, and Next Steps

Have the client summarize the session highlights to you. If this is one of your earliest modules, then it may be beneficial to model this summarizing for your client.

Therapist: Today, we worked on coming up with a list of pleasant activities. We've decided which ones were easier to do and have scheduled them for the upcoming week.

Ask the client for feedback regarding the session. This feedback allows you to know what is working in real time and what is not working as well. You may use this information to improve your subsequent sessions.

Therapist: How do you think today's session went? What worked well for you? What do you think was least helpful?

The final step to the session is to prime the client for the next steps in therapy. You may be covering behavioral activation again in the next session, or you may be moving on to another module. It is helpful to prime the child as to which next step is likely.

Therapist: Okay, so we just covered behavioral activation and the importance of doing pleasant activities. I know this area is particularly challenging, so we will be talking about it again at the next session. Do you have any questions?

Common Hurdles and Solutions for Therapists

The most common hurdle in behavioral activation is that clients often feel fatigued, feel lethargic, and have low energy; they believe they don't have the energy to participate in the assigned pleasant activity. Anhedonia (loss of interest in pleasurable activities), which is another depression symptom, may make it difficult for the child or adolescent to identify any activity she deems pleasant. This is when therapists may benefit from becoming much more directive in their session. You can highlight the rationale for why behavioral activation helps the child feel better, but because the child has anhedonia, you may need to be very directive in developing the weekly schedule and essentially *assign* your client the task of following the schedule. The child may not have any "buy-in," but as she completes her therapy assignment of following the schedule, she may find that her mood has been positively affected.

Summary

Because depressed children and adolescents tend to have anhedonia, they may withdraw from many pleasant and daily activities. This may result in a socially isolated adolescent who remains at home and doesn't experience any behavioral reinforcement that may help improve her mood. This module focused on behaviorally activating the child, with goal-oriented and socially oriented activities and a focus on pleasant activities. You may see an observable improvement in the child's mood as she increases her behavioral activation.

Brainstorming List of Pleasant Activities

Routine Activities	Goal-Oriented Activities	Socially Oriented Activities
Example: Taking a shower	*Example: Completing homework*	*Example: Texting with a friend*

Downloadable copies of this form are available online at http://www.newharbinger .com/31175. (See the very back of this book for more details.)

Weekly Schedule: Scheduling Pleasant Activities

	Monday	Tuesday	Wednesday	Thursday	Friday	Saturday	Sunday
Morning							
Midday							
Afternoon							
Evening							
Night							

Chapter 7

Addressing Maladaptive Cognitions

Red taillights reflect off your face as you wait at a stoplight; a bumper sticker glares back at you: "Don't believe everything you think." Normally, bumper stickers aren't fantastic fountains of insight, but this time the sticker may have a point. How often do you jump to conclusions about what other people are thinking? Have you told yourself, "I'm never going to figure it out!" but later discovered your fortune-telling skills were shaky that day? How many times after making a mistake have you amplified the error by telling yourself, "I'm so stupid!" only to realize that particular mistake was a stepping stone on the path to finding a solution?

Of course, we've all experienced these thinking errors, probably hundreds of times. It's clear these maladaptive thoughts often lead to negative outcomes. For depressed children and teens, maladaptive thinking becomes the lens through which they see and understand the world around them. From a CBT framework your clients can do something about it, and if they do, they reduce unnecessary difficulties in their lives. The bumper sticker phrase "Don't believe everything you think" invites two important questions: Which thoughts should we not believe? And how do we change those thoughts?

In preparation for using this module, and as you read this chapter, we encourage you to critically identify ways in which we all stumble on the maladaptive cognitions in our paths. Examples of maladaptive thoughts are common in your life and the lives of others around you. Thoughtfully understanding the pervasive and common impact of maladaptive cognitions in all of our lives will help you notice and intervene with your clients in meaningful ways.

Preparing the Module

Background

While developing cognitive therapy, Aaron T. Beck came across an interesting finding in his research and clinical work with depressed patients. Although many professionals believed emotional problems led to thinking deficits for depressed individuals, Beck believed depression was actually driven by thinking deficits. After interviews with fifty depressed patients and thirty-one nondepressed patients, he concluded that depressed individuals were uniquely prone to low self-regard, self-criticism, self-blame, overwhelming reactions to problems and duties, persistent self-commands and injunctions, and escapist and suicidal wishes (A. T. Beck, 1976). From these conclusions, Beck formed a fundamental premise of CBT: depression is evoked by maladaptive and erroneous thoughts. On the shoulders of this cognitive theme identified by Beck in the 1970s, understanding of maladaptive cognitions has expanded, and different types of cognitive distortions have been identified and used to help hundreds of thousands of individuals treated through CBT-based interventions.

To help prepare you to use this module, in this background section we discuss what maladaptive cognitions are, specifically for children and teens, as well as the role of maladaptive thoughts in the development of depression. We also cover how to elicit and identify maladaptive cognitions. In the "Using the Module" section we will discuss how to intervene and address maladaptive thoughts and support the success of the overall modular CBT approach.

It has been widely demonstrated that children and teenagers with emotional and behavioral problems experience persistent negative thinking about the self (Kendall & Braswell, 1993). For depressed kids, this thinking extends into thoughts about school performance, social and peer interactions, family relationships, self-worth, and confidence. Therapists will notice irrational guilt about the past and exaggerated or unrealistic worries about the future (Birmaher et al., 2007; Hammen, Rudolph, Weisz, Rao, & Burge, 1999; Rao & Chen, 2009). These thoughts are maladaptive because instead of being encouraged to try harder next time, give it another shot, or learn from his mistakes, the youth gives up, internalizes a negative self-image, or responds with sadness or agitation.

To be concise, maladaptive cognitions are thoughts that contribute to the presenting problem. For depressed people, these types of thoughts tend to be exaggerated or irrational negative ideas about the self, world, or future. From the start of treatment, CBT therapists are taking note of the influence of thoughts on the client's feelings and behaviors and specific comments that point toward maladaptive cognitions. Therapists will keep an open ear for amplified, irrational, or other distorted concepts in the client's language. Similarly, therapists will be attuned to persistent maladaptive messages in the client's life based on common parent, caregiver, or family messages (which are likely internalized by the young person).

Because cognitions are not directly observable by therapists, it is important that therapists find ways to attend to the internal experiences of their clients. Helping your clients address maladaptive cognitions requires an understanding of your client's thoughts. The best connection to a child's thoughts is language. Probing, open-ended questions paired with empathic affirmations, reflections, and summaries will be the first line of accessing your client's internal experiences. When clients feel understood without judgment, they typically feel more open to verbal expression.

Some depressed children are very shy or use language minimally. In these instances, writing or art projects may help elicit increased discussion about a client's internal experiences. Incomplete sentence blanks may be helpful in starting conversations. Providing a client with a prompt of several sentences about himself may be helpful. Give your client ten minutes to fill out an incomplete sentence blank form and then review each sentence with him. This may provide rich information about the way your client thinks and interprets the world around him. Some example prompts are provided in the "Incomplete Sentence Blanks" exercise, which is also available for download at http://www.newharbinger.com/31175.

Incomplete Sentence Blanks

Example Prompts:

- I am...

- I often think...

- I like that...

- Sometimes I worry...

- People think I'm...

- The worst thing...

- I'm embarrassed that...

- The best thing...

- Other kids think I'm...

- I don't like...

- I believe...

- Nobody knows that...

- My mom thinks I'm...

- I don't like to tell people that...

- It's hard to...

Other ways to understand your client's cognitions include through art or collages. When verbal expression limits a therapist's understanding of a client's cognitions, the therapist can ask the client to create art that "tells me something about you" during the session or as homework. The therapist should let the client know in advance that the goal of the art is to understand his thoughts and prepare the client to talk a little about what he creates.

Once you are able to elicit expression of your client's internal experiences, you can start to consider cognitive errors that he experiences. Be familiar with the common thinking errors that accompany depressed youth so you know what to look for. Below we provide a list of common thinking errors and cognitive distortions that can often be maladaptive and may contribute to depression. Note that each of us makes thinking errors hundreds, if not thousands, of times per week. Cognitive distortions are common in depressed and nondepressed individuals. We focus on these in treatment of depression because these distorted thoughts occur more frequently, more persistently, and more strongly for depressed individuals. The commonness of cognitive distortions, however, is a benefit to you as a therapist. The concept of cognitive distortions will make intuitive sense to family members, clients, and others involved in the child's treatment. Hopefully, you will also notice ways that you make thinking errors from time to time. Take advantage of the familiarity of this theme to talk about it with your clients and their families. If it resonates with you, you will be able to teach it to your clients in a more meaningful way. If your clients' parents are aware of their own cognitive distortions, they can help identify maladaptive thoughts within the family and at home.

The following list was built upon Aaron T. Beck's (1976) work on depression and associated cognitions, and the popular list of cognitive distortions from David Burns's (1989) anxiety and depression handbook for adults titled *The Feeling Good Handbook: Using the New Mood Therapy in Everyday Life*. It is provided to give therapists an in-depth understanding of cognitive distortions. A simplified version of this list will be provided later in this chapter with language and concepts that are more appropriate for young people.

Common Thinking Errors

All-or-Nothing Thinking: Seeing things in black-and-white categories. When performance falls short of perfect, seeing the overall effort as a total failure.

Overgeneralization: Seeing a single negative event as a never-ending pattern of defeat.

Labeling and Mislabeling: An extreme form of overgeneralization; instead of describing an error, a negative label is attached to the person: "I'm a loser." "He's stupid." Mislabeling tends to involve describing an event with language that is emotionally loaded.

Mental Filter: Picking out a single negative detail and dwelling on it exclusively so the vision of all reality becomes darkened, like the drop of ink that discolors the entire beaker of water.

Disqualifying the Positive: Rejecting positive experiences by insisting they "don't count" for some reason or other. Maintaining a negative belief that is contradicted by everyday experiences.

Jumping to Conclusions: Making a negative interpretation even though there are no definite facts that convincingly support the conclusion.

Mind Reading: Concluding that someone is reacting negatively without evidence and without bothering to check it out.

The Fortune-Teller Error: Anticipating that things will turn out badly and feeling convinced that the prediction is an already-established fact.

Magnification (Catastrophizing) or Minimization: Exaggerating the importance of things (such as a goof-up or someone else's achievement), or undermining the importance of things until they appear tiny (positive characteristics or another person's imperfections).

Emotional Reasoning: Assuming that negative emotions necessarily reflect the way things really are: "I feel it; therefore, it must be true."

Should Statements: Trying to motivate with *shoulds* and *shouldn'ts*. *Musts* and *oughts* are also offenders. These statements suggest a person is deficient if he or she should or must, but does not. The emotional consequence is guilt. When directed toward others, *shoulds* and *musts* lead to feeling angry, frustrated, and resentful toward others.

Personalization: Seeing yourself as the cause of some negative external event for which, in fact, you were not primarily responsible.

Using the cognitive model, maladaptive thoughts can be organized into three different types of beliefs or cognitions based on how entrenched they have become in the client's life: automatic thoughts, intermediate beliefs, and core beliefs (J. S. Beck, 1995). Automatic thoughts, the most accessible form of cognitions, are the internal self-statements or imageries that constantly stream through our consciousness. Automatic thoughts are the comments that our internal voice constantly makes throughout the day. After spilling a drink at a restaurant, what messages immediately run through your mind? *Got to get some towels, quick! Oops. Happens to all of us. That was dumb. I ruined the dinner—I'm so embarrassed!* Each of these is an automatic thought.

Intermediate beliefs, on the other hand, represent the transition of a persistent automatic thought to crystalized rules, attitudes, or assumptions. Intermediate beliefs are more global assumptions or attitudes about the self, how the world works, or what will happen in the future. These are expressed through patterns and persistent attitudes by clients and are not usually expressed directly by children and teens.

Core beliefs are even further formed stable beliefs and are less likely to be identified by young people without in-depth probing. Maladaptive core beliefs of depressed individuals tend to be broad, stable, pessimistic, and firmly held beliefs about the self, world, and future. For example, depressed individuals often hold beliefs that positive experiences are due to chance or luck and negative experiences caused by internal faults, and that they have little control over their lives (Benassi, Sweeney, & Dufour, 1988).

Automatic thoughts are the initial focus of this module. While it is entirely acceptable to address intermediate and core beliefs with young people, there are limitations to initially targeting those during this module. Depending on maturity and developmental level, core beliefs may not be firmly crystallized and therefore may be difficult to articulate. Focusing treatment on identifying core beliefs with a young person may be a time-intensive process, and the end results may have little meaning for the client since his "cognitive map" is continuously developing. With this in mind, therapists must use their judgment to understand how the maladaptive thought patterns contribute to each client's unique depressive symptoms. Focusing on automatic thoughts early in this process provides a starting point that is often effective for alleviating presenting symptoms. Success with addressing maladaptive automatic thoughts can also initiate a process of becoming aware of one's own cognitions that the client and family may continue after the treatment episode ends.

Now that we have described the conceptual framework for maladaptive cognitions, we can practice identifying these cognitions from statements made during the treatment session. Here are two examples of maladaptive cognitions from a twelve-year-old female client, Elsie. Can you notice any cognitive distortions?

Elsie: The other kids are stupid at my school.

Therapist: Stupid?

Elsie: Yeah. They all make fun of me, and nobody likes me there. I hate school.

What is the pattern of irrational thinking you noticed? She first says the other kids are stupid. As she elaborates, you may have noticed that *stupid* is mislabeling, and *frustrating* or *hopeless* probably better captures what the child is trying to convey. The therapist may take note of that first comment and be attentive for other examples of ways the word "stupid" is used too broadly. Maybe when the client makes a mistake, she calls herself stupid. Perhaps the client's family often uses the word "stupid" to describe frustrating people or situations. The therapist would probably start to recognize the need for improved affective expression if this pattern continues.

Next, she goes on to say that they *all* make fun of her and *nobody* likes her. This overgeneralization expands the problem to the entire school rather than a small, manageable group of peers. In reality, the child is probably correct in thinking there are social problems at school; however, it's unlikely that she is universally disliked (to be sure, the therapist can communicate with adults at the school, the parent, or caregiver, or possibly conduct a behavioral observation).

Like most maladaptive cognitions, this overgeneralization serves a purpose. In Elsie's mind, all these "stupid" kids have created a hopeless situation. It's a social dead end. Therefore, it's okay that she hasn't been able to fix the problem—it's unfixable. She's probably gone through her entire social skills repertoire to get kids to like her, with little success. Trying to resolve the problem at this point may make her feel ineffective, defective, and lonely. This cognitive distortion protects her from those terrible feelings because it allows her to accept the situation as hopeless and not related to her social ineptness, which she doesn't know how to fix.

It's no wonder she hates school. While hating school is also a distortion (black-and-white thinking; she probably enjoys one or two people or a few small parts of school, such as physical education or music), imagine struggling daily to fix a problem and to feel bombarded by damaging ridicule or perceived failure, believing your only two options are to (a) try and fail or (b) give up and feel hopelessly alone. The context for that struggle would be extremely uncomfortable for most people. Let's try another example with the same twelve-year-old girl and her mother, Roxy:

Roxy: Elsie just goes to her room right after school and stays there all afternoon. She doesn't want to come out, and I'm not going to make her spend time with me. If she doesn't ever want to be with me, what am I supposed to do? She's always been a loner and doesn't like me very much anymore.

What did you notice here? Did you see an overgeneralization? Roxy says Elsie stays in her room all afternoon. This could be true, but it would be worth questioning since it seems unlikely. Did you notice a potential personalization or mislabeling? It sounds as if Roxy thinks Elsie stays in her room because she doesn't like her. With just the information given in this example, we don't know for sure, but most depressed children have more than one reason for isolating; and even if Elsie is avoiding Roxy, it's not because she doesn't like Roxy. Perhaps she doesn't like being criticized by Roxy or hearing her parents fighting. In either case, Roxy has personalized the isolation, which has distracted her from finding a solution. If their time spent together is warm and supportive, Elsie's behavior is likely to change. Roxy also describes Elsie as a "loner." This mislabeling singles out her daughter's isolation as her defining characteristic. As a therapist working with the family, you would want to help Roxy recognize and highlight many other of the more positive characteristics in Elsie's personality.

Clinical Rationale for the Module

In the preceding sections, you learned about maladaptive cognitions and how thinking errors can be elicited and identified. In the next sections, we discuss how to intervene in order to reduce the frequency and intensity of these distortions and their contribution to the child's depression. Before discussing the use of the module, however, we provide a rationale for intervening to help guide effective use of the skills presented.

Maladaptive thinking is a major contributor to depressive feelings and maladaptive behaviors in depressed youth. CBT-based treatments have been found to encourage changes in the monitoring and modification of automatic thoughts, assumptions, and beliefs, especially cognitive distortions (Kolko, Brent, Baugher, Bridge, & Birmaher, 2000). Through the behavioral and cognitive interventions described in the next section, your clients and their family members will begin to challenge and change their maladaptive ways of thinking to be more realistic, which will promote positive changes in mood.

As discussed in detail in the psychoeducation and mood monitoring modules, thinking has an important impact on feelings and behaviors. While your client can take steps toward controlling his feelings and behaviors, his thoughts are constantly in his direct control. He has more immediate ability to change his thoughts than any other aspect of the cognitive triangle. This module is pivotal because it will help diminish concerns about past events and increase the client's sense of control and hopefulness, and the skills can quickly generalize and be useful to confront ongoing difficulties (DeRubeis, Tang, & A. T. Beck, 2009).

Individually Tailoring the Module

One of the challenges of using a CBT approach with young people is that their cognitions are sometime difficult to access. A benefit of modular CBT is that treatment can be adapted to fit the client's affective and cognitive insight and expression. The mood monitoring module can be leveraged to help the client improve his affective expression when needed.

Psychoeducation and mood monitoring are the only two modules that are directly connected to the skills needed to master this module. Timing of the module following addressing maladaptive cognitions, however, may require more consideration. Mastery of this module implies that the client has started to change his maladaptive thinking. However, this progress is tentative until it is behaviorally reinforced. Automatic thoughts are habits, and habits change in meaningful ways when they are accompanied by different reinforcing experiences. Therefore, true mastery does not occur until the skills of this module are coupled with effective behavioral skill development. If your client changes his thinking but does not have the skills to try something new or take a different approach, he will demonstrate similar behaviors and experience similar results. This familiar pattern will likely be followed by thoughts like *I knew I couldn't do it* or *I knew it wouldn't work*. Therefore, this module could be followed with behavioral activation, social skills training, or another specific skill-based module that the therapist has strategically decided to target as part of the treatment plan.

Let's take the example of Elsie, the twelve-year-old girl who hates school. The therapist, using a CBT case formulation, will use the information Elsie provided and his interpretation of her maladaptive cognitions to update his conceptualization. He will recognize the despair Elsie seems to feel about social interactions. With this updated conceptualization, the therapist will add social skills training to the treatment plan, but before that can be effective, he will need to address the perceived failure and hopelessness about social interactions and school. This will include addressing maladaptive cognitions. By changing the cognitions, hopelessness will be replaced by moderate feelings of hope that will fuel Elsie's ability to engage in social skills training. If she experiences rewarding and successful social experiences during the social skills training, these new adaptive cognitions will be strengthened or reinforced to replace the maladaptive thoughts. Similar strategies could be used to address anxiety, isolation, anger, or negative family patterns.

Using the Module

The targeted problem in this module is persistent negative thinking that leads to negative affect and mood. The goals for this module are to help the client identify and replace persistent negative thinking with adaptive thinking. In order to address maladaptive cognitions, your client will learn to identify cognitive distortions and practice replacing distortions with accurate thoughts.

When to Use This Module

In a typical treatment episode, this module will follow mastery of the psychoeducation and mood monitoring modules. Addressing maladaptive cognitions follows psychoeducation so the client understands how cognitions connect with thoughts and feelings and, therefore, the reason that addressing maladaptive cognitions is important. Addressing maladaptive cognitions follows mood monitoring so your client will understand the difference between thoughts and feelings and be better equipped to describe his internal experiences.

Involving Parents and Caregivers

For the first session of this module, you should meet with your client alone to best identify his cognitive distortions; however, this can be a relevant module for including family members at a subsequent session (though only if the child or adolescent is amenable) because the themes are relatable to all family members. It will also give your client the opportunity to show off his existing familiarity with the cognitive triangle in front of the other family members. Since thinking can be automatic and difficult to track initially, many children may benefit from the support of parents who can help them track homework at home. Sometimes you may include this module to support family collaboration. Certainly, if maladaptive thinking seems to be a pervasive struggle within the family or if your client receives messages in the home that contribute to his maladaptive cognitions (an unfortunately common occurrence), involving the family would be prudent.

Structuring the Session

Before each session, the clinician should write the session structure on a dry-erase board or poster. For some children, it may be helpful to have a timer for each section.

Example:

- *Check-In and Agenda Setting (5–10 minutes)*

- *Homework Review: Mood Monitoring (5 minutes)*

- *Skills Training: Addressing Maladaptive Cognitions (20 minutes)*

- *Current Concerns (5–10 minutes)*

- *Assigning Between-Session Practice (5 minutes)*

- *Summary, Feedback, and Next Steps (5 minutes)*

First Steps

Check In. Since it would be unusual to begin treatment with this module, the check-in portion of this module will include at least a brief review of the previous topics and any between-session practice, and should also include a brief discussion of the overall progress in treatment at this point and next steps. Therapists may also explain that this module will build on the skills mastered in the psychoeducation and mood monitoring modules.

Agenda Setting. The agenda for this module should include a significant portion of time for didactic teaching since the skills used to address maladaptive cognitions require an understanding of how to notice, identify, and then intervene with maladaptive thoughts. It may take more than one session to cover the necessary material, especially if the didactic teaching is broken up by practicing activities. Your client's ability to learn should direct the pace and prioritization of the agenda and may require flexibility in the amount of time used for each agenda item. Since this module is integral to the overall treatment process, take the necessary time to make the module useful for the client and family.

Homework Review. Spend time reviewing any between-session practices from the previous session and ensure that the client is prepared to move to the next module. Let your client know you expect him to be responsible for his progress in treatment by checking on his success, challenges, and progress as a result of the homework. Make sure your client is prepared to move forward with treatment, rather than moving forward on an artificial timeline. If no progress has been made, take time to problem solve around barriers and do more practice in session.

Skills Training

To explain maladaptive cognitions and how to identify them, you will probably begin with a refresher on the cognitive triangle (from chapter 4) and use examples to review the connection between thoughts, feelings, and actions (using examples relevant to your client's maladaptive thoughts whenever possible). In some cases, you may also need to strengthen your conceptualization of how maladaptive thoughts contribute to your client's depression. You might elicit your client's common thinking errors using the "Incomplete Sentence Blank" exercise with your client, or through discussion with your client and other adults familiar with your client. These thinking errors are scattered throughout his language and his understanding of challenges in his life. As he discusses experiences and challenges in his life, pay attention to the way he understands these challenges. As you attend to his understanding with the intenttion of spotting distortions, themes and patterns will emerge. In most cases, you will already have a conceptualization of your client's common maladaptive thoughts as you've noticed patterns throughout the preceding elements of his treatment. With this conceptualization, you can start the skills training with didactic teaching.

After briefly reviewing the psychoeducation topics that lay the foundation for this module, you can then introduce the concept of common thoughts that we may think but shouldn't believe.

Therapist: What if I thought *I don't need to wear a helmet. I'm safe without a helmet,* but then I fell off my bike? Would I be safe?

Client: (shakes head)

Therapist:	That's right. And what if I fell on my head? Would my head be safe? Would I be okay?
Client:	No
Therapist:	Exactly. Just because I thought I'd be safe without a helmet doesn't mean it's true. Sometimes we think things that aren't true, so if we believe them, it can be bad for us. There are certain types of thoughts that we all have that aren't true, and they can make us feel bad about ourselves or about other people. For example, if I thought you didn't like me, how would I feel?
Client:	Bad.
Therapist:	That's right. Maybe I would feel mad, or sad, or even lonely. But what if I *thought* you didn't like me, but you actually do like me? Then I would feel mad, sad, or lonely when I didn't even need to. Today I'm going to help you learn about a few ways that we tell ourselves thoughts that may not be true and that can make us feel bad. Not only do they change the way we feel, they also change the way we act. The feelings and actions that come from incorrect thoughts usually don't work very well. They create problems and make life more difficult. If we can change those incorrect thoughts and use correct thoughts instead, we make healthy habits that work better and we feel better. Then we become happier with our lives. You already know that thoughts are a big part of how we feel and how we act. If you learn to be in charge of your thoughts, you also learn to be in better control of how you feel, and that's one of the biggest reasons you're here: you've told me you want to be in charge of feeling better. This is a huge part of that. That's why I'm so excited about this module for you.

You can then introduce the list of common thinking errors. Based on developmental level, you may shorten or revise the list or focus on a specific few common thinking errors. A list of common thinking errors written for youth is provided in the box below (and available for download online at http://www.newharbinger.com/31175) to help explain these concepts in a way that is easier to understand. As you go through the list, provide examples of each. Ask your client to share examples as well. You might award some type of reinforcement (points or stickers) for examples (and double points for examples that are actual thoughts your client has).

Common Thinking Errors

Black-and-White Thinking: Seeing things as either perfect or terrible, seeing people as either all good or all bad. When you're doing this one, it's really hard to see things that are in the middle, or that there is some good and some bad.

Magnifying the Negative: Acting as if hard times or setbacks are horrible and that you should give up. When you magnify the negative, you feel like one mistake means that it's the end of the world, even though it's just one mistake and you can bounce back.

Jumping to Conclusions: Assuming the worst without checking it out. When you're doing this one, you may think you know what other people are thinking or you worry that bad things are going to happen. You're guessing the worst will happen, even though you don't really know.

Missing the Positive: Forgetting to notice the positive, or just paying attention to the negative. When you're doing this one, you act like the things that are happy, fun, exciting, or positive don't count, even though the positive things in your life really are happening and they truly are important.

If your client has trouble coming up with examples, provide help by setting up scenarios that seem to impact your client and ask him to describe what he thinks in those scenarios. Once you have a list of examples, you can discuss which feelings follow each one and how that influences his behavior. Talk through your conceptualization out loud. This will help your client learn to identify when he has thinking errors. Sometimes simply identifying the distortion in this way reveals the flawed thinking and causes a cognitive reframing (J. S. Beck, 1995). We all have difficulty seeing past our own views. By encouraging your clients to reexamine maladaptive thoughts, you are helping them break through their old ways of thinking.

The three-questions technique can also strengthen your client's recognition of thinking errors (DeRubeis, Tang, & A. T. Beck, 2009). The three-questions technique consists of challenging or questioning a thought: (1) "What makes me think it's true, and what makes me think it's not true?" (2) "What else might explain it?" and (3) "What would happen if it *is* true?" These questions are focused on a specific thinking error and will help your client reason through the distortion. This technique helps you model appropriate reasoning skills to evaluate one's own thoughts. As part of this technique you will encourage your client to see his thoughts as ideas that he can examine to determine whether they're true or not.

Through this process, you can also create a list of alternative, more accurate, and adaptive thoughts. The thought *They all make fun of me, and nobody likes me at school* may instead become *Some people tease me, some people are nice to me at school, and I'm working hard in therapy so I know how to have more of the nice people around me at school.* Or *I hate school* may be changed to *Some things at school are hard for me, but I'm working on them. I like my music class.* You may notice that the replacement thoughts are not irrationally optimistic. Instead, an accurate, hopeful statement is made that acknowledges the client's capacity to improve the situation (but not the prediction that the situation will improve without the client's effort and growth).

With youth, this process can be supported through an imagination practice exercise. Ask the client to describe a time he thought he hated school. Identify the circumstances and the triggering thoughts or experiences that brought this thought to mind. Write the alternative adaptive thought on the whiteboard: *Some things at school are hard for me, but I'm working on them. I like my music class.* Ask the client to close his eyes and imagine himself experiencing the triggering experiences or thoughts and to practice telling himself the new healthy thought instead of the old unhealthy thought. He can say the new healthy thought out loud. Provide lots of reinforcing feedback and specific praise for effective trials. Practice with the same new healthy thought several times before switching to a different scenario and a different new healthy thought. The repetition, and repeatedly hearing the new thought, will strengthen the client's ability to access this thought during the week. In addition, having him imagine responding to triggers with the new thought is a way for him to practice the skill.

When initially addressing maladaptive cognitions in therapy, automatic thoughts are the most appropriate place to start, since these are typically easier to identify and change. Throughout this process, you will check in with your client's learning and continually engage participation to make sure your teaching pace is aligned with his learning pace. A young person can gain mastery of this module without restructuring intermediate or core beliefs. Ultimately, you are teaching clients to examine their automatic thoughts and recognize inaccuracies in their thought processes.

Between-Session Practice

The targeted skill that between-session practice should encourage is either identifying automatic thoughts, thinking new healthy thoughts, or replacing old unhealthy thoughts with new healthy thoughts. Identifying automatic thoughts can be accomplished using a thought log. The "Checking My Thoughts" log, provided at the end of this chapter and online at http://www.newharbinger.com/31175, can help your client make note of automatic thoughts during the week and describe how the thoughts influenced his feelings and actions. To practice thinking new thoughts, your client can write down the example thoughts and the new healthy thoughts identified and practiced during the session. You and your client can determine a goal for imagining the old triggers and repeating the new thoughts out loud, just as he practiced in therapy. For a slightly more challenging practice between sessions, your client can practice using the new healthy thoughts in vivo, or when the actual triggers occur during the week. If your client feels comfortable independently identifying automatic thoughts, he can practice replacing unhealthy thoughts with healthy thoughts using the "Making New Healthy Thoughts" and "Tossing Bad Thoughts Overboard" worksheets provided at the end of this chapter (and online at http:// www.newharbinger.com/31175). These worksheets and between-session practice goals are provided as examples, but there are several other ways to promote your client's generalization of these cognitive restructuring skills. Mastery of this module will be demonstrated when your client is able to independently identify, describe, and substitute maladaptive cognitions with adaptive cognitions. For school-age children, this may include doing so with support from parents, caregivers, or other supportive adults.

Summary, Feedback, and Next Steps

Make sure to follow up the next session with a thorough discussion of your client's progress in the past week. Evaluate his ability to retain the information and generalize the skills. As mentioned, the stability of these skills will be enhanced when coupled with behavioral reinforcement. As your client becomes more at ease with identifying and challenging maladaptive cognitions, find ways that these new thoughts can be supported with alternative behaviors and the use of new skills. Maladaptive cognitions will reemerge over time when your client is confronted by challenges. Since relapse is a common step in addressing maladaptive cognitions, take time to check in on these skills and interweave these themes throughout the remainder of treatment.

Summary

To some degree, maladaptive cognitions accompany all of us throughout our lives. Our automatic thoughts, intermediate beliefs, and core beliefs may evolve throughout our lives, but we will continue to identify cognitive "blind spots" that remind us not to believe everything we think. For many of your clients, this will be their first opportunity to recognize that their thoughts are malleable. By teaching the skills from the module, you will be helping your clients develop the cognitive flexibility to take charge of the thoughts that lead them toward depression. By taking a step away from depressive thinking, your clients will be learning the power they possess and the skills they are able to cultivate that empower them to not feel depressed.

Checking My Thoughts

Trigger (what happened):

Automatic Thoughts (things that I assume are true):

Feelings (how the automatic thoughts made me feel):

Discomfort Level (0–10):

Actions (what I did):

Making New Healthy Thoughts

Trigger (what happened):

Old Unhealthy Thoughts (things that I assume are true):

New Healthy Thoughts (different, healthier thoughts):

Feelings (how the automatic thoughts made me feel):

Feelings (how the new thoughts made me feel):

Feeling Level (0–10):

New Feeling Level (0–10):

Actions (what I did):

New Plan or Actions:(what I did differently):

Tossing Bad Thoughts Overboard

Directions: Write or draw your negative thoughts inside or around the fish. Describe to your therapist these negative thoughts that you are tossing overboard into the ocean.

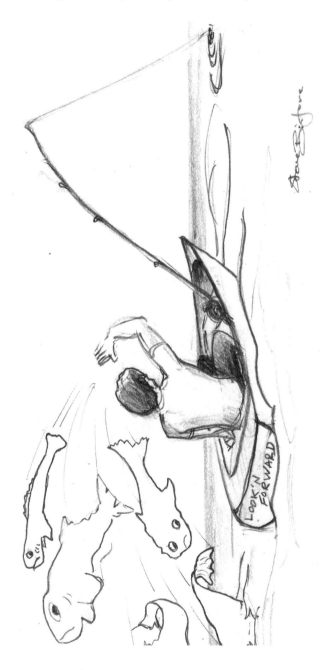

Chapter 8

Relaxation Training

It's bedtime. Grant's mother read him a favorite story, kissed him goodnight, and tucked him into bed with his favorite blanket. He is drowsy and comfortable in his warm bed; thus, he settled into his usual position on the soft mattress as his mother turned off the lights and closed his bedroom door. As the door closed softly, darkness flooded the bedroom. Grant heard the usual sounds of his mother's footsteps fading away, but he also heard the distant sound of a dog barking. He peeked out from under his blanket. While his eyes adjusted to the darkness, Grant saw shadows in the room. Suddenly, in a flash, he remembered a campfire story that was told by a friend during a recent camping trip—a story about the Shadow Man, a terrible villain who comes out at night and steals pets. Grant squeezed his eyes shut to avoid seeing the shadows in his dark bedroom, but it was too late—the story was vivid in his mind, and his heart pounded, goose bumps sprouting across his arms. His breathing became shallow, and his fingers and toes felt cold. In just a matter of seconds, upon imagining the story about the Shadow Man, Grant went from a happily drowsy state to a panicked, alert one.

This scenario illustrates the connection between your mind and body. Your mind can actively cause a response from your body, whether that is a panic reaction (e.g., heart racing, skin sweating) or a calming response (e.g., slower breaths, blood returning to your extremities). This active connection between your mind and body is the key to teaching children and adolescents how to train their body to relax. The first step in intervening with anxious or fear responses is for the child to understand the process in which it occurs. This chapter focuses on the basic, active skills that children need to effectively respond to the daily stresses that occur in their lives.

Preparing the Module

This chapter is heavily focused on both psychoeducation and active skills-building exercises. We discuss the background and clinical rationale for relaxation training. This background is intended to help therapists provide effective psychoeducation to children and adolescents while using this module. After discussion of the role of the mind-body connection in relaxation training, we describe how to use the relaxation training module. Implementing the module includes planning the agenda, providing psychoeducation, using interventions and teaching techniques, and finding ways to involve parents. In addition, there is an option in this module to utilize exposure techniques for children and adolescents who may have fears or anxiety and who may benefit from exposure treatment. Overall, this chapter will help support effective use of relaxation-training skills, as well as introduce exposure techniques, in the successful treatment of depressed children and adolescents in the context of modular CBT.

Background: Understanding the Mind-Body Connection

As shown in the example at the beginning of this chapter, research has demonstrated that when a child imagines an experience, she may experience the same physical sensations as if the experience were actually occurring in real life. A well-known imagery exercise that succinctly exemplifies this mind-body connection involves a guided imagery using a lemon. In chapter 4, we used the lemon example to demonstrate how your mind can impact your body. In this module, you will review the lemon imagery again, but with the goal of your client experientially understanding the mind-body connection. You ask your client to close her eyes and imagine a lemon on the counter. Ask your client to imagine that you cut the lemon in wedges, and she can now see the lemon juice dripping down the lemon wedges. She picks one up in her hand. Ask her to imagine holding the lemon in her hand, smelling the outside peel of the lemon, and feeling the lemon juice leaking into the palm of her hand. Then, you ask her to imagine that she is holding the lemon up to her mouth and squeezing the juice onto her tongue. Finally, you ask her to describe any physical responses that have occurred subsequent to the lemon imagery. Often clients will describe their mouth producing saliva in response to imagining the lemon juice dripping onto their tongue. This exercise can be used to demonstrate to children the mind-body connection—that the mind can imagine an event, and the body can respond to that imagined event as if it were an event occurring in real life. In this module, this imagery is used to educate children that while they can imagine events that may cause them to have a fearful response, they can also learn to imagine events that help them calm down and make the scared feelings go away.

You may have heard well-meaning friends tell you to "just live in the moment and experience every moment fully." While many relaxation-training techniques focus on teaching children how to clear their mind of anxious thoughts and worries about the future, this advice to "experience every moment fully" is overly simplified. If an individual went about her daily life trying to experience every moment fully, she would be flooded with too many senses, feelings, and thoughts, and likely overwhelmed by the plethora of sensations. On the other hand, if the individual went about her daily life with little awareness of how her cognitions impact her bodily responses, then she may experience unwanted physical reactions that, in turn, negatively impact her cognitions. In providing psychoeducation about the mind-body connection and in teaching active skills on how to capitalize on that connection, we are providing children and adolescents with the skills to understand and effectively use the mind-body connection in order to have a healthy response to stress-provoking or even feared stimuli.

Children are faced with many experiences throughout the day. How does the mind-body connection apply to children's day-to-day experiences? When a child is faced with a positive, negative, or ambiguous situation (e.g., going on a roller coaster ride, watching a movie, sitting in class), her mind is constantly producing thoughts that elicit physical responses. When the child's mind is faced with perceived danger, the flight-or-fight response occurs naturally and the child automatically and involuntarily experiences significant physical sensations such as heart racing, shallow breathing, and paling of the skin. Often children and adolescents are unaware of this entire process as it is happening in their mind and body. Thus, the first step in relaxation training is to provide psychoeducation to the child and her family about the mind-body connection and how having a good understanding of this process allows the child to take control of her reaction.

Developmental Considerations

It is important to consider the developmental level of the child or adolescent when providing psychoeducation about the mind-body connection. The therapist will tailor the vocabulary and instruction method based on the child's developmental level. For instance, for younger children, the therapist may use drawings (art), simplified language, and short psychoeducational videos. There are many developmentally appropriate video clips on the Internet free of charge and available to clinicians. Clinicians are recommended to be prudent and review these videos beforehand to determine their suitability for their clients. Videos that are produced by well-known academic institutions tend to be more accurate in their information. For children who respond to sessions that involve movement and art, you may use large rolls of poster paper and have the child draw an outline of her body. Then, the child may color in the parts of her body where she experiences certain physical sensations (e.g., color red at the heart to indicate pounding heart). This activity helps the child identify the physical sensations that occur in her body. For older adolescents, the therapist may employ a more verbally intensive method of instruction and use more elaborate or academic explanations. The key aspect here is to carefully consider the developmental level of the client and then tailor the psychoeducation of the mind-body connection in a manner that is most effective for the client. (A worksheet for this exercise is provided at the end of this chapter, and a downloadable copy is available online at http://www.newharbinger.com/31175.)

Clinical Rationale for the Module

In reviewing the *DSM* criteria for depression and anxiety, you will note that many of the symptoms overlap and are physical in nature. For instance, lethargy, lack of appetite, and changes in sleep are all bodily reactions in the context of a depressive disorder. It is even more so the case in anxiety disorders, where many of the symptoms (e.g., panic) are experienced primarily through bodily sensations. Because these physical responses can significantly impact a child's perception of her environment (and vice versa), teaching the child the mind-body connection and how to take control of her physical sensations can be some of the most effective tools the child learns in treatment.

Furthermore, for children who have coexisting fears, phobias, or anxious feelings, exposure therapy may be clinically indicated. The research literature has provided significant evidence that exposure-based behavior treatment is typically the most effective intervention for these symptoms (Chorpita, Daleiden, & Weisz, 2005; Feske & Chambless, 1995; Meyerbröker & Emmelkamp, 2010). Exposure-based treatment is defined as any treatment that encourages the systematic exposure to feared stimuli, with the goal of decreasing an anxious or fearful reaction. In some instances, such as with panic disorder, relaxation training may be counterproductive (Schmidt et al., 2000) as exposures have been shown to be the active ingredient for change in treatment. This chapter will briefly address the application of exposure therapy. There are multiple theoretical explanations for the mechanism behind exposure-based therapy; therapists who are interested in further information on the theoretical basis for exposure-based treatment are encouraged to read the works of Barlow et al. (2011), Foa and Kozak (1986), Kazdin (2001), Kendall (1994), and Rachman (1977). For an in-depth understanding and application of modular CBT for anxiety disorders, therapists are also encouraged to read the seminal work on the modular approach of CBT for childhood anxiety disorders by Chorpita and colleagues (2004). Chorpita (2006) has a comprehensive and clinically relevant book on modular CBT for anxiety that is highly applicable for youth with anxious disorders. Furthermore, Chorpita and Weisz (2009) have a scholarly and complex book with a comprehensive delineation of the modular approach for comorbid conditions in youth. Of particular relevance, clinicians delivering the modular approach of CBT are recommended to use the PracticeWise website (http://www.practicewise.com); this web-based resource offers clinicians clinical tools in treating youths with a variety of disorders. The Managing and Adapting Practice (MAP) tool available on that site provides clinical protocols along with recommendations for treatment. For children who require more intensive anxiety treatment, *Camp Cope-A-Lot* (an interactive CD) is an evidence-based option (Khanna & Kendall, 2008).

FIT OF TOPIC WITH OVERALL TREATMENT

Providing relaxation training can help the child follow through with subsequent modules. For instance, in the affect regulation module, the child learns how to regulate her emotional responses in situations. Being able to initiate a relaxation response and maintain a calm state (as taught in this module) can be an effective coping strategy that the child may use in regulating her emotions. Another example is with the mood monitoring module. In that module, the child learns to identify her mood states. For the depressed and anxious child, her mind may be racing with thoughts (e.g., fears, worries, ruminative thoughts), which can impair her ability to learn how to identify her mood states. A simple relaxation exercise may help the child clear her mind or slow down the ruminative and racing thoughts enough so she can follow through with her mood-monitoring task. Finally, as described in the problem-solving skills module, relaxation exercises are often the mechanism that children use in order to initiate the first step in accessing their problem-solving skills.

Using the Module

Equipped with the information from the "Preparing the Module" section, the various pieces of this module should be purposeful and feel cohesive with the other modules for your client. This section is designed to introduce and teach these relaxation skills effectively. We present some of the key pieces needed for a relaxation-training session, including structuring the session, approaches for psychoeducation, using the agenda, and strategies for building the skills. Ultimately, your goals with this module are to help your client understand why and how to use relaxation-training exercises, develop capacity to increase relaxation to reduce or avoid excessive anxiousness or anger, and strengthen her ability to progress toward the overarching treatment goals.

When to Include the Module

This module may be employed for depressed children who tend to have anxious or fearful responses to normal daily stressors. Children or adolescents with co-occuring anxiety or obsessive-compulsive disorder (OCD) may particularly benefit from use of this module early in treatment. For instance, in the behavioral activation module, the child may be assigned the task of playing basketball at the park; however, if the child has anxiety symptoms, then she may be too anxious to follow through with that assigned task. This is a prime example for the therapist to be mindful about whether to administer this relaxation training module early in the treatment sequence. In this example, the child learns relaxation-training skills or undergoes exposure-based treatment in order to help her successfully follow through with her behavioral activation–assigned tasks.

Cultural Considerations

Of all the skills in modular CBT, the skills in relaxation training may be considered the most universal. Given that all humans have the flight-or-fight response, along with the same sympathetic and parasympathetic nervous systems, relaxation training is arguably a skill that can be useful to people across cultures and ethnicities. Furthermore, there are religions in which forms of relaxation training are integral parts of the culture. For instance, in Buddhism, meditation (a form of relaxation training) is practiced on a daily basis and is an integral part of the living experience.

In Christianity, there are repetitive prayers that have a focus on breathing and specific phrases. In Islam, there is a similar procedure called *dhikr*, whereby the individual engages in a repetitive prayer that has a meditative component. It should be noted that there have been some recent studies on culturally adapted relaxation training for specific race and ethnicities, such as for Latino and Southeast Asian individuals (Hinton, Hofmann, Rivera, Otto, & Pollack, 2011; Hinton, Rivera, Hofmann, Barlow, & Otto, 2012; La Roche, Batista, & D'Angelo, 2011; La Roche, D'Angelo, Gualdron, & Leavell, 2011).

Alternatively, there are families who may live in a culture where meditation and relaxation exercises are not commonly used; thus, effective and convincing psychoeducation about the relevance of relaxation training in depression treatment is particularly important. For instance, for children whose families are from lower-socioeconomic backgrounds and whose parents are working long hours at multiple jobs, there may be a cultural belief that relaxation is unhelpful or downright "lazy." Prior to providing psychoeducation about relaxation training, therapists would benefit from assessing the child and her family's cultural perspective on relaxation training first, so that the psychoeducation content and delivery can be effectively tailored to address the family's concerns about the utility of relaxation.

Involving Parents and Caregivers

Relaxation exercises can feel foreign or even silly to children and adolescents who have not practiced these exercises previously. The key to relaxation training is repetition and practice between sessions. This is where parents and family members can be most helpful to the child. The therapist is recommended to provide psychoeducation to both the child and parents in order to obtain "buy-in" from all parties. In addition, the therapist should engage parents to help remind the child to practice her relaxation exercises at home (e.g., at bedtime). As with any new habits, parents can support their children in developing new habits by reminding them to practice the new behaviors. Parents may also help children by modeling the behavior and providing rewards or reinforcements for following through with the exercises. There are some excellent online videos with child-friendly breathing exercises, such as "Sesame Street: Belly Breathing with Elmo" (available on YouTube), as well as technology-oriented activities, such as the "Breathe, Think, Do with Sesame" app.

Structuring the Session

Before each session, the clinician may write the session structure on a dry-erase board or poster. For some children, it may be helpful to have a timer for each section.

Example:

- *Check-In and Agenda Setting (5–10 minutes)*

- *Homework Review: Addressing Maladaptive Cognitions (5 minutes)*

- *Skills Training: Relaxation Training (20 minutes)*

- *Current Concerns (5–10 minutes)*

- *Assigning Between-Session Practice (5 minutes)*

- *Summary, Feedback, and Next Steps (5 minutes)*

First Steps

Check-In. The first few minutes of the session may be spent checking in with the child. Refer to the dry-erase board and prime the client for the session structure.

Therapist: As you can see on the dry-erase board, we will be checking in on how you've been doing, reviewing how the mood charting has been going for you, and then talking about how to calm ourselves down when we get worried. Now, how are things going for you this week? Are there certain things that you'd like to make sure that we talk about today?

Agenda Setting. Any concerns or situations that were brought up during the check-in process may be placed on the agenda for later discussion. For many therapists, one of the challenges with manualized or structured treatment approaches is being able to effectively address the numerous situations or events that have occurred since the previous session. Clients or parents may bring in issues or incidents (commonly known as the "crisis of the week") that they want to discuss. While these issues may be relevant and important to discuss, if they occur too frequently, discussions of these issues may interfere with skills building and derail treatment progress. An effective way to address "crisis of the week" incidents is to incorporate the discussion into the skills-building exercise that is on the agenda for each particular week. For instance, an adolescent may wish to discuss an incident involving a failed exam that occurred over the past week. You may incorporate this discussion into relaxation training by highlighting how the adolescent may use progressive muscle relation or deep breathing to aid in her distress before an exam.

Therapist: You may remember from last week that we will be setting the agenda at the beginning of every session. You mentioned that you got so nervous in class that you "blanked out" on your exam and ended up failing it.

Client: Yes. I got so anxious at the beginning of class that by the time the teacher passed out the exams, I just blanked out and couldn't remember any of the stuff I had studied.

Therapist: Okay, let's put this on our agenda for today. We will talk about what happened with your exam and how the relaxation skills you learn today can help you with future ones.

Homework Review. The next few minutes should be spent reviewing the client's homework assignment from the previous session. It is important to hold the child or adolescent accountable by checking in with her regarding whether she has completed her therapy homework. If the adolescent did not complete her homework assignment, then it is recommended that you spend a little more time at this point in the session to help the client complete it. You may also engage the client in problem solving ways to overcome her barriers to completing future homework assignments. For instance, if your client reported that she keeps forgetting to practice her relaxation exercise every evening, you can ask her to set a daily alarm on her smartphone (you can have her do this during your session). You can also engage parents in reminding the child every evening to complete her therapy homework.

Skills Training

Didactic. Using your case conceptualization and the information provided in this chapter, explain the clinical rationale for relaxation training or exposure-based therapy with your client.

Therapist: Tell me what happened when you blanked out on your exam. What was going through your mind when the teacher first passed out the exam?

Client: I was thinking that I didn't study enough. I was thinking that I was going to fail the exam.

Therapist: And what happened when you had those anxious thoughts? How did your body react?

Client: I don't know. I guess my heart started pounding, and I felt like I couldn't breathe. My head started clouding up, and everything was just a blur on the exam.

Therapist: Remember the cognitive triangle that we talked about when we first started therapy? Sometimes, when we have anxious or worrisome thoughts, those thoughts can be unhelpful in that they cause our bodies to respond in a stressful way. It sounds like, in your situation, your anxious thoughts about failing the exam caused your body to respond physically. Your heart was pounding, and you felt like you couldn't breathe, so you found it hard to concentrate on the exam. One way to stop this from happening is to calm your body down as soon as you realize you are having anxious thoughts. And that's what we'll learn how to do today.

When teaching relaxation training and exposure-based intervention, it is helpful for the child to self-rate her current state of mood before and after each exercise. This can be done using a one-to-ten rating scale, where one equals no anxiety and ten equates to very anxious. This is called a SUDS rating (with SUDS standing for "subjective unit of distress/discomfort scale"). It may be helpful to spend a few minutes helping the child come up with real-life examples to anchor these ratings. For instance, you can ask the child, "Describe a time when you felt the most relaxed in your life," and instruct the child that this event is an example of a self-rating of one. You can ask the child, "Describe a time when you felt the most anxious ever in your life," then instruct the child that this event is an example of a self-rating of ten. These anchors, tied to actual events, may help the child self-rate more effectively.

Another reason for teaching the child how to self-rate her mood (e.g., anxiety, depression) is to demonstrate that there is a range of emotions. Often, when children are experiencing a depressive or anxious symptom, they feel the emotion strongly and erroneously perceive it as an all-or-none phenomenon. It is helpful to teach them that their emotions do have a range and that using relaxation strategies can impact where their emotions land on that range.

Modeling. Many children, when learning how to use relaxation training for the first time—for example, by focusing on their breath—find it to be an awkward experience. One effective tool the clinician may use is modeling. In the relaxation training module, you may use modeling by demonstrating how you use a relaxation exercise. It is helpful to be explicit in your thought process and practice.

Therapist: When I first started using deep breathing, I thought it was really silly! It felt weird to focus on my breathing, but then I got really good at it. Now, when I start getting nervous about something, I remind myself to take deep breaths, and it helps calm down my body.

Role-Play with Feedback. After modeling the relaxation strategy, elicit the child to practice the relaxation exercise. Role-plays should always begin with the therapist modeling the behavior; then the roles are switched and the child practices the behavior. The clinician should always provide praise as well as any needed corrective feedback.

Therapist: Okay, let's practice deep breathing. We are going to role-play that you are walking into class and the teacher is handing out the math exams. You begin to have anxious thoughts about failing the exam. What should you do at this point?

Client: I could take some deep breaths to calm myself down.

Therapist: That's right. Let's practice it now.

Relaxation Strategies and Exposures

The following is a list of relaxation strategies; it is not exhaustive. You may be creative in teaching relaxation strategies. If you have a child who enjoys using the computer and tends to be highly motivated by using one, you may decide to teach the child relaxation techniques by showing a video on YouTube that teaches about deep breathing. If the client enjoys play, you may use a puppet. It may be helpful to let the child know in advance that she may need to try numerous strategies before finding one that appeals to her. This is also why this module often requires more than one session. Printable instructions for these exercises and example scripts are provided at the end of this chapter and online at http://www.newharbinger.com/31175.

Deep Breathing: When we feel stressed, we often automatically breathe shallowly, which can cause us to feel more panicked. To counter this shallow breathing, you can learn how to take deep breaths.

One strategy to teach deep breathing to clients is to use *bubble breathing*. Have at least two bubble bottles with wands on hand and engage the child in a contest to see who can blow the biggest bubble. Teach the child that deep breaths (rather than shallow breaths) are required to blow the biggest bubbles.

A second game is to use *pinwheels*. Engage the child in a contest of who can spin the pinwheel the longest using their breath. Teach the child that in order to get the pinwheel to spin for an extended period of time, you have to take a deep breath and breathe out slowly. Always link the skill to a scenario in which the child could use the skill. In this instance, have the client identify situations in which deep breathing (or bubble breathing, or breathing to spin a pinwheel) may be used to help calm down the body. Clinicians are encouraged to be creative in how they teach children the skills. For instance, for adolescents who have an interest in singing or pop stars, you can engage them in a singing contest to see who can sing a note for the longest duration.

Therapist: Close your eyes and take some deep breaths. Imagine that your stomach is a balloon, and take in a big, deep, slow breath as if you are filling up that balloon. Your chest is not moving, just your stomach. Now, let out your breath slowly and watch as your stomach deflates like a balloon with a slow leak. And now, take in a big, deep breath, and keep breathing in until I count to five.

Visualization and Guided Imagery Sample Script: Learning how to visualize calming scenery may aid in decreasing anxious arousal or even stop anxious thoughts.

Therapist: What is your favorite place in the whole world?

Client: The beach. I love hanging on the beach.

Therapist: Okay, we are going to practice a relaxation exercise. Close your eyes and take some deep breaths. Imagine you are at the beach. You are sitting on the warm sand. You can feel the grainy sand between your toes, the warm sun against your face, and the salty smell of the ocean water in your nose. You feel the warm breeze against your skin. As you notice the waves crashing in front of you, you hear the sounds of the sea gulls flying by above. You take some more deep breaths. With each slow, deep breath, you realize that you are completely relaxed and calm. Your body is completely relaxed while you are sitting on the sand.

Progressive Muscle Relaxation (PMR) Sample Script: PMR has been demonstrated to relax the body. It entails the systematic tensing and releasing of various muscle groups in order to relax the body. The sample script below uses the theme of a warm laser light, but you can individualize the theme to your client (e.g., a butterfly flying slowly up each section of the body as those muscles are tightened and relaxed).

Therapist: Close your eyes, and take some deep breaths. Now, imagine a warm light is entering your body through your toes. As the warm laser light moves through your body slowly, you tighten the section of your body that is touched by the warm light. The light is entering your toes; tighten your toes as hard as you can. Now release. The light is moving up your feet, through your calves. Now tighten your calf muscles, then release. You feel the warm light moving up through your thighs to your hips. Tighten your thighs really, really strongly, and now let go. Remember to keep breathing deeply. As the warm laser light moves up through your bottom and hips, squeeze them tight, now release. The light is moving up through your stomach; tighten your tummy muscles, really tight, and now release. From your stomach all the way down, your body feels warm and relaxed. Now the laser light is moving up through your chest and arms. Tighten these muscles, then let go, and relax all your muscles. The warm laser light is now moving through your face. Squeeze your cheeks, your chin, your nose, and your eyes really, really tight. Now release. You feel the warm laser light leave your body through the top of your head, and from the top of your head all the way to the bottom of your toes, you feel warm, relaxed, and calm.

Other strategies include meditation and yoga, which can be done via classes or by viewing and following developmentally appropriate videos online.

Prior to completing exposure-based treatment, therapists are reminded to refer to Bruce Chorpita's book *Modular Cognitive-Behavioral Therapy for Childhood Anxiety Disorders* (2006) or Khanna and Kendall's *Camp Cope-A-Lot* (2008) that outlines the procedures in detail. Below is an overview of basic steps; however, clinicians are encouraged to obtain clinical training in exposure-based behavioral treatment and to have ongoing clinical supervision or consultation for the treatment application until they are adequately trained. While relaxation training is covered in this chapter, therapists should be mindful that relaxation techniques can be counterproductive to exposures.

1. Develop an exposure hierarchy. (A worksheet for this task is provided at the end of this chapter and online at http://www.newharbinger.com/31175.)

   a. This may be a list of fears, phobias, or anxiety-provoking items and experiences (e.g, elevator, heights, test-taking situations).

   b. Have the adolescent provide a subjective unit of distress/discomfort scale (SUDS) rating for each item.

   c. Reorder the list based on SUDS rating, with the lowest number at the bottom of the hierarchy and the highest SUDS rating at the top of the hierarchy. (A worksheet for this exercise is provided at the end of this chapter, and a downloadable copy of that worksheet is available online at http://www.newharbinger.com/31175.)

2. Conduct exposures in a systematic, gradual manner.

   a. Start at the bottom of the list and do not move up until each step is successful in reducing the child's fear of that particular item or experience.

   b. At the beginning and end of each exposure, have the client provide a SUDS rating.

   c. The active ingredient of change is new learning. After each exposure, the client must learn that the feared outcome does not occur in response to each exposure trial, or if it does, it isn't as terrible as she originally imagined.

   d. Be careful of "safety behaviors"—those behaviors that clients (sometimes secretly, sometimes unconsciously) engage in to prevent feared outcomes. These safety behaviors are thought to be harmful to the success of exposure-based treatment because they prevent the child from learning new outcomes. Safety behaviors may prevent the child from disconfirming her faulty belief about the feared stimuli and cause exacerbation of the anxiety or fears (Deacon & Maack, 2007).

   e. Identifying and addressing maladaptive cognitions (refer to that module) related to these feared stimuli or outcomes may also be helpful as part of exposure-based treatment.

Working on Current Concerns

Any topics that were brought up by the child or caregiver at the beginning of the session may be discussed in this part of the session. If the current concerns were adequately addressed during the skills-training segment, then this section may be skipped.

Between-Session Practice

The key aspect to learning how to use relaxation strategies effectively when one is feeling anxious is to practice, practice, practice. The child should practice these relaxation strategies on a routine basis (e.g., nightly before bedtime) so the behavior becomes habitual. Once the strategies are part of the child's repertoire of coping skills, then the child will be better equipped to use the strategies when she finds herself in an anxiety-provoking situation.

Summary, Feedback, and Next Steps

Have the client summarize the session highlights to you.

Therapist: Today, we learned how to use some relaxation skills. In what kinds of situations might you use these skills?

Ask the adolescent for feedback regarding the session. This feedback allows you to know what is working in real time and what is not working as well.

Therapist: How do you think today's session went? Which relaxation strategy was most helpful to you? Which one was least helpful?

The final step to the session is to prime the child or adolescent as to the next steps in therapy. You may be covering relaxation training again at the next session, or you may be moving on to another module. It is helpful to prime the child as to which next step is likely.

Therapist: Okay, so we just learned some relaxation strategies and the importance of knowing how to calm down our body's responses. I know that you only liked one of the relaxation exercises that we learned today. I do have some other good ones that I'd like to teach you next week. I think you might like those strategies, so let's try those strategies at the next session. Thank you for being honest with me with your feedback. Do you have any questions?

Common Hurdles and Solutions for Therapists

The most common hurdle for relaxation training is how awkward or silly the exercises may initially seem; however, these strategies usually appear less awkward as the client practices them in session or between sessions. One of the best ways to address the initial awkwardness is to acknowledge it at the beginning. Tell your client that these relaxation exercises may seem silly, but the more she practices them, the more likely she will eventually feel comfortable with and benefit from them. Another common hurdle in this module is the client's potential reticence to participate in exposures; after all, these are the very stimuli that the client had identified as anxiety-provoking. The best way to address this hurdle is by highlighting the rationale for doing exposures. You can provide a more in-depth psychoeducation on the consequences of avoidance (e.g., the more you avoid school, the more you feel anxious when confronted with it). Finally, another hurdle may be the therapist's own reticence to complete exposures. This is one reason it is beneficial to consult with an experienced clinician who can help you on these issues.

Summary

In this module, we addressed the crosscutting symptoms of depression and anxiety. Because these two are often paired, we offer relaxation-training strategies and behavioral-based exposures to aid in helping depressed children develop constructive coping skills for when they feel anxious, frustrated, or stressed. The goal of this module is to give clients adaptive skills that they can use to help them overcome anxiousness or fear so they are able to complete essential components of cognitive behavioral therapy (such as behavioral activation).

Feelings Identification: Where Do I Feel My Emotions In My Body?

Directions: Instruct the child to color in where he or she experiences emotions (e.g., red around the head for feeling angry).

Downloadable copies of this form are available online at http://www.newharbinger .com/31175. (See the very back of this book for more details.)

_____'s Exposure Hierarchy

Anchoring Examples	SUDS Ratings
	10: Most Anxious
	5: Medium Anxious
	1: Least Anxious, or Not Anxious At All

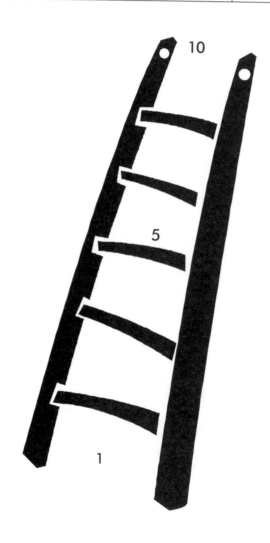

What makes me anxious?	SUDS Rating
	10
	9
	8
	7
	6
	5
	4
	3
	2
	1

Downloadable copies of this form are available online at http://www.newharbinger .com/31175. (See the very back of this book for more details.)

Relaxation Strategies and Scripts

Relaxation Strategies

Bubble Breathing: Have at least two bubble bottles with wands on hand and engage the child in a contest to see who can blow the biggest bubble. Teach the child that deep breaths (rather than shallow breaths) are required to blow the biggest bubbles.

Pinwheels: Engage the child in a contest of who can spin the pinwheel the longest. Teach the child that in order to get the pinwheel to spin for an extended period of time, you have to take a deep breath and breathe out slowly.

Singing Contest: See who can sing a note for the longest duration.

Video Clips: Play an instructional video clip for the client while she practices along. For instance, "Sesame Street: Belly Breathing with Elmo" (available on YouTube) is a helpful tool for young children.

Relaxation Scripts

Deep Breathing Script: Close your eyes and take some deep breaths. Imagine your stomach is a balloon, and take in a big, deep, slow breath as if you are filling up your stomach like a big balloon. Your chest is not moving, just your stomach. Then, let out your breath slowly and watch as your stomach deflates like a balloon with a slow leak. Now, take in a big, deep breath, and keep breathing in until I count to five.

Visualization and Guided Imagery Sample Script: What is your favorite place in the whole world? *(In this sample script, the child chose the beach.)* Close your eyes and take some deep breaths. Imagine you are at the beach. You are sitting on the warm sand. You can feel the grainy sand between your toes, the warm sun against your face, and the salty smell of the ocean water in your nose. You feel the warm breeze against your skin. As you notice the waves crashing in front of you, you hear the sounds of the sea gulls flying by above. You take some more deep breaths. With each slow, deep breath, you realize that you are completely relaxed and calm. Your body is completely relaxed while you are sitting on the sand.

Progressive Muscle Relaxation (PMR) Sample Script: Close your eyes, and take some deep breaths. Now, imagine a warm light is entering your body through your toes. As the warm laser light moves through your body slowly, you tighten the section of your body that is touched by the warm light. The light is entering your toes; tighten your toes as hard as you can. Now release. The light is moving up your feet, through your calves. Now tighten your calf muscles, then release. You feel the warm light moving up through your thighs to your hips. Tighten your thighs really, really strongly, and now let go. Remember to keep breathing deeply. As the warm laser light moves up through your bottom and hips, squeeze them tight, now release. The light is moving up through your stomach; tighten your tummy muscles, really tight, and now release. From your stomach all the way down, your body feels warm and relaxed. Now the laser light is moving up through your chest and arms. Tighten these muscles, then let go, and relax all your muscles. The warm laser light is now moving through your face. Squeeze your cheeks, your chin, your nose, and your eyes really, really tight. Now release. You feel the warm laser light leave your body through the top of your head, and from the top of your head all the way to the bottom of your toes, you feel warm, relaxed, and calm.

Downloadable copies of these strategies and scripts are available online at http://www.newharbinger.com/31175. (See the very back of this book for more details.)

Chapter 9

Social Skills Training

The first week of school has started and five-year-old Cole is excited to make new friends. As he arrives to class, he runs up to a group of students and stands next to them. Not sure how to enter the group conversation, he stands there for a few minutes and then proceeds to "accidentally" bump into one of the boys. The boy yells out in annoyance, so Cole runs over to another side of the classroom where other children are milling about.

The above scenario is a common interaction that occurs daily in many schools and playgrounds. As a new kindergartener, five-year-old Cole is still learning how to interact with others and how to make friends appropriately. But what happens if over the next several years he never develops appropriate social skills? What you have is a twelve-year-old boy without the appropriate social skills to make new friends.

One of the primary undertakings during childhood and adolescence is to develop socially. Between school, sports, day care, and family time, children and adolescents are developing their ability to understand and respond to the social cues around them. The importance of social development popularized by Piaget in the 1930s and later supported by numerous researchers (Chandler, 1973; Crick & Dodge, 1994; Damon & Killen, 1982; Jaffari-Bimmel et al., 2006; Rubin, Bukowski, & Parker, 1998; Selman & Schultz, 1998), has been an area of ongoing emphasis among developmental psychologists.

Preparing the Module

Background: Depression and Social Skills

The path of social development is marked by countless interactions that reinforce, punish, and shape attitudes about social exchanges. From a boy teased for wearing his fanny pack and a teenager who gains a reputation as "nice to everyone" to a girl who tells a joke that gets the entire class to laugh and a young man who is rejected by peers after posting an embarrassing photo online, children and adolescents are constantly shaping behaviors and developing their beliefs about themselves in the process. Social interactions represent essential developmental processes that improve our resilience throughout life. On the other hand, social isolation can be extremely painful for children and adolescents and can contribute to the maintenance of depressive symptoms.

Researchers have suggested that repeated failed social interactions contribute to the learned helplessness of a young person (Goetz & Dweck, 1980). Rubin and Asendorpf (1993) provided evidence that expanded this theory based on the Waterloo Longitudinal Project, a seminal ten-year study of social withdrawal among children. They found that very withdrawn children attribute social failures to their own internal, stable traits. Additional research has supported the finding that socially withdrawn children will have "negative self-perceptions of their social skills and relationships" (Rubin, Burgess, Kennedy, & Stewart, 2003, p. 385).

Social Skills Training Snapshot: Juan

Juan is a Mexican American eight-year-old who gets bullied during recess. His dad attempted suicide two years ago. Although Juan didn't see what happened, he has heard family members talking about his father's suicide attempt. Juan presents as sad, worried, fearful, and reserved. He has flat affect, cries often with no clear reason, doesn't talk much, and is very timid at school. His older brother thinks he is a "wimp" and criticizes him often.

When he gets bullied, Juan tries to back down quickly, but he still gets teased by bullies regularly. Backing down has only made him more of a target for teasing and bullying.

Lately, he has been refusing to go to class when his dad drops him off at school. He also refuses to go out at recess. He avoids social settings except in his classroom and hides in the bathroom when he is forced to leave the classroom at lunch.

Some of Juan's automatic thoughts are *Other kids don't like me, I'm a wimp,* and *There's nothing I can do.* Some of Juan's beliefs include *My dad doesn't love me, Nobody cares that much about me,* and *I'm no good.*

Depressed children and adolescents often have increased exposure to social failure and peer rejection, and are at risk for developing negative, self-critical beliefs. Over time, these beliefs may become central to a child's self-perceptions or view of the world. As researchers have discovered, depressed children with friendship difficulties are more likely to experience persistent depression (Goodyer, Germany, Gowrusankur, & Altham, 1991; Goodyer, Herbert, Tamplin, Secher, & Pearson, 1997) and recurrence of depression (Warner, Weissman, Fendrick, Wickramaratne, & Moreau, 1992). In addition, depressed young people are often exposed to environmental and contextual experiences that exacerbate their social deficits, such as a higher level of peer-related stressors (Rudolph & Hammen, 1999). For example, depressed children are expected to experience a higher level of teasing (Puig-Antich et al., 1985).

Children and teenagers who struggle with peers tend to come to the logical conclusion that it is easier in the short run to avoid social interactions. Repeated social failures over time have likely contributed to internalized blame, self-criticism, hopelessness, or helplessness about social exchanges, and lead to further social withdrawal.

Avoiding or withdrawing from social interactions paired with negative cognitions will block opportunities to develop the skills that lead to successful social initiations. Unfortunately, withdrawal and social avoidance with a strong negative internalized affect cannot lead to improved social skills. In the absence of intervention, this negative feedback loop can easily develop into an entrenched pattern, rooted deeply in the person's view of himself, the world, and others.

Social Skills Training Snapshot: Maddy

Maddy is a fourteen-year-old European American ninth-grader. Since her parents' divorce five years ago, she has been primarily living with her father. Maddy is artistic and intelligent, but is not involved in extracurricular activities or sports. She usually has a slightly disheveled appearance.

Two years ago, her father was diagnosed with cancer, which caused him to lose his job and undergo aggressive treatment. Recently, Maddy's father has started to respond well to cancer treatment and is beginning to feel better. He is now able to put more time and attention into her needs but is finding that she is not interested in spending more time with him.

During the course of her father's treatment, Maddy has isolated more and more. Her grades have steadily declined, and her adjustment to high school has been poor. She has one or two "kind of" friends at school, but they don't hang out except when they eat during lunch. Natalie is fascinated with teen vampire books and will spend hours in her room alone.

When Maddy's father talks about school, friends, or getting involved in clubs, she becomes quickly agitated and yells at her father. She refuses to join new activities or even take care of basic personal hygiene chores like brushing her teeth or washing her clothes.

Clinical Rationale for the Module

Social isolation or withdrawal may lead to increased severity of the child's or adolescent's depression. Adolescents are particularly vulnerable to the damaging effects of social isolation and withdrawal because of the heightened importance of the role of peer groups during the adolescent developmental period. As noted earlier, increasing pleasant activities (behavioral activation) is one of the most effective tools in treating depressed mood. Recall the cognitive triangle that was introduced in the first module: changing one's behaviors can directly impact one's mood. Furthermore, the best types of pleasant activities for behavioral activation are socially oriented ones. Because depressed children and adolescents may have poorly developed social skills, it is important to assess their social skills and include the social skills training (SST) module in their treatment if their skills need improvement.

Case Conceptualization of Child's Social Functioning

Prior to determining which social skills training activities to use as part of this module, a therapist must be armed with a clear and thoughtful understanding of the role of depressive symptomology in the presenting concerns, the key barriers to the client's positive social development, and the strengths and protective factors that will help the child successfully adopt the new skills. This clear understanding requires the therapist to continually consider the immediate processes of the therapy session while maintaining a focus on the broader, evolving picture of the client. In other words, by seeing the forest for the trees, a therapist will understand the current intervention in the context of the module and the overall treatment arc, or the client's current social skills barriers in terms of the entire client picture.

This conceptualization will typically include several layers. Substance abuse, post-traumatic stress, and developmental delays complicate this unique client picture even further. In CBT, emphasis is placed on the behavioral and cognitive factors that contribute to the presentation and maintenance of the current behaviors. When creating your client conceptualization, we urge you to remind yourself of the question, how is this affecting him now? Although a child may become more socially withdrawn because of the divorce of his parents, what are the current thoughts and attitudes that contribute to his ongoing isolation? You will develop a client conceptualization early in the treatment process, but the picture is constantly evolving as you learn more. The following sections highlight the essential topics of particular consideration for SST that will help to inform your intervention.

Individually Tailoring the Module

The first thing that will provide a framework for moving forward is the answer to the following question: What is the purpose of this intervention, and how does it fit in the broader modular CBT treatment context? Although somewhat obvious, the point with this easily overlooked question is to encourage therapists to be attentive to the client's needs and the maintenance of the presenting problem.

Instead of starting SST because the client has few friends, a thoughtful therapist will look deeper into the conditions that cause the client to have limited friendships. This will include considering the function of the symptoms, as well as the thoughts, feelings, and behaviors associated with this problem. Social skills training for school-age bullying is very different from social skills training for a peer-rejected teen. Vaguely defined interventions will have vague results as the therapist and client move toward indistinct goals. Specifically designed, individualized interventions, on the other hand, will focus the client and therapist's efforts toward the same goal.

Social Skills Training Snapshot: Maddy

Maddy loves vampire books and loves talking about vampires. She also shared that her two "kind of" friends at school are also interested in vampire books. The SST intervention for Maddy will likely include starting with peer interactions related to vampire books and later working on broadening conversation topics. The therapist may also consider ways Maddy and her father could have warm, positive interactions based on this interest.

Social Skills Training Snapshot: Juan

Early in treatment, Juan was very motivated by stickers and seemed concerned about performing well in therapy. In addition, his father was willing to attend every session. With these strengths in mind, Juan's SST intervention will likely include reinforcement for successful role-play with several stickers and praise as well as using a sticker chart during the week to track his practice of the intervention. His father will be enlisted as a champion for the plan, and he will be monitoring the sticker chart between sessions.

Using the Module

The underlying foundation of the social skills training module is that social skills can be developed and improved with practice. Many depressed children have maladaptive cognitions: *I will never make friends. Some people are just good at making friends; I'm not one of them.* These cognitive distortions should be addressed by relating back to the earlier module on addressing maladaptive cognitions and underscoring that social skills can be learned and improved with practice and feedback (much like riding a bicycle). Ultimately, the goals of this module are to help the client develop active and effective engagement in social interactions to strengthen his comfort with assertiveness, communication, and social interaction skills in social settings and among peers. He will learn to use assertiveness training autonomously to respond to teasing social situations and use communication skills to strengthen friendships and increase time engaged in social activities.

When to Include the Module

How does this intervention fit with the overall progress that has been made at this point and with the client's existing strengths and skills? Early on in treatment, children and adolescents have already developed an understanding of CBT themes coupled with mood monitoring. Psychoeducation, behavioral activation, and addressing maladaptive cognitions are typically helpful building blocks for this module. If the client has mastered mood-monitoring skills, for example, you have a significant strength to build on. Similarly, if the client understands the cognitive triangle from past treatment modules, he can move toward addressing maladaptive cognitions about social interactions in this module. Acknowledging this progress and pointing out the use of these strengths for the next module to the client is an opportunity for bootstrapping to improve relapse-prevention skills and fortify emerging strengths.

In considering when to use this module, you want to consider the level of impairment in your client's social skills functioning and how severely it is impacting his level of depression. For instance, if your client has difficulty engaging in pleasant activities with peers because he does not know how to ask them in an appropriate manner, then you may wish to consider including this module early in treatment. Likewise, if your client's core belief is *Nobody likes me; I'm unlikeable* because he doesn't know how to start and sustain a conversation when attempting to make new friends, then you will want to add this module early in the sequence. Alternatively, if your client has adequate social skills and making and keeping friends is not an area of deficit for him, then you may leave this module entirely out of your treatment course.

Cultural Considerations

When laying the foundation for a CBT intervention, it would be careless to solely consider the child's thoughts, feelings, and actions. Clearly, family, peer, community, and cultural factors influence a young person's attitudes, thoughts, and beliefs, as well as his behaviors. Thinking more broadly, a child's social capacity will be dramatically strengthened or limited based on key environmental cues.

Researchers have consistently supported the notion that parents' behaviors are affected by their thoughts and feelings and that these behaviors will affect the social development of their child (Bugental & Goodnow, 1998). Specifically, Baumrind's pioneering research on parenting styles categorized parenting styles across two dimensions: "warmth/responsiveness" and "control/demandingness" (1967, 1971). A parenting style with high warmth and high control (authoritative) was found to be related to healthy social interactions. Conversely, parents with a high-control and low-warmth (authoritarian) style were more likely to have socially anxious children (a finding that has been replicated several times since the original study; Rubin, Burgess, Kennedy, & Stewart, 2003). With the important role of parenting in social skills, successful clinicians will find ways to introduce interventions with strong collaboration and engagement among caregivers. Involving caregivers in social skills training provides an extra opportunity to integrate therapy beyond the session, which will help the child or adolescent generalize his skills into other settings.

Similarly, understanding the client's school, home, and neighborhood characteristics will allow for a more accurate translation of session topics to real-world practice and utilization. Generalization of an intervention is strongly dependent on the intervention fit in those contexts. For instance, collaboration with teachers and conducting school observations are two strategies that will likely strengthen the relevance of an intervention.

Furthermore, clinicians should take into consideration culturally specific issues. It is important to check in with parents to assess their cultural expectations of the child's social behaviors. For instance, the family may value or prefer the child's shyness. They may be reluctant to schedule playdates because it's not commonly done in their culture. These cultural expectations should be addressed early on during the first session of this module; it may be necessary to adapt and individualize the social skills training based on these cultural expectations.

Session Structure

Before each session, the clinician may write the session structure on a dry-erase board or poster. For some children, it may be helpful to have a timer for each section.

Example:

- *Check-In and Agenda Setting (5 minutes)*

- *Homework Review: Relaxation Training (5 minutes)*

- *Skills Training: Social Skills Training (25 minutes)*

- *Current Concerns (5 minutes)*

- *Assigning Between-Session Practice (5 minutes)*

- *Summary, Feedback, and Next Steps (5 minutes)*

First Steps

Check-In. The first few minutes of the session may be spent checking in with the child. Refer to the dry-erase board and prime the client for the session structure.

Therapist: As you can see on the dry-erase board, we will be checking in on how you've been doing, reviewing how the relaxation training has been going for you at home and school, and then talking about how to learn to make and keep friends. Now, how are things going for you this week? Are there certain things that you'd like to make sure that we talk about today?

Agenda Setting. Any concerns or situations that were brought up during the check-in process may be placed on the agenda for later discussion.

Homework Review. The next few minutes should be spent reviewing the client's homework assignment from the previous session. It is important to hold the child or adolescent accountable by checking in with him regarding whether he has completed his therapy homework. If the adolescent did not complete his homework assignment, then it is recommended that you spend a little more time at this point in the session to help the client complete it. For instance, if the client did not practice his deep breathing exercise, then you will lead him in a deep breathing exercise before moving on in the session.

Provide Children and Teens with a Rationale for Social Skills Training

As with previous modules, it is important to always begin with the rationale for learning or improving a skill. Particularly with children and adolescents, it is important to recognize the "benefits" that they may experience from being socially isolated. Social withdrawal may be accompanied with an emotional payoff. A teenager might avoid club meetings because of the harsh self-criticism he experiences internally at these events, followed by second-guessing and shame about perceived mistakes as he reviews his actions after the event. In this case, the payoff of avoiding such criticism may appear "worth" the isolation. Using the cognitive triangle, the clinician may demonstrate how the depression is maintained due to this cycle of avoidance and shame. Social skills training would then be offered as a potential remedy to break this cycle of social avoidance.

Skills Training

The following table provides an outline of the key elements that describe the categories of social skills training. Specific SST strategies are provided, and two example cases illustrate the real-world application of SST. The types of skills you are likely to target with this module include the following:

Social Interactions	Assertiveness Training	Communication Skills
Appropriate Body Language	Responding to Teasing	Responding to Peers
Interpreting Cues	Responding to Bullies	Initiating Conversation
Perspective Taking	Asking for Needs	Asking for Help
Initiating Interactions	Responding to Others When Angry	Telling Others How You Feel

SOCIAL INTERACTIONS

Appropriate Body Language: This intervention includes practicing eye contact, facial reactions, speech volume and pace, and body posture, and can be integrated into other skills, such as responding to teasing.

Interpreting Cues: This strategy involves understanding facial gestures but also recognizing automatic thoughts that contribute to the perception of malicious intentions or hurtful behaviors with minimal information. The cognitive triangle can often be helpful in uncovering these maladaptive cognitions among teenagers (who might irrationally decide their teacher is evil or that their parents want them to fail without considering alternative explanations).

Perspective Taking: Often a challenge for depressed youth, this intervention strategy entails the identification of the automatic thoughts that accompany misinterpretations of cues. Developmental limitations make this social skill a challenge for young children; however, it is a skill that can be developed through identifying automatic thoughts, thought stopping, and cognitive restructuring.

Initiating Interactions: This intervention focuses on how to join a game or activity with peers and can be used in connection to initiating conversation. Among teenagers, initiating interactions can include longer-term social interactions, such as developing friendships to eventually spend time outside of school.

ASSERTIVENESS TRAINING

Responding to Teasing: Based on the level of severity of the teasing, this intervention may entail how to respond assertively, how to laugh along with a joke, and how to join a conversation. Teenagers who have a low tolerance for laughing at their mistakes, for example, may have difficulty adjusting to high school.

Responding to Bullies: This intervention strategy may be somewhat tricky, depending on the severity of the bullying. The notion that the child should tell the teacher when he is bullied is widespread but is often met with limited effectiveness. Teaching a child to strategically, assertively, and calmly respond to a bully, on the other hand, can be a more realistic and lasting solution if there is low risk for physical harm. Take time to assess the scenario carefully and design a role-play that is well suited for the specific needs of the child or adolescent.

Asking for Needs: Children working on this skill may have problems with expecting others to understand their internal needs. Identifying cognitions that play a role in this behavior may help to promote appropriate assertiveness so that children ask for what they need from caregivers, friends, or teachers.

Responding to Others When Angry: Depression in children and adolescents may likely include anger. Teaching the client how to use assertiveness skills, to tell others how he feels, and to use mood-regulation skills will help to address the needs of a child whose temper can get out of control.

COMMUNICATION SKILLS

Responding to Peers: Role-play activities will give clients the opportunity to practice responding to peers, especially if they have recent experiences of responding inappropriately. For example, if a child lashed out at his friend and said, "I hate you," a therapist can offer a chance to "re-do" and respond in a more appropriate manner, which includes preparing the client to practice bringing up the issue.

Initiating Conversation: To develop this skill, the therapist (in collaboration with the client) creates a list of scenarios and randomly chooses different scenarios for the client to practice initiating conversation. As in previous modules, the therapist models the behavior first, and then the client practices via role-plays with feedback.

Asking for Help: The therapist develops a list of times when the client feels he could use help from his friends, parents, or teacher. After creating the list, the client practices asking for help in these scenarios via role-play with feedback.

Telling Others How You Feel: Telling others how they feel is often a very important but difficult skill for children and adolescents with internalizing problems, as discussed in chapter 5. For a child, the therapist may use an emotions chart (poster illustrating faces with varied emotions) to help him identify his feelings. For an adolescent, it may be helpful to describe how internalizing emotions may impact his mood and behaviors and to identify situations in which he tends to internalize. Then, the adolescent develops strategies and practices this skill. He may accomplish this skill via mood-tracking tools or setting a goal to check in with someone each day about how he's been feeling.

The "Sentences About Me" and the "Positive Personal Qualities" worksheets—which you'll find at the end of this chapter and in downloadable format at http://www.newharbinger.com/31175—can be useful to help children and teens consider how others see them, how they see themselves, and how to strengthen their social confidence. These worksheets may be used to enhance several of the strategies listed above.

ACTIVE LEARNING SEQUENCE

When training a social skill, CBT therapists use an active learning sequence. This includes the therapist describing the skills, modeling the skills, role-playing with the client, and providing feedback to refine the skills. A helpful model to keep in mind is "tell, show, do."

Tell: The therapist describes the new skill the client will be learning.

Why is he learning it?

How does the skill fit within his life and the things important to him?

What are the key parts of this skill that will make it work?

Show: The therapist demonstrates the skill.

What does it look like?

In which setting is it used?

What is the body language like?

How does it sound or feel?

Do: Now it's the client's turn to show what he understood.

Did he use the essential components?

Is his role-play likely to work if he were on his own?

How much support did he need doing the skill in session?

After the client completes the role-play, make sure to offer lots of positive reinforcement for his attempt. Praise as many behaviors as he was able to complete correctly. This will help the client be willing to role-play again; will model good, warm behaviors for the caregiver if he or she is present; and will help you notice the positive things the child achieved.

Creating a role-play intervention that will generalize to the child's or adolescent's life requires scenarios that are as realistic as possible. Do your best to make the role-play practices similar to real-life situations. You may rearrange furniture, use props, and have family members contribute to different roles. When possible, use scenarios that were previously brought up by the child or adolescent.

Providing corrective feedback is also an imperative step following the role-plays. It allows the child to recognize the important elements of the skill and shapes the desired behavior. Corrective feedback, however, can also be difficult to deliver to a depressed child or adolescent (who can be prone to internalizing criticism). As mentioned above, praise specific positive behaviors at a high ratio (keep a "five praises to one corrective comment" ratio in mind). When providing corrective feedback, offer clear, specific pointers or offer the feedback as coaching.

Therapist: Jeni! That was fantastic! I really liked the way you looked me straight in the eyes, stood up straight with strong body language, and told me exactly how you felt. That was so good! I'd bet if you said that to your friend Jordan, she'd understand so much better about how you felt. Let's try it again, okay?

Jeni: (nods)

Therapist: Okay, this time, I want you to do all of those great things you did the first time: strong body language, strong eye contact, and saying the same words you said. I have one thing I'd like you to try a little differently. On a scale of one-to-ten, how strong do you think your voice was in that practice?

Jeni: A four or five…?

Therapist: Okay, that's really good. When we started, you said you usually don't say how you feel. A four or five is way more than not saying anything. You already went from a zero to a four or five! Before we start, show me what your voice would sound like if you said it at a seven.

Jeni: *(in somewhat louder voice)* Jordan, it makes me mad when you take my chips without asking!

Therapist: Amazing strong voice, Jeni! What would it sound like at a nine?

(Jeni's tone of voice is more assertive at this point.)

Therapist: That was fantastic. I really liked your strong voice. That was perfect, so let's try again, this time with your voice at a nine. Okay?

Between-Session Practice

A typical therapy session is 1 hour of the child's or adolescent's 168-hour week. That's less than 1 percent of his time! Maximizing the potency of that clinical hour will require extra work by the client. Successful interventions will include repetition of treatment themes through homework or between-session practice. Effective therapists find ways to promote action outside of the therapy sessions as the client makes weekly progress toward mastery of the new skills. With children and teenagers, there are very realistic barriers to remembering to work on therapy homework. In these cases, successful interventions take advantage of key players in the child's or teen's life. Parents can be important "champions" outside of the session to remind, role-play, reinforce, practice, or otherwise be involved in social skills training.

Now that your client has effectively performed the skill with coaching, he will need to practice the behavior. Describe the rationale for practicing; let him know you'd like him to show you how well he can do it next time you see him. Take advantage of the champions in his life that will be able to role-play, follow up, and remind him of his homework. Let your client know that the first thing you'll ask about when you see him is how his homework went, and offer him a chart to keep track of his progress.

As a general guideline, you will know that your client has developed a mastery of the specific skill you are training when he begins to utilize the skill without prompting or coaching from others. Regularly asking your client to teach you or his family members about the skill or psychoeducation portion of the intervention is also a useful homework assignment to help him connect the therapy activity with his own life.

Several tools are available for clients that can help with therapy homework and skill building. If your client has a smartphone, there are several apps to help with emotional recognition, mood monitoring, and relaxation skills. Using apps can be a fun way for your client to practice different voice pacing or tone skills in or outside of the session. Using games, technology, or family members can add creative spins to the intervention approaches that you use to reinforce new social skills.

Social Skills Training Snapshot: Juan

Based on his conceptualization, Juan's therapist chose to use two intervention steps. First, she provided psychoeducation about how avoiding the bully problem by hiding in the bathroom can lead to more problems and probably won't lead to a solution. With the cognitive triangle, she helped Juan list several thoughts that run through his mind when he thinks about the bullies. These included *They're going to beat me up*, *Everyone will think I'm a wimp*, and *I hate school*.

During the psychoeducation exercise, Juan, his father, and his therapist discussed the feelings that arise when he has those thoughts (e.g., scared, alone, worried, and embarrassed) and how those thoughts and feelings can lead to a pattern of social avoidance over time. The therapist then enlisted Juan and his father to list alternative thoughts. They came up with *I can be strong* and *I won't let them bother me*, and the therapist added the thought *I know what to do*.

Based on their conversation, the feelings that went along with these thoughts were strong, prepared, and brave. Following this first intervention step, the therapist then asked Juan and his father to come up with ideas about what to do when the bullies confront Juan.

In this way, the therapist moved toward her second intervention step of assertiveness training to help Juan respond to bullies. The group created a list of ways to respond, like "Tell the teacher" and "Run away." Juan's father mentioned that Juan could "Be strong…stand up to them," and the group discussed what that might look like. Everyone agreed that fighting probably wouldn't work and telling the teacher about the bullies has led to Juan being bullied even more in the past.

The therapist then, using a key comment from Juan and his father, described how to stand up straight, look someone in the eyes, hold up a finger in front of oneself, and state in a firm, loud voice, "Stay away from me." She modeled the behavior with Juan's dad, having him pretend to take the ball away (an example that had actually happened to Juan). When the therapist first said the phrase, Juan seemed somewhat alarmed, and the therapist took this opportunity to say, "Did you notice how I caught your attention? What was my voice like?" She continued, "Part of the reason I used a loud, firm voice is so that other kids see what's going on, so the bully knows I'm being strong, and because other people are going to notice what he's doing."

The therapist had told and showed, and it was now Juan's turn to do.

After three to five tries with corrective feedback, Juan was able to demonstrate the key skills. The therapist modeled good praise throughout the session for Juan's father and encouraged him to talk about what he noticed and liked about Juan's practice. After each role-play, she gave Juan a sticker and asked him to do it three more times, "just like the last one!" After successfully demonstrating that he could use the skill with minimal feedback, the family developed a plan for using the skill during the next week. Since the session time was running out and Juan seemed to have just started to use the skill effectively, the therapist decided Juan would role-play the activity and skill at least one time per day for the next week, with his father acting as the bully. This would give him a chance to practice before using it at school. Juan seemed enthusiastic about practicing and filling out a sticker chart to show how well he could do. The therapist asked Juan to also give himself a grade on how well he used the skill each time that he practiced it, in hopes that he would earn all As to help build his confidence and also to let her know how comfortable he felt using the new skill.

Summary, Feedback, and Next Steps

At the end of the SST session, take time to notice genuine strengths that emerged during the session, practiced by the client and by any family members. Be sure to offer specific praise for new skills your client started to develop. Even if the client's practices seemed poor (which rarely happens), having the motivation and courage to attempt new skills and challenge old behaviors is admirable. While emphasizing strengths, find out which strengths the client noticed in himself. In which areas did he notice feeling comfortable? Which areas did he feel were more challenging? Finally, review the plan for continuing to develop social skills in the upcoming week. Discuss potential pitfalls, problem solve, and enlist encouragement from supportive individuals in the client's life. Make sure your client and his participating family members are clear on the goals of the between-session practice and this module in general. Help them understand how the client will reach mastery and how you'll know that he's mastered the social skills you are targeting with them.

Common Hurdles and Solutions for Therapists

One common challenge in this module is resistance from clients to discuss and practice new social skills. One of the frequent barriers to developing social skills is anxiety. As described in chapter 8, the relaxation training module, anxiety is often exacerbated by avoidance; however, gradual exposure is an antidote for this type of anxiety. When confronting a client who is resistant to working on new social skills and seems to be hesitant because of anxiety, keep a hierarchy of his fears or anxiety in mind. If he is resistant, move down a rung on the hierarchy of fears and find a starting point that is approachable from his point of view. While he may not be willing to try new skills with someone, he may be willing to simply imagine using those new skills and describe that to you. Whatever willingness you are able to spark will allow your client to realize his fears are irrational, and with encouragement, he will naturally feel better equipped to try a more challenging step next.

When the hesitation is not related to anxiety, it can instead be caused by depression (and generally low motivation or low activity) or resistance to treatment in general. In both cases, the behavioral activation module (chapter 6) and treatment engagement module (chapter 12) may be used to encourage progress through this module to develop mastery of new social skills.

Summary

Learning social skills can seem like an unassuming element of effective treatment for depression; however, there is strong evidence for the critical importance of the nature, quality, and frequency of social interactions for depressed children and teens. Most therapists will encounter clients whose treatment largely depends on improving social interactions. Positive social interactions are a cornerstone for many other meaningful aspects of our lives and play a pivotal role in experiencing happiness. As you build social interaction, assertiveness, and communication skills, various individuals in your client's life will contribute to more frequent positive and less frequent aversive interactions throughout his day. Over time, helping a child unlock his capacity to encourage these experiences simultaneously unlocks new avenues leading away from depression. The themes discussed in this chapter will help you teach, train, practice, and expand these skills for your clients and ultimately contribute to the overall success of treatment.

Sentences About Me

Complete each of these sentences to describe you. Use as much space as you need.

1. When I'm talking with other kids, I usually feel _____.

2. At school, I really worry that _____.

3. One thing I think others kids like about me is _____.

4. One thing I can do to be a good friend is _____.

5. Other kids say that I'm _____.

6. I like talking with other kids about _____.

7. One thing other kids think about me is _____.

8. One thing I like about myself is _____.

9. I like being alone because _____.

10. One thing that makes me different from other kids is _____.

Downloadable copies of this form are available online at http://www.newharbinger .com/31175. (See the very back of this book for more details.)

Positive Personal Qualities

Name of Friend, Family Member, Teacher, or Someone Else I Know	Positive Qualities He or She Thinks I Have	Level that I Agree (Circle; 1 = Totally Disagree, 10 = Totally Agree)
		1 2 3 4 5 6 7 8 9 10
		1 2 3 4 5 6 7 8 9 10
		1 2 3 4 5 6 7 8 9 10
		1 2 3 4 5 6 7 8 9 10

When people say nice things about me, it makes me feel:

_____

_____

_____

Downloadable copies of this form are available online at http://www.newharbinger .com/31175. (See the very back of this book for more details.)

Chapter 10

Affect Regulation

For the third time in the same week, headlines about an unruly airplane passenger were plastered all over the US media. In the last episode, a passenger on an airplane attempted to recline her seat. The woman behind her responded by yelling and swearing. When the flight attendant intervened, both women yelled at the flight attendant and became so agitated that the pilot had to divert the plane and land at the nearest airport so they could be escorted off the plane by law enforcement. In a separate incident involving road rage caught on video, a man became angered at two young occupants in another car on the freeway because they were allegedly distracted. The man used his truck to force the two young women off the road. He pounded on their window and hollered at the young women for an extended period of time while the frightened occupants recorded his tantrum using a smartphone.

How many times have you felt the same emotions as the aggressors in the above two incidents? It is a normal and common human experience to feel strong emotions. How many times have you experienced frustration, anger, or irritability when taking a flight on a crowded airplane? Or experienced anger at another driver for his distracted or poor driving skills? Although many individuals experience strong emotions, they are able to regulate and behaviorally demonstrate their emotions in socially acceptable or constructive ways. When we see someone who cannot control his or her emotions and acts up behaviorally, it is often viewed as socially unacceptable, and there are usually negative consequences. In both examples, the aggressors' behavior resulted in them being arrested, socially ostracized, and the brunt of a firestorm of negative news media coverage. Other consequences can include marital problems, job instability, housing problems from neighbor conflicts, and many more. Learning to regulate one's emotions is arguably one of the most important skills children and adolescents can develop in order to function successfully throughout their lives.

Preparing the Module

Background

A child's ability to regulate her emotions can significantly impact her functioning. In a commentary, C. C. Bell and McBride (2010) defined *affect* as the behavioral expression of emotion and *affect regulation* as a set of processes individuals use to manage emotions and achieve goal-directed outcomes. Research studies have linked affect regulation with depression. In one particular study comparing depressed and nondepressed children and young adolescents, children who endorsed higher levels of depressive symptoms reported using affect regulation strategies significantly less often than did nondepressed children (Garber et al., 1995). Furthermore, adolescents who endorsed having suicidal ideations reported having more difficulty using affect-regulation skills compared to nonsuicidal adolescents (Fritsch, Donaldson, Spirito, & Plummer, 2000).

In a review of clinical, behavioral, and functional neuroimaging studies of dysphoria and its regulation in depressed children and adolescents, Kovacs and Yaroslavsky (2014) found that depressed children and adolescents exhibited affective lability in their day-to-day functioning. In Brent and Poling's (1997) treatment manual for depressed and suicidal youth, they indicated that depressed children and adolescents may have difficulty using their adaptive coping skills when confronted with affective arousal. Thus, it may be useful to teach depressed youth, who are prone to affective dysregulation skills, the skills necessary to adequately regulate their affect.

Clinical Rationale for the Module

Children and adolescents who have adaptive affect regulation have learned how to cope with intense emotions in a manner that contributes to their healthy functioning. They typically have a variety of constructive methods they can use in different emotional situations, which aid these individuals in achieving their goals and living with adaptive functioning. In contrast, some depressed children have maladaptive affect-regulation skills. Given that irritability is a primary symptom of depression in youth, depressed children with irritable mood in particular may be prone to affect dysregulation. Because affect dysregulation tends to result in impaired functioning in multiple domains, it is included as a supplementary module in this treatment manual. In this module, the goal is to teach children and adolescents how to cope with their emotions and regulate their affect in order to improve their ability to use their problem-solving or coping skills.

Case Conceptualization of a Child's Affective Dysregulation

If you have selected this supplementary module to be included in your client's treatment, you have presumably assessed your client to have an affect-regulation problem. At this point, it is important to review your case conceptualization and have a clear understanding as to why your client has difficulty with controlling her response to intense emotions. Did she have a parent who modeled poor affect regulation? Was she abused as a child by a parent who expressed anger by hitting her? Is she receiving attention and inadvertent reinforcement each time she engages in an emotional outburst? Or do others predictably leave her alone when she yells and screams, which provides her with desired alone time? Does the client have a co-occuring psychiatric disorder? Having a good case conceptualization of your client's behaviors and affect dysregulation—along with the antecedents, beliefs, and consequences—will allow you to individualize this module and address potential barriers to treatment.

> Twelve-year-old Emmi is sitting in the backseat of her mother's car. As her mother pulls up into the alley to park in her garage spot, another car is blocking her way. Seconds tick by, and Emmi's mother has quickly become visibly upset at the occupant of the other car. She puts down her window and yells at the other driver. Upon seeing her, the other driver points to another car in front of him to indicate that he is waiting for the lane to clear. Unassuaged by this message, Emmi's mother storms to the other car and bangs on the driver's window. She screams profanities at him and kicks his car. Emmi has a clear view of her mother's affective outburst and is concerned that a police car has now pulled up alongside her mother.

This example, derived from Emmi's case conceptualization, reveals that Emmi's mother modeled temper tantrums to Emmi via these outbursts. Additionally, Emmi's mother has been diagnosed with bipolar disorder, so there may be a genetic component to the behaviors, like anger outbursts, that Emmi displays now. With this information about Emmi's mother, her therapist would continue to look for areas in Emmi's environment that could be changed to reduce anger outbursts and encourage new affect-regulation strategies. The therapist would keep in mind the family dynamics as well as the family history of bipolar disorder as he prepares for this module.

Individually Tailoring the Module

Consistent with other modules in this treatment approach, you should always be thinking about ways you can flexibly and creatively teach the skills so that the skills-based learning is maximized in the child or adolescent. Ask yourself, "How can I teach affect identification in a way that encourages this child to be interested and to listen?" You should take into consideration the child's developmental level and any specialized areas of interest. For instance, does the child have a mature understanding of emotions? If so, you may move along quickly and spend less time on teaching her how to identify affect. Does she have an interest in superheroes? If so, then you may want to use superhero action figures in the activities for teaching the skill. You may ask the child what the superhero is feeling when she is confronted with a villain. What about an adolescent who has received a long-awaited smartphone? How can you elicit the use of the smartphone in teaching the adolescent affect-regulation skills? You may consider an app that allows her to identify emotions of characters in the app. There are feeling-thermometer apps that allow the adolescent to rate her emotions directly on the device while the app records it.

Using the Module

This module is targeted to clients who have intrusive anger or mood instability problems that are contributing to their depression. The goals of this module are to develop capacity to respond to triggers and regulate emotions to improve mood stability. Your client will learn to demonstrate the use of affect-regulation skills to promote stable mood when confronted by usual triggers, to effectively and autonomously utilize reappraisal strategies to correct cognitive distortions, and to enhance mood stability.

When to Use This Module

This module is considered supplementary and is not used with all depressed clients. If you have a client who has difficulty regulating her affect, then you will want to include this module as part of your treatment course. This module is intended to be used after the child has already learned mood monitoring. This is because the first step to learning how to regulate one's affect is being able to identify one's emotional state. The mood monitoring module teaches the child how to identify and rate her emotions and understand that there is a range (e.g., mild to moderate to severe) to the experiencing of emotions. Prior to learning the skills in the mood monitoring module, the adolescent may experience emotions in an "all-or-none" manner. Learning how to monitor her mood allows her to perceive the varying intensity of her emotions. To rate the intensity of her emotion, the adolescent may use either the feeling thermometer, which was described in the mood monitoring module, or an emotion ladder (see the worksheet at the end of the chapter, which is also available online at http://www.newharbinger.com/31175), which is used in a similar fashion.

With the emotion ladder, similar to the feeling thermometer, you use a range of numbers on a one-to-ten scale to indicate an increasing range of severity of emotion. You write the number one next to the first rung on the ladder to indicate a neutral emotion such as "calm." You then write the number ten at the top of the ladder rungs, with a strong emotion such as "explosive anger" next to it. Finally, you write the number five next to the middle rung, and write a midrange emotion such as "frustrated." Next to each of the emotions, you will have the child write a real-life example of when she felt each of those emotions. For instance, for number ten, "explosive anger," you can ask the child, "When did you feel the most angry you've ever felt in your life, when you couldn't control your emotions at all?" Her answer would be written down next to number ten to serve as an anchor.

Therapist: Remember when we used the feeling thermometer a few sessions ago? You learned how to rate your mood level using the one-to-ten scale. We are going to use that feeling thermometer again in this session; however, one will represent feeling calm—no anger at all—and ten will represent the most angry you've ever felt in your life. Think of a time when you've felt that way.

Cultural Considerations

While affect and emotions are universal phenomena, they are impacted deeply by culture. Affect (the behavioral manifestation of an emotion) is often steeped in cultural context. It is recommended that clinicians consider the cultural context of the client's environment when assessing for affect dysregulation. In a study that looked at the processes of emotion regulation in twenty-three countries, differences in these processes were found based on cultures (Matsumoto, Yoo, & Nakagawa, 2008). You are encouraged to take a cultural humility approach and follow the family's lead in learning about how emotions and affect are expressed and viewed in their family culture. For instance, in one family's culture, it may be generally more acceptable or expected for individuals to yell or show strong emotion, whereas another family's culture may expect their family members to exert strong control over demonstration of emotions.

Involving Parents and Caregivers

This module requires the involvement of parents or caregivers because the child or adolescent with affect-regulation problems often needs their scaffolding. Parents may be helpful in identifying triggers or cues that the child experiences (e.g., clenched fists, raised voice) when initially becoming upset. Sometimes the adolescent is unaware of these cues, and parents can offer insight and information based on previous experiences when she was affectively dysregulated. Moreover, during the psychoeducation component of this module, you want to elicit the parents' agreement and cooperation in supporting the adolescent's selected coping strategies. Without this agreement, you may find the parents inadvertently creating a barrier for the child to follow her plan to maintain affect regulation. For instance, an adolescent begins arguing with her parents and becomes affectively dysregulated as indicated by raising her voice and clenching her fist. She then recalls her affect-regulation skills that she learned in session with her therapist. She decides to take a "chill-out" break from the situation in order to help her calm down. As she walks to her room, her parents, if they were not involved in the affect-regulation work during the session (where they would have learned about the "chill-out" coping strategy), may unintentionally escalate the situation by perceiving her walking away as insolence and demanding that she return to the situation to finish resolving the conflict by talking it out.

Structuring the Session

Before each session, the clinician may write the session structure on a dry-erase board or poster. For some children, it may be helpful to have a timer for each section.

Example:

- *Check-In and Agenda Setting (5–10 minutes)*

- *Homework Review: Social Skills Training (5 minutes)*

- *Skills Training: Affect Regulation (20 minutes)*

- *Current Concerns (5–10 minutes)*

- *Assigning Between-Session Practice (5 minutes)*

- *Summary, Feedback, and Next Steps (5 minutes)*

First Steps

Check-In. The first few minutes of the session may be spent checking in with the adolescent. Refer to the dry-erase board and prime the client for the session structure.

Therapist: As you can see on the dry-erase board, we will be checking in on how you've been doing, reviewing how the social skills between-session practice has been going for you, and then talking about how to cope when we have strong emotional responses to situations. Now, are there certain things that you'd like to make sure that we talk about today?

Agenda Setting. Any concerns or situations that were brought up during the check-in process may be placed on the agenda for later discussion. As a reminder, an effective way to address any "crisis of the week" incidents is to incorporate the discussion into the skills-building exercise that is on the agenda for the particular week. For instance, an adolescent may wish to discuss an incident during which she had a bad break-up with a boyfriend that occurred at school over the past week. You may incorporate this discussion in the skills-building section of affect regulation by using the situation as an example as you're teaching the skills.

Therapist: You may remember from last week that we will be setting the agenda at the beginning of every session. I'm really sorry to hear how upset you are about your break-up with Richard.

Client: Yes, it was a big blowout after school. I get so angry when I think about what happened.

Therapist: Okay, let's put that on our agenda for today. We will talk about what happened with Richard and how to deal with your emotions about what happened.

Homework Review. The next few minutes should be spent reviewing the client's homework assignment from the previous session. You want to consistently hold the child or adolescent accountable by checking in with her regarding whether she has completed the therapy homework. If the adolescent did not complete her homework assignment, then it is recommended that you spend a little more time at this point in the session to help the client complete her homework assignment. You can engage parents in reminding the child every evening to complete her therapy homework.

Skills Training

PROVIDING A RATIONALE FOR AFFECT REGULATION

Using your case conceptualization and the information provided in this chapter, explain the clinical rationale for affect-regulation skills building with the adolescent. Particularly with children and adolescents, it is important to recognize the function of the affect dysregulation. Is the child receiving any reinforcement for the affective outbursts? Is the temper tantrum the only way she has learned to express her emotions? Understanding the function of her behavior will allow you to help her select the appropriate and most effective coping skills to use when she is affectively labile. As part of the psychoeducation component, you want to elicit the child's or adolescent's motivation for learning to control her affect. One way to increase this motivation is to ask the child to identify the unpleasant consequences that have resulted from her affect-regulation problem. For instance, has she been suspended from school? Lost a friend? Been alienated from a peer group? Had privileges taken away? Had her girlfriend leave her? You want to highlight the direct connection between her emotional dysregulation and the subsequent consequences. Then, you can employ Socratic questioning to teach her that learning to regulate her affect can help her avoid or mitigate these consequences in the future. As a reminder, Socratic questioning is the use of questions to guide the adolescent's discovery.

ACTIVE LEARNING SEQUENCE

When teaching affect-regulation skills, CBT therapists use an active learning sequence. This includes the therapist describing the skills, modeling the skills, role-playing with the client, and providing feedback to refine the skills. A helpful model to keep in mind is the model-practice-corrective-feedback process. You may use an imaginal script to elicit the strong emotions in session (e.g., describe a situation that was upsetting to the child). Another way to elicit strong emotions in session is to watch a video that shows a situation that tends to upset the client. You may also engage a parent in the role-plays; this can be especially helpful if the child tends to become affectively dysregulated during interactions with the parent.

The five basic steps to learning affect regulation involve the following:

1. Recognize and identify when your emotional state becomes increasingly aroused (e.g., frustrated, angry, sad). This is where parents may offer insight into the adolescent's specific behavioral cues, such as the adolescent sighing loudly, clenching her fist, or slamming the door. The key issue here is to bring these cues into awareness early in the stage of emotional arousal.

Client: I notice that whenever I start getting really angry, my breathing becomes faster and my face feels really tense.

Therapist: When your breathing becomes shallow and you tense up your facial muscles, where on the emotion ladder would you say you are? (*Therapist points to emotion ladder depicted on the worksheet or drawn on a whiteboard.*)

Client: (*points to the third rung of emotion ladder*) I'd say, maybe a three.

2. Identify the number (on the feeling thermometer or emotion ladder associated with the emotion self-rating) that is associated with the adolescent feeling out of control of her emotions. For this part, it may be helpful to use examples from previous episodes of affect dysregulation.

Therapist: Let's look at the emotion ladder; you said that when you start feeling angry, your breathing becomes shallow, your face tenses up, and you would rate that to be a three (points at third rung on emotion ladder). I want you to think about the point at which you felt out of control of your behaviors because of your strong emotions. For example, when you got angry during the break-up with your boyfriend last week, at which point did you feel so out of control of your emotions that you slapped him?

Client: I'd say, when I get to a seven (*points to seventh rung on the emotion ladder*). Once I get that angry, it's really hard for me to control myself.

Therapist: Okay, that's good; now that we know the point at which you feel out of control, we can learn how to back down from that point so you can learn how to control your behavior when you get really angry. Look at the emotion ladder—I think of the point at which you get out of control as the point at which you climb up the ladder and fall off and get really hurt. If you know which rung on the ladder is a safe point to stop, then you can pause, look at your surroundings while standing on that rung, and then make a plan for how to go back down the ladder safely once you have a good awareness of your predicament.

3. Make a plan to avoid an emotions rating of seven (as designated by the client) on the emotion ladder. Select a number that is several points below that "out-of-control point" and have a plan for specific actions to help the adolescent return to a lower number where she feels more in control of her affect.

Therapist: Okay, so you said that when you get to a seven on the emotion ladder, you feel out of control of your behavior. You said that you were at a seven when you slapped your boyfriend last week. Would you say that you could have controlled your behavior if you were still at a five on the emotion ladder?

Client: Yes, at a five I probably would have not slapped him.

Therapist: Let's think of ways that you can deal with your emotions when you get near five, so you move down the ladder, instead of up to seven. What actions can you take to help your emotions go from a five to a four?

Client: I don't know. I can't think of any.

Therapist: What about the time a couple of weeks ago when your sister pushed you and you were able to keep in control of your feelings? You didn't push her back, and instead you went to your room.

Client: Oh, yeah, when I get really upset, sometimes it helps me to go to my room and listen to music.

Therapist: Okay, so when you get to a five on the emotion ladder, do you think it might be helpful to grab your headphones and iPod and listen to some music? Or walk away from the situation? Would that help your emotions rating go down to a four or three? What else might be helpful? What about taking some deep breaths? Can you think of any other coping skills?

4. Enact the action plan for affect regulation. The action plan should include multiple options so that the adolescent can systematically try each coping strategy until one is effective. A common error here is identifying too few options or including unrealistic options. For instance, an adolescent may identify "texting a friend" as a coping strategy. In the incident with her boyfriend, having just one identified coping strategy on her action plan is likely insufficient. The risk of having too few options for coping strategies or including unrealistic options is that the adolescent or family may come to believe, erroneously, that affect regulation isn't effective for the adolescent. In the above example, you may see the adolescent come into session, express feedback that she failed, and feel disheartened about therapy working for her. Thus, it is important to ensure that the action plan includes multiple coping strategies, and that the adolescent is instructed to try each of the coping strategies until one is effective. In the example of the adolescent who was in the altercation with her boyfriend, if texting a friend didn't work, then the adolescent may move on to the next coping strategy, such as walking away and taking a break from the situation while listening to music on her iPod.

5. Identify the number (on the feeling thermometer or emotion ladder) that is associated with the adolescent feeling more in control of her emotions. This last step also includes a brief self-assessment into which coping strategies were most effective, in order to inform her future action plans.

This supplemental module assumes that mood monitoring has already been discussed previously with the child or adolescent. You may wish to review the feeling thermometer from the mood monitoring module with the client. If you individualized the mood monitoring module and used another concept (e.g., the emotion ladder), then you want to be consistent and use the same concept for this module. The key issue for this section is that you can review the client's ability to rate her emotional state. Using the thermometer (or any appropriate analogy), describe the range of emotions; that is, that people often experience a range of emotional states such as "calm to mildly irritated to moderately frustrated to severe anger."

Modeling. Many children and adolescents, when learning how to use affect regulation for the first time, find it to be difficult. One effective tool the clinician may use is modeling. For example, in this module, you may use modeling by demonstrating how you identify cues about your emotional state. It is helpful to be overt in your thought process and practice.

Therapist: I notice that whenever I'm around David and I see him using my things without asking me first, I become upset. I can tell that I'm getting upset because my voice raises, my heart feels like it's pounding, and I have the strong urge to yell at him.

Role-Play with Feedback. After modeling the affect regulation, elicit the adolescent to practice the coping strategies. Role-plays should always begin with the therapist modeling the behavior; then the roles are switched and the adolescent practices the behavior. The clinician should always provide praise, as well as any needed corrective feedback.

Therapist: Okay, let's imagine that I'm your mom and I just removed your computer privileges because of a poor report card. You are feeling angry. What should you do?

Client: Well, I think I'd be pretty mad since that's not fair. It's not my fault that my teachers don't like me.

Therapist: Let's practice what you can do when you feel really angry and you want to stay in control of your behaviors despite feeling so angry. Janelle, your grades are terrible—you got four Cs and a D! Like I told you before, if you get any Ds then you don't get to use the computer for two weeks.

Client: Okay, so I'm gonna say I'm at a four on the emotion ladder because my voice is getting louder. My face is feeling hot, which happens when I get angrier. I know that seven is my point of feeling out of control, and I don't want to hit my mom or do anything that will make her ground me more, like taking away my cell phone.

Therapist: Janelle, I'm really mad about these grades. I can tell that you are getting really angry because you're starting to yell. Do you want to go to your room and take a break?

The adolescent should role-play the action of walking out of the room, perhaps even sighing loudly if that is part of her behavioral repertoire. The idea here is to mimic real-life situations to enhance learning new behaviors. You should encourage her to practice additional identified coping strategies during this role-play.

Between-Session Practice

The key aspect to learning how to regulate one's affect effectively is to practice during role-plays, as well as to practice these skills when the emotion is moderately strong. You want to strongly encourage the client to practice frequently so the behaviors become habitual. Once the strategies become very familiar and easily accessible, then the child or adolescent will be better equipped to use the strategies when she finds herself in a strong emotional state.

Summary, Feedback, and Next Steps

Have the client summarize the session highlights to you.

Therapist: Today, we learned how to take control of our emotions. In what kinds of situations might you use these skills?

Ask the client and family for feedback regarding the session. This feedback allows you to know what is working in real time and what is not working as well.

Therapist: How do you think today's session went? What was most helpful to you?

The final step to the session is to prime the client as to the next steps in therapy. Affect regulation can be a difficult skill to learn and generalize in real-world situations, so it is likely that you may need to conduct this module over several therapy sessions. Do not move on to another module until the client has demonstrated the ability to use the action plan in a real-world incident. As always, you should prime the client as to which next step is likely.

Therapist: Today, we talked about the emotion ladder, and you did an excellent job of coming up with real-world examples linked to each number on the emotion ladder. We talked about the point of feeling out of control of your behaviors because of your strong emotions, and we also talked about the kinds of strong emotions you tend to have in various situations. You said that you feel really frustrated when your sister goes into your room without asking, and you feel angry when your boyfriend doesn't respond to your texts within the hour. We also talked about cues that occur during strong feelings, and these cues can be signs like your voice raising or clenching your fist. For your between-session practice, whenever you start feeling a strong emotion, like frustration or anger, I would like you to take notice and be aware of cues that are connected with your number on the emotion ladder going up. What cues in your body or behaviors occur when you go from a one to a four? Go ahead and record those cues on your smartphone app. Next week, we will come up with ways to help you control your strong feelings so you can avoid getting into more trouble. Do you have any questions?

Common Hurdles and Solutions for Therapists

Affect regulation is a skill that is easily practiced during therapy sessions, but can be quite difficult to implement in real-world practice. This is a common complaint that you may hear: "I see that she can practice the coping skills during the therapy session, but at home, when something upsets her, she doesn't use those skills. She throws a tantrum instead!" Thus, it may be helpful to acknowledge this difficulty ahead of time and provide psychoeducation to both the adolescent and parent about the importance of practicing these skills frequently so they become habitual and easier to use in moments when the adolescent is faced with intense emotional arousal. The following example uses the concept of learning how to ride a bike. But again, you want to always use examples that are relevant to your client. For instance, if your client's preferred activity is video games, then you may want to replace the bicycling example with a video game one.

Therapist: Learning how to cope with our emotions when we get upset is a lot like learning how to ride a bike. When you first learn how to ride a bike, you practice all the movements and it can seem awkward, right? Where do you put your feet? When do you push on the pedals? How do you hold on to the handles to steer? You have to think about a lot of movements, and you're likely to move very slowly and fall often. This is just like learning how to cope with your emotions. When you are first learning how to use helpful coping strategies, it will seem awkward or even silly. Practicing how to take deep breaths, walking away, counting to ten, taking a "chill-out" break, and engaging in progressive muscle relaxation exercises may be difficult to use when you are first learning, and especially when you are feeling an intense emotion like frustration or anger. Just like how it was awkward when you were learning how to ride the bike, it will feel awkward when you are learning how to use these coping skills. However, if you keep practicing, there comes a time when riding the bike will become easy. When you hop on a bike in a hurry to get home, your muscle memory will retain the skills, and you can ride home without thinking about each and every movement required to ride the bike. The same is true for these strategies that help you cope with your emotions. If you keep practicing, there will come a time when using the coping skill will become easy, like a habit. And then when you are faced with a strong emotion, your "muscle memory" will remember what to do, and you will be able to use the coping skill without thinking about each and every movement required to complete that coping skill. It'll become easy, just like riding a bike!

Summary

This module is considered supplementary and is used with clients who have difficulty regulating their affect. Prior to learning this module, the adolescent may experience emotions in an "all-or-none" manner. Learning how to monitor her mood, recognize the cues of her emotions getting stronger, and use her coping strategies before she loses control will help your client improve her relationships and interpersonal interactions with others.

Emotion Ladder:
Learning How to Cope with Anger
or Frustration

Emotion Ladder Worksheet Goals: To develop affect regulation, to recognize the range of an emotional state, and to identify when and how to cope with strong emotions.

Instructions (refer to chapter 10 for full instructions):

1. Personalize the anchors.

    a. For 1 (*point to bottom rung of ladder*): "Think of a time when you were very relaxed." Write the client's answer next to the bottom rung of the ladder image. If the client has difficulty thinking of a situation, then you may elicit one from the parent (if present) or offer examples.

    b. For 10 (*point to top rung of ladder*): "Think of a time or situation when you have felt the most angry or frustrated ever, when you felt really mad or frustrated." Write the situation next to the top rung of the ladder.

2. Recognize and identify when your emotional state becomes increasingly aroused (e.g., frustrated, angry, sad). This is where parents may offer insight into the client's specific behavioral cues, such as sighing loudly, clenching his fist, or slamming the door. The goal is to bring these cues into awareness early in the stage of emotional arousal.

    a. "Think of when you start to feel angry [or other emotion]. How do you know that it is happening?" Engage the client to identify physical cues (e.g., heart racing, shallow breathing, face feeling hot).

    b. "When you start to feel upset, at what number on the ladder do you notice these physical sensations?" For instance, if the client responds with the number 3, then write the client's identified physical cues next to the rung associated with number 3.

3. Identify the number (on the emotion ladder) that is associated with the child or adolescent feeling out of control of his emotions.

    a. "Let's look at the emotion ladder. You said that when you start feeling angry, your breathing becomes shallow, your face tenses up, and you would rate that to be a 3 (*point to third rung of ladder*). I want you to think about the point at which you felt out of control of your behavior because of your strong emotions."

    b. Write "Out-of-Control Point" or "Danger Point" next to the number identified by the client.

4. Select a number that is several points below that out-of-control point and discuss a plan for specific actions to help the client return to a lower number where he feels more in control of his affect. This may be the same as the number identified in step 2b, or it may be slightly higher.

    a. "Now that we know the point at which you feel out of control, we can learn how to back down from that point so you can learn how to control your behavior when you get really angry. Look at the emotion ladder. Think of the point at which you get out of control like the point at which you climb up a ladder and fall off and get really hurt. If you know which rung on the ladder is a safe point to stop, then you can pause, look at your surroundings while standing on that rung, and then make a plan for how to go back down."

    b. Write these strategies next to the number (the point at which the client first notices that he is starting to get increasingly upset and is potentially nearing the out-of-control point).

5. Discuss and practice using the identified adaptive coping strategies. Ensure that parents are aware and in support of these strategies.

Downloadable copies of this form are available online at http://www.newharbinger .com/31175. (See the very back of this book for more details.)

Chapter 11

Family Collaboration

Imagine you had five sentences to introduce yourself to someone. Take a moment to think how you would fill in the blanks here with five different answers.

I am _____ .

I am _____ .

I am _____ .

I am _____ .

I am _____ .

What could you say? *I am a student. I am funny. I am thoughtful. I am a boyfriend. I am working on being a better person. I am Latino. I am frustrated by all the hurdles of getting licensed. I am a woman. I am interested in helping people who struggle with depression. I am trying to be a better mother.* It might be a challenge to make five statements that really give a good introduction to you as a person. We might feel only partially understood without the chance to describe the contexts of our lives. The contexts in our lives are the layers of who we are. One layer that contributes to our identity is family. Each person has a unique story, which is constantly changing or evolving with different types of family relationships.

Now imagine asking a child or teenager to choose five statements to describe himself. What would he say? With less time to develop an individual identity, family layers are inseparably connected with who children and teenagers are. Trying to help depressed children and teenagers without involving this important aspect of their lives can sometimes mean the difference between success and stagnation. In this chapter we discuss the role families can play in modular CBT to collaborate and expand the impact of treatment.

Preparing the Module

In the treatment of children and youth struggling with depression, you will encounter family patterns, family interactions, and family connections that contribute to your client's well-being and symptomology. Starting with the initial assessment, the therapist is cued in to the different pieces of the client's life that contribute to the treatment process. If interventions are going to be successful, families will play a role in that success, at least to some degree. Often, family collaboration is essential to treatment success. Using the ongoing assessment and conceptualization of the case, you will identify ways family involvement will contribute to solutions. Most commonly, parent behaviors and family patterns can be strengthened in order to help your client progress toward successful treatment. In this chapter, we discuss the role of families in modular CBT for depressed children and youth. After a brief background, we offer specific skills-building approaches for enhancing family collaboration in treatment.

Background

Early learned experiences are widely believed to significantly contribute to the psychological vulnerability that leads to emotional disorders (Barlow, 2000), as well as the psychological resilience associated with effectively coping with emotional challenges. The early learned experiences that contribute to depression can include chaotic or unresponsive home environments, modeling of an external locus of control or ineffective coping reactions to stress, and childrearing in a way that increases negative cognitions and emotions (Benjamin et al., 2011; Epstein & Schlesinger, 1996).

Parenting behaviors that can elevate the risk for depression in children and youth include high interparent conflict and inconsistent discipline, as well as parents consistently offering low warmth (i.e., providing little support or affection) and low autonomy (i.e., providing children few opportunities to consider decisions and make choices for themselves). In connection to low warmth, risk for depression is increased when parents adopt a parenting style that is very directive, demanding of unquestioning obedience, and highly punitive. Also, parents who are overinvolved might use hostile or coercive techniques to intrude on opportunities for autonomy and increase the risk for depression (Yap, Pilkington, Ryan, & Jorm, 2014). Parenting styles and practices are therefore very important in the treatment of depression. Children with parents who have consistent and significant problems balancing control and warmth are more likely to experience cognitive, emotional, and behavioral problems, despite the progress they might make individually in a session.

While early learning and parenting practices can increase the risk of depression, family collaboration can contribute to disrupting ineffective family patterns, changing the status quo, and improving cognitive, emotional, and behavioral coping. There are many ways family members can support clients as they replace ineffective patterns with new skills and strengths (Dattilio, Epstein, & Baucom, 1998; Teichman, 1992), and therapists can build on family strengths to encourage the success of different interventions.

Clinical Rationale for the Module

As families have become increasingly recognized as integral to treatment success, ecological or family-based approaches to CBT have gradually emerged to strengthen interventions (Benjamin et al., 2011; Dattilio, 1998, 2001, 2014). Children and youth successful in modular CBT for depression must be successful in translating new skills, new ways of thinking, and new behavioral patterns outside of the therapy session. This includes at school, with peers, and at home. The home environment in particular seems to be the most impactful for many clients and the setting in which therapists have the greatest ability to create change through collaboration with family members. Family collaboration in modular CBT incorporates parent training and behavioral modification by parents, as well as enhanced contextual support for the child to reach mastery of new skills.

From a modular CBT–informed conceptualization, children, siblings, and parents can benefit from learning about how thoughts, feelings, and behaviors are connected and contribute to mood. For example, parents may learn to reduce their modeling of depressive thinking as they participate in the psychoeducation module, or siblings may reduce their aggression toward your client as they learn he is struggling with negative mood symptoms as a result of the aggression. Families may also develop solutions and problem-solving skills together as they learn about these skills. A sister may remind her mother about the between-session activity that was planned in session, or a father may remind his son to communicate his feelings more openly or to use the feeling thermometer.

When parents participate in modular CBT for depression, one additional and important benefit is that the treatment process is transparent. When parents are not involved, therapy may seem like a "black box." They have little understanding of what has happened to help their child's mood improve. When involved, however, parents can see and learn from the interventions and how they contribute to improving their child's mental health. This opportunity for modeling makes it more likely that parents will be successful if they try to help their child in the future if he has difficulty sustaining changes or if symptoms return. The child's depressive behaviors will not seem as puzzling or inflexible.

Family Collaboration

Therapists, clients, and families have several options for involvement in therapy. The process tends to move smoother when these decisions are discussed early and are based on the conceptualization and treatment plan formulation, with the understanding that needs may change as the process continues. Perhaps the first decision will be to decide who should be involved in treatment. This can be a very practical consideration about who is available and will be responsible for transportation. Beyond practical considerations like transportation, however, this question can have a big impact on the tone and effectiveness of treatment.

Mothers are the most common therapy companions for young people. Although there is evidence that father involvement contributes to positive long-term outcomes in mental health treatment, fathers are often overlooked and passively excluded from the treatment process (Pahl & Barrett, 2010). Similarly, foster parents, siblings, and extended family members are sometimes ignored as potential resources to strengthen the treatment process. However, in order for treatment to be successful, the session must translate into the child's life. When significant family dynamics and relationships are brought into the treatment session, the factors that contribute to the client's depression will also be accessible to the therapist and the treatment process. Including as many family members as possible usually benefits the therapist since she will have a much better understanding of how different individuals interact with the client, leading to a more complete conceptualization and treatment plan.

Similarly, family collaboration helps better inform therapists about family needs. For example, therapists will be more likely to understand if there are financial strains, developmental needs of other family members, or significant parenting deficits. In these cases, therapists can identify needs for supplementary services such as case management, parenting classes, referrals for developmental evaluations, and so forth. Many times these stressors on the family play a primary or secondary role on the child's experience of depression. Some reasonable flexibility by the therapist may help open opportunities to include multiple family members. Therapists might consider their flexibility with schedules as well as their flexibility toward meeting by phone, at schools, in homes, or at other locations in the community.

A few important considerations when involving family members include each individual's mental health status, the individual's contribution and influence in the session, the individual's role or potential role in generalizing skills, and the available services that might complement the treatment process. If family members demonstrate significant mental health impairment, it is important to make a referral for treatment and to take steps to help those individuals initiate treatment. This step can often have significant effects on the child's symptomology—increased parental functioning, for example, can simultaneously improve the child's functioning (Epstein & Schlesinger, 1996). If family members are disruptive to the session, this family dynamic is an important piece of information that may inform your conceptualization of the client. Rather than merely excluding or avoiding that disruptive individual, a therapist should consider this part of the family functioning in her conceptualization and treatment plan. She might address the disruption clinically, particularly if it contributes to the child's depression.

When family members are present, the therapist is also better able to assess family strengths. Positive qualities and examples of resilience will emerge as you learn about family history, the ways individuals interact, and the roles that exist. You may find that an older sibling or an aunt has a strong, positive relationship with your client. You may find that a mother is willing to try new skills and really wants her son's depression to improve. If there are individuals who can help your client develop new skills, a therapist may enlist these individuals as champions to support changes in between sessions. Collaborate with these family-member champions to understand how your client is impacted by depression, to offer encouragement and support for new skills, and to model new behaviors themselves. These champions can often have a much stronger impact on your client's ongoing success than you might have via weekly therapy sessions.

Individually Tailoring the Module

The timing and use of this module can vary widely based on the family structure, the therapist's conceptualization of the child's depression, and the role of the family in reducing the depression. In some cases, family collaboration will simply mean the therapist works with the client, his brother, and his father in each of the sessions to address depression from a family-based approach. In others, the specific parenting skills provided in this chapter will be useful for the parents, and the therapist will schedule additional sessions with just the parents to help them develop their capacity to support the client and change patterns in the family that seem to exacerbate symptoms. The parenting-skill activities presented in this module may include the client and siblings or might be more useful with the caregivers alone (at least initially). The case conceptualization will drive these decisions about individualizing this module and the treatment plan.

Using the Module

This module emphasizes ways to incorporate family members in the treatment of a child's or teenager's depression. The most common way that family members contribute to modular CBT for depression is by participation in the modules or by building new skills that will augment the treatment process. Throughout each chapter, we've discussed ways family members can participate in specific modules. In this chapter, we outline ways family members can augment the overall treatment process. This chapter focuses on strengthening parenting skills (including parent communication) and the use of parental behavioral management as primary techniques for including family members and enhancing treatment success.

Structuring the Session

Before each session, the clinician may write the session structure on a dry-erase board or poster. As with other modules, you will begin with a check-in on treatment-relevant client or family changes since the previous session. This is followed by setting the agenda, reviewing previous session topics and practices, and checking in about the treatment plan to discuss current progress and next steps.

Example:

- *Check-In and Agenda Setting (5 minutes)*

- *Homework Review: Affect Regulation (3 minutes)*

- *Skills Training: Family Collaboration (30 minutes)*

- *Current Concerns (3 minutes)*

- *Assigning Between-Session Practice (3–4 minutes)*

- *Summary, Feedback, and Next Steps (5 minutes)*

First Steps

Check-In. Take time to assess progress and changes between sessions and to ensure the client is ready to transition to the next module.

Agenda Setting. Write the session agenda in a place that the client and family members can see it. Include homework review, didactic and skills training, current concerns, between-session practice, and summary, feedback, and next steps. You might then prioritize the agenda by discussing which topics are most important and creating a road map to proceed. The parent-training portion could extend beyond three sessions depending on how parents progress. Parenting behaviors can be fairly entrenched, and parents may need ongoing practice, separate meetings, or phone calls with the therapist, or additional support from other service providers for the skills to crystallize.

Homework Review. Depending on how the client is involved in this module, you may need to meet separately with him for approximately ten minutes to review homework and prepare him for ongoing practice while his parents participate in this module. The client can be simultaneously working on developing mastery of the skills from other modules while his parents develop the skills discussed in this module. For example, when parents are working to strengthen their ability to use discipline strategies, it's usually better for teenagers not to know their parents are working on these new skills since they are likely to challenge or resist the parents' attempts at enforcing new rules. In other cases, the family will work together on this module and the homework review will be similar to other modules.

Skills Training

Psychoeducation about parenting styles helps lay the groundwork for parents to understand the skills you will be presenting. With a conversation focused on parenting styles, you are encouraging parents to consider their behaviors in a non-confrontational way. Nearly all parents are trying to do their best for their children, and all parents encounter roadblocks along the way. It can be very hurtful to suggest parents are using ineffective skills or detrimental practices since for most parents, the last thing they want to do is cause difficulty for their kids. Psychoeducation about parenting styles encourages parents to let you know in what ways they hope to make progress.

PARENTING STYLES

As described in the background section of this chapter, parenting practices have been found to contribute to a child's risk of experiencing depression. The parenting practices that are most closely connected with depression in young people center around the parent's balance of control and warmth. In the 1970s, Baumrind (1971, 1975) categorized four parenting styles based on research on parenting practice and child development. These parenting styles are driven by the parent's balance of control and warmth with his or her children.

Authoritarian parenting is characterized by low warmth and high control. Authoritarian parents are overcontrolling or unreasonably demanding for the child's developmental level, with inadequate affection or acknowledgment of appropriate behavior. With highly demanding parents, children rarely feel adequate and see themselves as constantly failing as they experience continuing displeasure from their parents. The lack of warmth results in feelings of rejection and low nurturance. Children with authoritarian parents more commonly struggle with aggression, social withdrawal, low self-confidence, and distress, and are at risk for depression. The most authoritarian parents can be highly critical and controlling to the point of being emotionally or physically abusive, which will heighten your awareness of the potential need for child protection services as well as the potential impact of traumatic stress for the child.

Permissive parenting, on the other hand, involves parenting with low control and high warmth. Permissive parents resist taking an appropriately assertive role with the child. Without appropriate control, children in these families miss opportunities to develop frustration tolerance and have difficulty adhering to basic social norms connected to authority. Parents can be overly responsive to the child's needs, including those needs that are unreasonable or developmentally inappropriate. Sometimes these parents strive to be the child's "best friend" by avoiding conflict, structure, or discipline. These children often struggle with aggression, low responsibility, and impulsivity. In extremes, these children can be at risk for delinquency.

Neglectful parenting is characterized by low warmth and low control. Neglectful parents often struggle with their own behavioral health problems, such as depression, substance use, traumatic stress, or anxiety. Without warmth or control, children of neglectful parents tend to be at highest risk for distress, delinquency, substance use, and low functioning, and have poorer outcomes into adolescence and adulthood.

Neglectful parents also raise concerns about maltreatment, the need for child protection services, and the impact of traumatic stress.

Authoritative parenting is a balance of warmth and control, exemplified by responsiveness to a child's developmentally appropriate needs while maintaining developmentally appropriate, clear, and consistent discipline, demands, and expectations. Authoritative parenting is associated with numerous positive child and teen behaviors, such as responsibility, good academic achievement, and positive peer relationships (Henggeler, Schoenwald, Borduin, Rowland, & Cunningham, 1998; Steinberg, Fletcher, & Darling, 1994).

PARENTING STYLES PSYCHOEDUCATION

While it isn't important that parents learn the names of each parenting style, it is important to help them understand the concepts that underlie them. Many parents are unaware of the interplay of control and warmth in their parenting. Providing psychoeducation about parenting styles can immediately help parents dispel cognitive distortions about their own parenting practices. This information can open the door to new parenting practices that will help them better balance their use of control and warmth. The concepts often make sense to parents as you discuss them. Opening this discussion can be a fun experience as parents start to think about their parenting styles in new ways. The example script and figures that follow offer one approach to providing psychoeducation about parenting styles.

Therapist: Researchers have been really interested in parenting since it's such an important part of how we all grow. Over the past several decades, they have studied parenting styles with hundreds and thousands of kids and families, and it turns out certain parenting styles can lead to different behaviors in kids. That's the first piece of good news: parents can learn certain skills that can help their children be healthy, be responsible, and do well. The other piece of good news is that we've learned which parenting styles help kids the most, and I'd like to talk a little about those now. Does that sound all right?

Parent: (*nods*)

Therapist: Okay, so what we've learned over the years is that two of the most important parts of parenting style are control and warmth (*writes "control" and "warmth" on opposite ends of a dry-erase board*). Warmth is about affection, love, and kindness. Parents who praise their kids by saying, "I love and appreciate you for helping at home," or "Nice job doing your chores," when their kids do the right thing are being warm. Parents who are warm are teaching their kids that they matter, that they are able to do some things well, that it feels good to do things you're supposed to do, and that they are not only loved, but lovable. Control means teaching your children about rules, having expectations for them, and being firm with them sometimes about what they're allowed to do. Parents who use control are teaching kids about responsibility, the value of work, and how to stick with something even when it's tough. Does that make sense?

Parent: Yeah. That's good so far.

Therapist: Great! So, if you imagine these things on a spectrum, along this line, we can picture a parent using too much warmth or too much control. Let's talk about a parent who's way over here on the control side. *(Therapist draws a line near "control.")* So over here is a parent who's good at control but isn't warm with her child. What do you think might happen? What would that child learn and how might that child act? *(Elicits parent conversation as she describes authoritarian parenting, using the information provided in this chapter and in the "Authoritarian Parents" figure below.)*

Authoritarian Parents

Authoritarian Parents
Directive, overcontrolling, and expecting unquestioning obedience, but not responsive to child's needs. Often show little acknowledgment of positive behaviors.

Authoritarian parenting is associated with aggression, social withdrawal, poor self-confidence, feeling distressed, and depression.

Control		Warmth

Therapist: Now let's imagine a parent who's way over on the opposite end, on the warmth side. *(Therapist erases first line and draws a line near "warmth.")* This parent is super warm and loving with his child. In fact, he barely has any rules or control. What do you think that would be like? How might that child feel and act? *(Elicits parent conversation as she describes permissive parenting, using information provided in this chapter and in the "Permissive Parents" figure that follows.)*

Permissive Parents

> **Permissive Parents**
> Low structure or discipline but high warmth. Often not overly concerned about setting boundaries or challenging their children at appropriate levels.

> Permissive parenting is associated with aggression, low responsibility, and impulsivity.

Control		Warmth

Therapist: Okay. So we've talked about parents who are way on either side of control or warmth. There are some parents who aren't controlling or warm. Those parents are using a "neglectful style," which may be one of the most difficult styles for a child, and it leads to long-term problems for kids. I already know that's not an issue for you because I've seen how much you care about your child and how you try to teach him responsibility. So I'm not going to talk much about the neglectful parenting style.

Now let's talk about parents who are in the middle, somewhere in between controlling and warm. These are parents who use a style of some warmth and some control, but not too much on either side. What do you think that would be like? How might that child feel and act? (*Elicits parent conversation as she describes authoritative parenting, using information provided in this chapter and in the "Authoritative Parents" figure below.*)

Authoritative Parents

> **Authoritative Parents**
> Responsive to child's reasonable needs and desires, with reasonable demands on child's obedience and development through clear expectations and rules.

> Authoritative parenting is associated with positive achievement at school, responsibility, and good peer relationships.

Control		Warmth

Therapist: There's a lot of information that shows a balance of control and warmth leads to kids who are cooperative (for the most part), responsible (for the most part), and doing well with school and friends. Kids are never perfect, just like parents are never perfect—that's why this balance is a general idea. You don't have to find the perfect balance to have a healthy kid, but just enough. Just doing your best at balancing control and warmth usually leads to kids who are healthy. A lot of times it's really about parents moving just a little more toward the other direction—for example, if they're really controlling, they can learn to be a little warmer.

At this point, therapists can probe into the parent's own style, which can be done a number of ways. You might hand over the pen and ask a parent to mark where on the spectrum between control and warmth her parenting style lands right now. Through a discussion you can eventually ask her where she wants her parenting style to be, which would direct the next steps in the session.

A useful conversation that can emerge from this psychoeducation is about the intergenerational parenting patterns in the family. Some parents will be thinking about their own parents when they learn about these styles. Starting a conversation about the difference between a parent's style and her experiences as a child may help identify patterns that could be changed or improved. When parents mark a style that is different from the therapist's or other family member's expectations, you can ask members of the family to mark where their impression of the parent's style is and discuss if and why there are differences. In either approach to discussing these themes, once a parenting style direction is identified—to either increase warmth or increase control—you are able to proceed from psychoeducation to skills training and use behavioral management to increase warmth or control.

BEHAVIORAL MANAGEMENT PARENTING INTERVENTIONS

Behavioral-focused parenting interventions can be tremendously useful to increase desired behaviors and reduce or eliminate undesired behaviors in children and youth. For depressed children and youth, behavioral interventions will most likely center around reinforcing proactive and prosocial behaviors in cooperation with other cognitive-focused interventions. This can include increasing specific behaviors such as homework completion, positive communication, cooperative social interactions, and obedience to house and family rules, as well as increasing involvement in activities and hobbies or reducing anger outbursts.

In the following section, we offer a foundation for therapists to help parents and caregivers use behavioral interventions. We encourage therapists to also gain familiarity and clinical training using behavioral interventions in order to convey this knowledge to parents. While behavioral interventions can be highly effective for a number of behaviors targeted in treatment, they can be nuanced and are often developed through experience. More so than other interventions described in this guide, behavioral interventions can be thrown off by seemingly small details or will need adjustments throughout the process. The type of behavioral intervention you might use will either include increasing or reducing a certain stimulus to either increase or decrease a targeted behavior. Keeping the stimuli and targeted behaviors clear and specific in your conceptualizations will strengthen your interventions.

Positive reinforcement is increasing a targeted behavior by adding a stimulus. For example, a rewards chart for doing chores is a type of positive reinforcement since doing chores is the targeted behavior and adding rewards (the stimulus) increases the likelihood of the chores getting done. Other examples include providing praise when siblings cooperate, or hugging a child after he completes a difficult homework problem. Positive reinforcement is effective to the degree that the stimulus is desirable to the child, and based on the frequency of reinforcement. For example, if the reward for completing chores is TV time but the child already gets unrestricted TV time or doesn't like TV, the behavioral plan probably won't work. Similarly, if the child is given praise for a desired behavior, but only rarely, the behavioral plan probably won't work. When the stimulus is desirable and offered with good frequency, positive reinforcement is the most influential of the four behavioral categories provided here and is often used in therapy.

Negative reinforcement is increasing a targeted behavior by removing a stimulus. For example, to avoid nagging (the stimulus) a child may complete his chores (the targeted behavior). Another example could be a child starting a pattern of saying he is sick or crying to avoid school (and bullies at school).

Positive punishment is decreasing a targeted behavior by adding a stimulus. An example of this might be additional math questions (stimulus) if a child refuses to focus on his math questions during homework time (the targeted behavior). Another commonly encountered example of positive punishment is spanking.

Negative punishment is decreasing targeted behavior by removing a stimulus. A common example is using grounding or time-outs (e.g., removing stimuli such as toys, TV time, or video games) in response to a child disobeying a rule (targeted behavior to decrease). Negative punishment is another behavioral concept that is often used in therapy.

	Increase Targeted Behavior	Decrease Targeted Behavior
Add Stimulus	Positive Reinforcement	Positive Punishment
Remove Stimulus	Negative Reinforcement	Negative Punishment

USING BEHAVIORAL MANAGEMENT PARENTING INTERVENTIONS

Behavioral management interventions will become more and more effective as therapists gain experience in teaching parents to use these interventions. To effectively coach parents to use behavioral management with their children, it helps therapists to be clear on the current problematic patterns (antecedents, targeted behaviors to change, and consequences of the targeted behaviors) and the specific changes the therapist will coach the parent to make (either adding or removing specific stimuli). Behavioral parenting interventions are most commonly used with preschool- and elementary school–age children. With middle school– and high school–age youth, behavioral interventions tend to be more effective when the teenager clearly understands the behavioral plan (i.e., the rules he is expected to follow and rewards he will earn) or even helps to develop the plan. In both cases, and particularly when therapists see limited progress, support from behavioral specialists and in-home coaches can be tremendously helpful and sometimes necessary for catching the minor modifications that are often needed in the home.

If home-based supports aren't available, we recommend therapists follow up with parents shortly after starting to implement a behavioral plan (perhaps by phone if sessions occur every week) to discuss how the process is going and any necessary modifications. Slight modifications are common with these interventions, and sometimes parents need support and encouragement in order to trust and stick to the plan.

Many of the skills developed through modular CBT are naturally reinforcing, meaning they automatically produce positive, desirable consequences. For example, expressing thoughts and feelings when feeling depressed (even though it may be difficult at first) naturally allows most individuals to feel relieved, less isolated, or better understood. However, ensuring family members respond appropriately to new skills can "sweeten the deal" and boost the naturally positive consequences of using new skills. Therefore, behavioral interventions, such as reward charts, family rules, and selective attention, are not always necessary but can strengthen and encourage new skill development.

Reward Charts. Reward charts are commonly used in behavioral management. Reward charts consist of making marks or adding stickers on a chart to indicate when specific tasks or behaviors are completed. Once a certain number of marks has been reached, a predetermined reward is provided. An Internet search of "reward charts" will produce countless examples, and there is a lot of room for therapists to be creative with these charts. There are several essential components that will help improve the success of a reward chart. First, the reward must be desirable to the child (the more desirable, the more motivated he will be). Second, the parameters of the reward should be clearly laid out so there is less risk for negotiation or argument. Third, the reward must be timely and offered reasonably soon after the behaviors have been met. Finally, reward charts should not eclipse the intrinsic reward associated with the behavior. That is to say, when a child completes his chores, parents still need to provide praise and point out, "It feels so good to get something done. I'm so proud of you for doing it on your own! It looks like you're proud of yourself!" This final element is essential since the goal is to eventually wean and transition children off of reward charts and toward experiencing the natural reward of doing well.

Family Rules. If the family is able to establish three to five clear family rules and determine straightforward, natural consequences for breaking those rules, parents will have opportunities to practice the balance of warmth and control. Each week or between sessions, therapists can check in with parents and identify ways that the family members were successful with the rules, ways the parents were successful adding consequences, and ways the use of family rules may improve. Therapists can be very helpful by guiding the family to establish one to three "easy" family rules to start and then to gradually incorporate more challenging family rules. Family rules that might help depressed clients include the following: the family will participate in a fun activity one or two times each week; if a family member yells, he or she must take a quick break; and limiting the amount of time any family member stays isolated in his or her room.

Selective Attention. Sharing the concept of selective attention with parents can be very powerful for reframing some of their frustrations at home and reshaping the way they interact with their children. Many times, corporal punishment (like spanking) or even abuse is the result of parents feeling frustrated and not knowing what else they can do. Selective attention equips parents with a powerful parenting cache. Parents who effectively use selective attention are calmer, less frustrated, and less likely to revert to ineffective or harmful parenting behaviors.

Selective attention relies on positive reinforcement and negative punishment. Essentially, selective attention means intentionally providing plentiful positive attention for positive behaviors and little or no attention for negative behaviors. First, the most simple and potent behavioral intervention provided by parents tends to be the use of affirmations or praise (a form of positive reinforcement). Praise or affirmations are brief positive phrases about the child or youth that draw attention to desired behaviors. There are general praises, like "Nice job" or "Good work," and there are specific, more effective praises, like "Nice job telling me how you feel about going to school." Meaningful praises are specific, sincere, and accurate. Praising insignificant behaviors, haphazardly praising any old thing, or praising general behaviors will have a less powerful impact and can sometimes contribute to behavior problems. On the other hand, it's difficult to overstate the value of parents consistently providing accurate, sincere, and specific praises to children. This form of positive reinforcement has several pivotal outcomes for the depressed child or youth, and also for the parent.

First, praises (general or specific) result in the child temporarily feeling good. This result is a brief period of positive affect. Moreover, specific praises help the child recognize that he has done something well and will increase the likelihood that the behavior will happen again in the future. Parents using specific praises are essentially teaching children to do that behavior more often. More importantly, children will internalize these messages over time. To a great extent, these praises become their cognitions. That means that parents who use specific praises appropriately (when the behavior is genuinely meaningful and healthy) will also have children who are more likely to hear specific praises internally at appropriate times. These children are more likely to have accurate and healthy cognitions. Parents who attend to these healthy behaviors are also modeling how to notice strengths, and which behaviors matter and should get attention. Finally, praising also creates positive changes for the parent. Parents who consistently praise are looking for and noticing positive behaviors. Over time, noticing these positive behaviors leads to improved cognitions about the child and the ability to see the child in a more positive light, and increases the warmth and connection the parent experiences with the child (and vice versa).

Remember that some parents will need practice offering praise. There may be an intergenerational family pattern of not offering praise or of frequent criticism. Just as with building other skills, coaching and practice will help strengthen these new "muscles."

Effective use of praise relies on a ratio of frequent meaningful praises to very few criticisms. A criticism is a negative statement about a person, like "You're stupid" or "I wish you weren't so lazy." Interestingly, criticisms do not tend to reduce the frequency of a behavior. Most children are hungry for parental attention. They will naturally prefer praise, but will settle for criticism. This is why a toddler will continue to do a behavior when the parent is telling him to stop. He is getting attention (the stimulus), so the behavior increases (is positively reinforced) as he learns how to draw the parent's interest. During adolescence, youth become less interested in parent attention and will learn to avoid the parent in order to avoid criticism. Therefore, criticisms often increase the likelihood of a behavior or lead to the youth avoiding the parent.

Criticisms can rapidly undermine the value of praises as these negative messages overtake the child's internal messages or cognitions, draw attention to failures or mistakes, and contribute to dysphoric mood. Persistently criticized children and youth will learn that negative behaviors (mistakes, problems, shortcomings) deserve more attention and focus than positive behaviors. When positive messages outweigh the criticisms (usually at a ratio of five- or ten-to-one) children and youth will learn to pay attention to positive behaviors rather than focus on negative behaviors. In order to avoid using criticisms, parents may need to learn alternative ways to respond to inappropriate behaviors. Sometimes criticizing makes parents feel as though they are in control or taking action with the child or youth. They will need new skills to replace this perceived control with actual control.

Many parents will misperceive their own ratio of praises to criticisms. It can be eye-opening for parents to learn how frequently they actually criticize their children. With permission beforehand, therapists may observe an interaction or conversation between the child and parent on a challenging topic, count the number of criticisms and praises, and provide that feedback. Alternatively, therapists could ask parents to simply keep track of their praises and criticisms during the week by keeping tally or by asking a co-parent about the ratio. Each of these techniques can help raise parents' awareness of their use of attention and start the process of parents developing selective attention. When parents use specific and accurate praises often and use few criticisms, there is a powerful effect on combating depressive symptomology.

Some parents confuse selective attention with not being firm or not having control with their children. In reality, using selective attention offers parents more control and helps them effectively balance control and warmth. Parents who avoid criticisms still use discipline strategies. As an example of the difference between criticisms and discipline, a criticism might be "You didn't do your homework today! You're so lazy." Discipline for this same issue might include "Because you didn't do your homework today, you will only be able to use your phone starting after school tomorrow once your homework is done. I hope you get your homework done quickly so you can get your phone back as soon as possible." This example of discipline avoids negative judgments about the teen but clearly communicates that missing homework is unacceptable. The parent constructively offers a solution to fix the mistake of skipping homework.

Negative reinforcement strategies can offer effective alternatives to criticism by removing any reinforcement for acting-out behavior. Once the therapist and parent are able to identify the reward or payoff for an inappropriate behavior, they can brainstorm ways to remove that reward. For example, if a child is acting out to gain attention, the parent can proactively and strategically remove this attention and instead clearly say, "Once Tyler tells me calmly what he needs, I will help him." Or when a child engages in a negative behavior, like skipping homework to play video games, a parent can remove video games until homework is completed. Collaborating with parents to identify opportunities to remove privileges refocuses parent feedback away from the negative behaviors and toward the desired behaviors. Instead of criticizing a child for playing video games, the parent can let the child know that once his homework is done, he can play video games.

One important consideration to using negative reinforcement strategies is the concept of extinction burst. When removing a stimulus to change a targeted behavior, often the targeted behavior will spike prior to going away. For example, if a parent begins ignoring a child's whining behavior at the store to get a treat, the child will whine more, thinking to himself, *Hey, whining usually works. What's the deal?* As the parent ignores the whining but continues to teach the child how to appropriately get what he wants (e.g., telling the child in the car, "If we go through the store and you keep your happy attitude and talk nicely with me the whole time, we can have an extra fifteen minutes of playtime together when we get home"), the whining behavior will disappear after the brief burst. This alarming burst of the targeted behavior often makes parents feel as though they're failing, but it is actually an indication that they are successfully using negative reinforcement and that soon the frequency of the targeted behavior will diminish or disappear.

A comment on spanking. The use of spanking as a method of control in parenting is common in the United States. Based on a nationwide sample, 57 percent of mothers and 40 percent of fathers of three-year-olds engaged in spanking, and 52 percent of mothers and 33 percent of fathers used spanking when children were five years old (MacKenzie, Nicklas, Waldfogel, & Brooks-Gunn, 2013). Despite its widespread use, spanking is not more effective than alternative methods of parental control. To the contrary, there is good evidence that spanking causes detrimental effects over time. Longitudinal research suggests maternal spanking at age five (even at low levels) is connected to externalizing (e.g., oppositional, aggressive) behaviors at age nine. Frequent paternal spanking at age five seems to also be linked to impaired vocabulary development (MacKenzie et al., 2013). While there is little evidence supporting this parenting practice and strong evidence that spanking causes harm over time, it continues to be a common parenting practice.

We acknowledge the controversy surrounding this age-old parenting method, as well as the cultural values connected to many parenting methods. However, there is little controversy among researchers that spanking contributes to increased childhood aggression. The American Academy of Pediatrics warns against spanking as a form of discipline because of the detrimental effects (1998), and the increasing body of research on spanking reiterates this caution. As we learn more, we are able to do better. Sharing this information with parents in a nonconfrontational manner may help them seek out more effective and less detrimental methods of control.

Between-Session Practice

There are several family-collaboration-related goals that can be emphasized through between-session practices, including cultivating parenting skills, bolstering collective family strengths, simultaneous skill building (e.g., encouraging siblings or parents to individually work on the same skill between sessions), and encouraging clients to develop new skills with support from other family members. Dattilio (2002) categorized different types of between-session practices for family therapy, including (a) *bibliotherapy assignments* like reading from handouts, books, or websites; (b) *recording out-of-session interactions* to later review in session (either audio or video); (c) *activity scheduling* to encourage individual or family activities that might reinforce skills or behaviors; (d) *self-monitoring* to keep track of thoughts, feelings, or behaviors; (e) *behavioral task assignments* to practice the use of a specific behavior or a new skill; and (f) *cognitive restructuring* to challenge and change dysfunctional thoughts. Use creativity as you prepare any of these types of assignments. For behavioral management parenting skills, parents may appreciate one or two booster phone calls between sessions from the therapist to help make adjustments as they practice and develop new skills. When two or more family members are working on similar assignments, they may be able to check in with each other between sessions to encourage accountability and cooperative learning.

Summary, Feedback, and Next Steps

At the close of family collaboration module sessions, take time to discuss family strengths that emerged during the session. Acknowledge the bravery and determination that contributes to adjusting parenting practices or the status quo of the family. Therapists may encourage other family members to also acknowledge each other and their strengths as a whole. Therapists or family members should summarize the topics discussed, the action items for each member of the family, the between-session practice assignments, and the purposes of the between-session assignments (immediate and long-term). Therapists may also take a moment to discuss next steps for treatment, to point out any changes in the targeted symptoms at this point, and to describe how they are evaluating the client's and family's progress in treatment.

Common Hurdles and Solutions for Therapists

The two most common barriers for family collaboration are difficulty coordinating schedules so key family members can participate and involving family members who struggle with their own mental health problems. Information in the treatment engagement (chapter 12) module may help involve family members when scheduling is a challenge. Having engagement-focused discussions about the purpose of their involvement may help them feel more engaged in finding solutions. The therapist's scheduling flexibility, or providing services in the home or community when possible, may also help to remedy this issue. Sometimes there is no clear solution, so next-best alternatives, such as touching base via phone or meeting with family members intermittently, may be the best available options. These options are typically better than no involvement at all.

Family members who struggle with their own mental health issues can be very challenging for the treatment process. However, therapist frustration with these mental health problems might embody the frustration experienced by the client on a day-to-day basis and the ways the family member contributes to ongoing symptomology of your client. Making referrals to mental health treatment or taking steps to help family members attend sessions is a worthwhile use of treatment time. Follow up about family members' experiences with treatment, offer support when they encounter barriers, and (with proper permission and signed releases of information) collaborate with any family member's mental health professional. These steps will help individual family members, the family as a whole, and your client.

Summary

For many clients, focusing on individual factors will only partially help reduce depressive symptoms. The family setting can be thought of as the soil in which their new thoughts, feelings, and behaviors will grow. By inviting family collaboration in treatment through involvement in different modules or encouraging parents and families to learn new skills, therapists are able to cultivate treatment progress. Examining parenting styles and developing behavioral management parenting skills can have long-term benefits for the overall family and individual client. When appropriate (based on your conceptualization of your client's depression), use this module to expand the reach of the interventions so your client has warmth and structure in the home environment and support from family members. Through family collaboration, therapists can promote individual and contextual treatment progress.

Chapter 12

Treatment Engagement

You would probably step right over it if you didn't know it was there. At the corner of Christopher Street and Seventh Avenue South in New York City's West Village, you'll find a concrete triangle with a cracked and worn mosaic slightly larger than a slice of pizza. The Hess Triangle declares the defiance of the Hess Estate: "Property of the Hess Estate Which Has Never Been Dedicated for Public Purposes." In the early 1900s the adjacent land and seven-story Voorhis apartment building with a little park in the front were owned by David Hess. The property was one of 253 properties that were expropriated and demolished through eminent domain, making way for the expansion of Seventh Avenue and construction of the IRT subway. The city asked the Hess Estate to donate the tiny remaining plot for use as public sidewalk, but the request was refused. Instead, in 1922 the Estate memorialized its longstanding noncooperation with the city seizure via a mosaic on the diminutive plot (Atlas Obscura, 2014; Whong, 2014).

Photo courtesy of Jana Crandal.

Architectural or property holdouts are not entirely uncommon. There was the "Million Dollar Corner" in New York City and Edith Macefield's iconic home in Seattle. In China, a holdout property is called *dingzihu* or "nail house," in reference to the nails that are intractably embedded in wood. Under tremendous pressure, these owners stand their ground against all odds. Despite seemingly better alternatives, what makes these owners tenaciously, stubbornly, and sometimes heroically resist? You might ask, what happened to start this? How did it get to a point of such disagreement?

Any experienced therapist has encountered the therapeutic equivalent of a "nail house." Clients and families who resist or reluctantly engage in treatment are common and can sometimes inculcate frustration for therapists. Researchers have reported that as many as 50 to 75 percent of referred youth do not initiate treatment or drop out prematurely if they begin, and that 40 to 60 percent of families stop attending treatment prior to termination (Kazdin, 1997; McKay, Nudelman, McCadam, & Gonzales, 1996).

Like the property holdout examples above, resistance can sometimes be caused by opposing goals. Fortunately, the goals of the client and the goals of the therapist don't need to be at odds. Children, adolescents, and families participating in modular CBT are typically experiencing distress and looking for help. The best interests of the client and family usually align with the intentions and goals of a therapist. When the goals are in conflict, it is often simply through miscommunication or misunderstanding, and solutions are reachable. While there are rare cases where an intentionally destructive individual is seeking therapy, it is more common that a therapist will misperceive this exception than encounter it. More commonly, therapists can use specific engagement-focused skills to bring the therapeutic process back on track. Treatment engagement and motivation are discussed in this chapter to prepare you to use this module and adopt an engagement-focused lens throughout the treatment process.

Preparing the Module

Despite the commonly encountered barriers to treatment engagement, there are effective skills and tools that can be used to enhance treatment engagement and promote the involvement of clients and families in the treatment process. In the following sections, you will develop a conceptual understanding of how these skills fit with your case conceptualization.

Background

In therapy's not-too-distant past, clients who interrupted, denied obstacles, or argued were commonly labeled "unmotivated." The responsibility of treatment engagement was placed squarely on the shoulders of clients and families. A shift in these assumptions was led by research from Patterson and Forgatch in 1985. Therapists at the Oregon Social Learning Center were asked to conduct sessions using different therapeutic styles in ten-minute intervals. They switched between a "teach-and-confront" therapeutic style and a "facilitate-and-support" style. The sessions were recorded and coded based on caregiver compliance or noncompliance. Researchers found that with these two styles, they could essentially turn parent compliance on and off in the treatment session like a light switch. The teach-and-confront style led to increased noncompliance while the support-and-facilitate style led to better treatment compliance. This discovery changed the way therapists approached client engagement and motivation and sparked the development of motivational interviewing (MI), a widely used and strongly supported motivational-focused treatment developed to address substance abuse. Client engagement in treatment is more complicated than randomly encountering a mix of motivated or unmotivated clients in your caseload. As described by Miller, the codeveloper of MI, "Resistance is not a client problem; it is a therapist skill" (Miller, Moyers, & Rollnick, 2010).

This module will help you strengthen family and client engagement in treatment by adopting a lens that acknowledges and emphasizes client and caregiver autonomy and capacity for change through *collaboration*, *evocation*, and *affirmation of autonomy*. We also discuss *stages of change* and ways to encourage families to *identify and overcome barriers*. Several therapeutic skills and techniques are presented to help you intentionally use engagement-focused therapeutic interventions to encourage client and family commitment to engage in therapy. These skills will help you develop and subsequently convey a sincere confidence in the caregivers' and client's strengths.

Clinical Rationale for Module

In chapter 2, we discussed the importance of developing a treatment plan that is consistent with the client's and family's goals for treatment. In each module, we comment on the importance of explaining the treatment process and linking each module back to the initial goals of treatment. These steps are important to help families connect activities from the therapy sessions and between-session practices with the changes they hope to achieve by coming to therapy. By emphasizing a family-focused and transparent therapeutic style, you can encourage client and family engagement in treatment. However, every therapist faces obstacles with client engagement in treatment. Every therapist encounters clients and families who are minimally responsive to certain modules or the overall treatment process.

Like other modules, the skills and techniques presented here are intended to be implemented as a module when the therapist identifies engagement as an important part of the treatment plan. Just as with other modules, these interventions may also be useful during other modules. You may find yourself using these interventions at different points in treatment, but a focus and foundation can be established with this module. On the other hand, this module is different from the others since we also provide information to help you develop an engagement-focused therapeutic lens. We expect the principles and essence of the module will permeate other parts of the treatment process as you use an engagement-focused therapeutic lens, even at times when this module is not included in the treatment plan.

Engagement-Focused Modular CBT

If modular CBT heavily relies on teaching, and Patterson and Forgatch's (1985) research suggests a teach-and-confront style leads to noncompliance in the session, how does modular CBT fit with engaging families and clients in treatment?

MODULAR CBT AND ENGAGEMENT

The conceptual background for modular CBT includes promoting change through teaching. The therapist is a supportive teacher and guide who helps clients and families develop new skills and new ways of approaching difficulties. Inherent in this framework is an assumption that children and youth struggling with depression lack specific cognitive, affective, and behavioral skills that, when learned, can help reduce the role of depression in their lives. Learning and practicing new skills during and especially between sessions requires a high level of buy-in. Clients and families who are not engaged in the skill-building process have a much more limited chance of succeeding in modular CBT.

The most common engagement problems in modular CBT have to do with therapists moving through the therapy process (including teaching, practicing, and skill development) while the client or family perceives the treatment as disconnected with their needs. Common missteps include therapists moving too quickly, ignoring immediate needs and concerns, and failing to help families understand the rationale for each step. These missed opportunities for collaboration distance the client and family from seeing how the steps of modular CBT address their needs. The essential teaching components of modular CBT transform into "support and facilitation" when clients and families believe the teaching is directly connected to their own therapy goals and treatment needs.

There are common reactions for families who have trouble understanding how therapy connects with their goals. Using the cognitive triangle, imagine a caregiver or teenager having the thoughts *This isn't going to help* or *This isn't working.* These thoughts likely lead to pessimism, hopelessness, or feeling misunderstood. These feelings often lead to giving less effort, not participating in between-session practices, missing appointments, and giving up with therapy (see the "Cognitive Triangle of Family Disengagement in Therapy" figure). Depressed children, youth, and caregivers can be prone to pessimistic thoughts. There are often existing thought, feeling, and behavioral habits that place them at risk for this cognitive pattern. Be attentive to these thoughts, actively discuss engagement-related thoughts, use engagement-related examples when describing the cognitive triangle, and describe potential engagement pitfalls and cognitive patterns to families and youth and why they matter.

Taking steps to acknowledge this potential obstacle as soon as it enters the treatment process can help you intervene early and promote engagement.

After years of graduate training or clinical experience, modular CBT treatment steps may seem familiar to you—even part of common sense; however, you are often introducing an entirely new framework to families. Most families are not familiar with the relationship between thoughts, feelings, and actions. Many families do not commonly talk about their thoughts, keep track of their moods, or practice deep breathing. Talking about feelings can seem like an unimportant step or just the "touchy-feely" therapy they've heard about in popular culture. At first, many of the ideas and topics introduced in modular CBT can seem downright absurd for those with a perspective that is not Western-oriented. The challenge for therapists is to keep this in mind as they introduce new topics. The intake assessment should start a process of establishing trust and meaningful mutual understanding between therapists and families. From this point forward, families should begin to take steps with you as a guide, but only if you keep in pace with them and reinforce the trust they place in you.

Cognitive Triangle of Family Disengagement in Therapy

Feelings
Hesitant
Skeptical
Apprehensive
Confused
Bored
Hopeless
Frustrated
Disengaged

Thoughts	**Actions**
This is strange.	Avoid between-session practice
She's not going to help.	Not attend therapy sessions
She's not listening to me.	Not return calls
Therapy doesn't work—it didn't work last time.	Be distracted in the session
She doesn't understand what we're asking.	Often bring up unrelated topics
She doesn't understand the issues.	Tell others therapy is not helping
She can't help us.	Behave passively or combatively

Modular CBT is a treatment modality rich with interventions and tools for therapists. Each module includes psychoeducation about several topics and various techniques to help families develop new skills. If your clients and their families are not engaged in treatment, however, these tools are essentially useless. Therapists may sometimes continue to teach and guide with psychoeducation and skill building even when there are clear indicators the family is not open to those steps. It brings to mind Kaplan's Law of the Instrument: "Give a small boy a hammer, and he will find that everything he encounters needs pounding" (1964, p. 28). Before you are able to access the array of therapeutic tools offered through modular CBT, make sure families are willing and able to accept those tools. In other words, client and family engagement is a prerequisite for utilizing modular CBT interventions. The only exception would be in times of crisis, where safety and harm reduction take priority. Therefore, before you can teach and guide, ensure clients and families are ready to learn and step forward.

ENGAGEMENT-FOCUSED APPROACHES

Of the established strategies for bolstering engagement in treatment, MI, identifying barriers and problem solving, and brief early discussions about treatment engagement while strengthening family coping and support, seem to be the most promising (Ingoldsby, 2010; McKay et al., 1996; McKay, Stoewe, McCadam, & Gonzales, 1998).

The engagement-focused principles rooted in MI encourage therapists to acknowledge and affirm client autonomy from a collaborative position, while supporting efficacy and eliciting change. From an MI framework, therapists may step back from modular CBT teaching or skill building in order to refocus on understanding the client, emphasizing the client and family role in the solution, and promoting a spirit of collaboration to address depression. Specific skills are associated with the foundation of MI; however, a therapist's attitude toward client progress allows the specific skills to be used in a genuine and effective manner. The developers of MI refer to this as the "spirit of MI" (Miller et al., 2010).

A major part of the spirit of MI is expression of accurate empathy. Fundamentally, this skill involves actively understanding the client's perspective without judgment through reflective listening. Accurate empathy has a number of advantages, including reducing client resistance, clarifying specifically what the client means, demonstrating respect and caring, building the therapeutic alliance, and encouraging clients to continue to explore the topic (Miller, Zweben, DiClemente, & Rychtarik, 1992). As Miller and Rollnick have pointed out, empathy is not an easy skill, although it can be easily misrepresented or done poorly (2012). Like the strings of a guitar, this skill requires continuous fine-tuning throughout a therapist's career.

Effective use of empathy includes selective reflective listening. In MI, listening with empathy includes emphasizing reflections of self-motivational statements so clients hear themselves saying these statements. For treatment engagement, therapists actively reflect client comments that emphasize changes to the status quo. An example could be "It sounds like you've really been looking for ways to help your daughter," or "It's been hard to help your son in the past because you've been on your own, but you're willing to try."

Acknowledging autonomy is also an important aspect of engagement-focused MI. Miller has commented, "A nice thing about acknowledging autonomy is that you're telling the truth" (Miller et al., 2010). It could similarly be said that the nice thing about believing each individual has the capacity to grow is that it's true. People have a tendency to live up to the expectations around them. When intake sessions are scheduled, families are demonstrating a significant step toward change. A prodding, pushing, and pulling therapist is sending the message that she does not trust her clients or families to make changes and that instead she is accepting that responsibility. In reality, it is a false assumption that therapists have the capacity to accept responsibility for the entire treatment process. Prodding, pushing, and pulling is likely to make clients and families follow suit by playing a passive or resistant role in treatment. When the treatment process includes shared, collaborative responsibilities and support to accomplish goals, both the therapist and the clients and families play distinct but interrelated roles in moving forward. Instead of struggling against each other, they are working together.

Even when clients, families, and therapists are working well together, treatment noncooperation can come up. From an MI perspective, resistance is a signal to the therapist that the client perceives the therapist as misunderstanding how the client is actually feeling. The MI model encourages therapists to "roll with resistance" (Miller & Rollnick, 2012). From this point of view, therapists use these signals as opportunities to better understand and support the client with the use of reflection and nonjudgmental understanding. Your reflections emphasize acknowledgment of the client's point of view while prompting the client to further explore her thoughts and feelings without resistance.

Finally, the MI framework also involves understanding stages of change. DiClemente and colleagues (1991) identified these stages when studying how individuals quit smoking, but they also offer a framework to ascertain a client's or family's readiness to engage in modular CBT for depression. Based on the stages of change, individuals move from precontemplation, contemplation, preparation, and action to maintenance in the process of adopting change. The *precontemplation* (or denial) stage is the stage in which an individual does not intend to change and does not acknowledge any problem (individuals deeply embedded in this stage rarely attend therapy sessions). During the *contemplation* stage, the individual considers making a change because of some problem, but has not yet either identified a specific change or committed to a specific change. During the *preparation* phase, the individual intends to make a change in the foreseeable future and is gathering information to develop a change plan. During the *action* stage, the individual is committed and takes steps to make changes. The *maintenance* stage is a continuation of the action stage, but the change has been achieved, so the individual is taking steps to sustain the change. Clients and families are continuously moving within these stages, either progressing or regressing.

Active modular CBT work typically occurs when clients and families are in the preparation, action, and maintenance phases. Many clients will initiate therapy after already moving through precontemplation, contemplation, and preparation, and are ready for action. Several, however, come to treatment in the contemplation and preparation stages; they are not seeking specific tools but instead are satisfying a referral made by someone else or investigating the suitability of therapy to help with the identified problem. Some families vacillate between stages. In either case, therapists who are conscious of these stages tend to be better attuned to their client's engagement. Questions you can use to assess the client and family's stage of change for therapy include the following:

- What are your goals for therapy?

- What are your expectations for therapy?

- What are you hoping will happen as a result of therapy?

- What are your past experiences with therapy?

- What concerns do you have about therapy?

- How does what I've told you align with what you're hoping will happen?

These questions could be easily adapted to focus on the client and family's stage of change for between-session practice or specific modules (e.g., What are your expectations for this between-session practice? or What are you hoping will happen as a result of this module?). A therapist who understands the client and family in terms of the stages of change and who acknowledges the autonomy of individuals involved in the treatment process will start to develop an engagement-focused lens. This lens will enhance the success of specific engagement-focused techniques described in the "Using the Module" portion of this chapter.

Since the mid-1990s, researchers have looked deeper into the factors that contribute to treatment engagement, found ways to enhance motivation and promote commitment, and tried to increase the likelihood that young people and caregivers will overcome barriers, identify solutions, and benefit from mental health treatment. Beyond the foundation provided by MI, McKay and colleagues' work on engaging families in treatment has drawn attention to the process of identifying barriers to treatment and problem solving around those barriers (McKay et al., 1996; McKay et al., 1998). One important idea introduced by McKay is to clarify different types of barriers a caregiver may encounter when initiating treatment (2013). These include *concrete barriers*, such as transportation, child care, or availability, and *perceptual barriers*, such as attitudes about therapy, stigma, fear, or past negative experiences with therapy. Interestingly, research seems to suggest perceptual barriers are the most influential barriers to treatment (Bannon & McKay, 2005; Harrison, McKay, & Bannon, 2004; Kazdin & Wassell, 2000; McKay, Pennington, Lynn, & McCadam, 2001). Even when caregivers are paid to attend sessions in order to reduce concrete barriers, results are not promising (Heinrichs, 2006). Therefore, although concrete barriers are certainly relevant, perceptual barriers may be the appropriate initial focus when discussing treatment engagement. Finding out about attitudes, assumptions, expectations, past experiences with therapy, and concerns early in the process will draw out perceptual barriers. Asking questions about both types of barriers and discussing solutions can be an important part of promoting engagement prior to skills training.

Taken together, a blend of motivational interviewing principles and an understanding of the concrete and perceptual barriers will help strengthen your engagement lens and ability to enhance treatment engagement in order to move forward with modular CBT teaching and skill building. When you utilize engagement-focused interventions, you can create a treatment environment where families are ready for the steps and skills provided in the modular CBT approach. Engagement focused treatment alone is not adequate for addressing symptoms of depression. Similarly, modular CBT alone, without attention to engagement, is not sufficient for most children, youth, and families struggling with depression. Therefore, it is not enough to simply support or simply teach. Providing modular CBT with an engagement focus allows therapists to expand caregiver and youth capacity for accessing the information and skills provided in modular CBT through supportive teaching and guiding. When you encounter treatment barriers in the form of thoughts, feelings, or actions, you can initiate this module or lean toward engagement-focused therapy skills until you and your clients and their families are aligned, and your clients and families are ready to take advantage of modular CBT psychoeducation and skills training.

ENGAGEMENT-FOCUSED ORGANIZATIONS AND THERAPISTS

As we discussed in chapter 1, your conceptualization of a child struggling with depression is incomplete without understanding family, social, school, and community contexts. There are significant barriers when a teenager tries to challenge her pessimistic thoughts in a pessimistic environment. Similarly, when a therapist tries to promote treatment engagement in an unsupportive organization or when she herself is disengaged, there are significant barriers. There is a strong relationship between the engagement of a child in therapy, the therapist's engagement, and the organizational context in which treatment is provided.

ORGANIZATIONAL CULTURE AND CLIMATE

Organizational culture refers to the way things are done in an organization, while organizational climate refers to the staff attitudes and perceptions about their work environment (Glisson, 2007). Researchers have found that organizations with staff reporting positive organizational climate and culture tend to also have clients who are more engaged in treatment. This finding has been consistently identified in health care settings (Moos & Schaefer, 1987; Schaefer & Moos, 1996; Weisman & Nathanson, 1985) as well as mental health and substance use treatment settings (Glisson, 2002; Moos & Moos, 1998; Schoenwald & Hoagwood, 2001). In particular, positive work culture and work attitudes have been found to contribute to a stronger therapeutic alliance, higher quality of services, and increased openness and adherence to efficacious treatments by therapists (Glisson, 2002). Therapists who feel supported, are adequately trained, and work in a collaborative and interactive work setting tend to be more effective at engaging clients (Broome, Flynn, Knight, & Simpson, 2007). In addition, Greener, Joe, Simpson, Rowan-Szal, and Lehman (2007) found that positive organizational functioning was associated with higher ratings of client engagement (i.e., rapport, satisfaction, or participation) in treatment.

We introduce organizational culture and climate in this clinician's guidebook to illustrate the multidimensional nature of client engagement. Each therapist is a part of an organization that contributes to the broad culture and climate encountered by clients seeking treatment. Even in private practice settings, there is an overarching tone that impacts client experiences of trust, commitment, and motivation. This culture and climate is reflected in the paperwork, the intake scheduling, the cancellation and no-show policy, business hours, general treatment practices, and attitudes of all individuals who interact with clients. Allowing your engagement lens to extend beyond individual families and to the context in which treatment occurs will promote your effectiveness and the success of your clients.

COMPASSION FATIGUE AND SATISFACTION

Since therapists have begun to appreciate their capacity to enhance treatment engagement, they have also uncovered the responsibility tied to that capacity. Most therapists are glad to know they can help their caseload thrive. At the same time, there is greater responsibility to nurture their attitudes and behaviors to promote engagement. The good and bad news is that your own engagement with each client and family (including your expectations and beliefs) contributes to how well they will do in therapy.

Being a therapist to children, youth, and families is an extraordinary profession. Young people and families open their most challenging and frightening weaknesses to you in therapy, with the hope and trust that you can help. Therapists, overall, comprise a very special group of individuals who are dedicated to helping others grow. This requires compassion, acceptance, openness, empathy, and many other emotionally demanding traits. Any therapist with experience is familiar with the toll that comes with this remarkable line of work. This toll wears on a therapist's emotional fortitude, and as a result, feelings of fatigue or burnout are not uncommon.

Many use the term "rustout" in place of "burnout," which perhaps better captures the gradual effects of providing therapy over time. The weight of paperwork and constantly discussing challenging emotional problems (like depression) can gradually make you feel as though you are gathering rust like the Tin Man from *The Wizard of Oz*. Researchers sometimes refer to this gradual wear and tear that accompanies helping professions as *compassion fatigue* (Figley, 2002). At one point or another, therapists will feel fatigued, drained, or disengaged from the treatment process.

Common indicators include feeling overwhelmed by paperwork; feeling resistant when preparing to go to work; feeling resentful, cynical, or critical toward clients; feeling drained or depressed; and feeling that you're fighting a losing battle. You may catch yourself having pessimistic thoughts like *Therapy won't work, People don't change,* or *I can't make a difference.* It's no surprise that when therapists feel this way, their clients have a less positive outlook.

The alternative to compassion fatigue is compassion satisfaction, which involves feeling that you are making a difference, feeling efficacious (that you can help meaningful changes happen with your clients), appreciating your job, feeling proud of your work, and feeling appreciated by coworkers, leaders, and other people in your life. Compassion satisfaction is gaining value and gratification by providing care for others (Ray, Wong, White, & Heaslip, 2013; Sprang, Clark, & Whitt-Woosley, 2007; Stamm, 2002). Thoughts that accompany compassion satisfaction might be *This is a family that will probably benefit from therapy, I bet we can make a lot of progress together,* and *I know this family is struggling, and I think I can help make a difference.*

Whether you are trying to address compassion fatigue and burnout, or grow your feelings of compassion satisfaction, recognizing your thoughts and paying attention to indicators will help you move in that direction. Your attention is like a spotlight. The things to which you pay attention will be the things you think about and appreciate. Your internal, personal experiences of your clients can help you emphasize opportunities for growth or emphasize barriers and shortcomings. Avoiding burnout and experiencing satisfaction with your work is an active process of which you are chiefly in control.

Individually Tailoring the Module

So far in this chapter, we've emphasized the therapist's role in engagement. There are also client and family characteristics that may increase risk for low engagement or encountering treatment barriers. There has been substantial evidence that youth who are seriously impacted by mental health problems or who are culturally diverse are more likely to not utilize services, drop out of treatment after the first session, or drop out prior to termination (Bui & Takeuchi, 1992; Cauce et al., 2002; P. Cohen & Hesselbart, 1993; Griffin, Cicchetti, & Leaf, 1993; McKay et al., 1998). McKay and Bannon identified a "triple threat" to treatment engagement: single-parent status, high stress, and poverty (McKay, 2013; McKay & Bannon, 2004). In other words, single parents who experience high stress and are impoverished are at particularly high risk for dropout or underutilization of treatment services. Assessing these factors during the intake process and paying particular attention to engagement when these risk factors come up will help you identify potential barriers and be better prepared to problem solve throughout the treatment process.

This module should be included in the treatment plan when risk factors or engagement problems are identified during the assessment process. Depending on the impact of these barriers, this module could be added to the treatment plan, or the therapist may decide to weave engagement techniques with other modules. The benefit of including this module in the treatment plan is that it offers an opportunity for the client, family, and therapist to discuss the importance of engagement in a straightforward way early in the process. It will also embed a conversation about engagement in the treatment process when the treatment plan and treatment progress is reviewed.

Engagement in treatment is often connected to caregivers, and it is usually very important for caregivers to be involved in this module. For example, discussing consistent attendance with a teenager has little meaning if the caregiver provides transportation to therapy. In some cases a teenager is driving the process and is primarily responsible for treatment. Even in those cases, for new skills to generalize beyond the weekly session hour, the youth will need support from the adults involved in her life. Therefore, in most cases, this module will include caregivers and families. Indeed, many times the barrier to engagement is the lack of involvement by caregivers. This module provides the opportunity to address this during treatment planning or during treatment. When necessary, therapists can put other modules on hold and use this module until the engagement barriers are addressed and resolved and caregivers can become involved in treatment solutions.

Using the Module

With the framework provided above, you are prepared to utilize techniques that are consistent with an engagement-focused approach to modular CBT. The following sections will discuss the ways you can initiate and utilize the treatment engagement module. This will include the specific therapeutic and communication skills introduced through MI (i.e., expressing accurate empathy, developing discrepancy, rolling with resistance, supporting self-efficacy, recognizing and eliciting change talk) as well as other engagement-focused techniques (e.g., problem solving around barriers) and activities to strengthen client, therapist, and organizational capacity to enhance treatment engagement.

First Steps

Since barriers to engagement are often the result of clients or caregivers having thoughts and feelings that are not open in the therapeutic relationship, the first steps of an engagement conversation should include helping the client or caregiver feel understood. Therefore, the focus early in this module is on opening conversation led by clients and caregivers. Instead of reviewing homework (which may be a source of resistance) or setting an agenda, therapists may briefly "set the table" by checking in and providing context for the session.

Therapist: Today, I'd like to focus on making sure I understand your needs and goals for therapy and making sure I help in the ways you need. To do

199

that, I'd like to take some time to find out what brought you to therapy, how things have been so far, and how you'd like them to go as we move forward.

If this module is part of the treatment plan, you may briefly review the treatment plan and how it fits in the broader context. Instead of didactic teaching, you will be eliciting a conversation about engagement from clients and families. By stepping back from actively teaching or skill building, the therapist is opening the therapeutic process to the client and family autonomy. Below we provide skills to support this discussion as well as activities that can enhance these discussions and encourage engagement.

OARS

A crucial set of skills used to initiate engagement-focused discussions is referred to by Miller and Rollnick (2012) as OARS. OARS stands for ask open-ended questions, affirm, reflectively listen, and summarize. The OARS skills are key interpersonal communication techniques that refocus the session emphasis on understanding and supporting the client. These OARS skills are the frontline skills a therapist can use to quickly and consistently reduce immediate resistance or tension she may encounter with clients.

Open-Ended Questions. Asking questions that start with "how," "what," or "tell me about" promote open discussion and conversation and signal to clients and families that you would like to hear from them. Initially, general open-ended questions can be used to encourage conversation (e.g., "What brings you to therapy?" and "How is therapy going for you so far?"), while specific open-ended questions will help move the conversation toward more salient themes (e.g., "What has been getting in the way of practicing at home?" and "Tell me about the biggest concerns you have with this module").

Affirm. Affirming is a way of acknowledging and validating thoughts, feelings, comments, and experiences. To be effective, affirmations must be sincere. Like open-ended questions, affirmations may be used to emphasize general or specific strengths and experiences to promote self-efficacy and treatment engagement (e.g., "It's important to you that you help your daughter" or "In the past you've taken a lot of important steps to make sure your daughter is safe and doing well").

Reflectively listen. When you reflect language, you repeat, rephrase, or paraphrase what the client or caregiver has said or what you believe the client or caregiver is trying to communicate. Reflections communicate that you are listening, interested, and understanding what is being said. Reflections help demonstrate empathy and provide opportunities for clients or caregivers to gently let you know when you do not quite accurately understand. It's usually helpful when a client corrects your reflections because it gives you an opportunity to understand more clearly. There are simple reflections as well as double-sided reflections. Double-sided reflections include shifting focus or agreement with a twist, emphasizing personal choice, and reframing. Some examples of reflections could include "Sometimes you feel so busy that it's hard to know when it would be the right time to make a change," or "While you feel really busy and it's been hard to make a change, it's still something that's on your mind and that's important to you." The first example here reflects the caregiver's frustration while the second acknowledges the frustration but then emphasizes the caregiver's reason to engage in treatment.

Summarize. Summaries provide important opportunities to shift topics or move on from a given topic, while also reinforcing what has been said. They are useful when used to transition from one theme to the next. The client or caregiver will see that you have been listening and understanding accurately, and you can also emphasize topics from the conversation that you think are important. Often thoughtful summaries will include resistant topics or ambivalence identified by the client or caregiver, but therapists will also include themes that demonstrate the client's or caregiver's desire to make changes or to engage in treatment.

Therapist: To make sure I understand you correctly: It sounds as if you have been aware of Elsie's depression for quite some time. You've noticed that Elsie seems to have some of the same struggles you had at her age, like wanting to be alone, crying a lot, and feeling sad. On one hand, you never went to therapy when you were young, but on the other hand, you want Elsie to be happier than you were. Even though at first you didn't think it'd help, you brought Elsie to therapy to get the school staff off your back. It's been hard to have the school staff tell you what to do. They don't seem to realize how much you love Elsie and that you would do anything to help her. Even with your early hesitation toward therapy, you brought her. You really hope something will help her, and you're open to trying therapy to see if it can help. What's most important to you is that Elsie is doing well and is happy. You are willing to do whatever you can if it will actually help. Is that right?

Typically you will end a summary with a question ("Is that right?" or "Anything else?"). Once the client or caregiver lets you know you understand, you can move on to the next topic.

Each of the OARS skills is first used to engage clients in conversation and to demonstrate understanding and openness. Therapists who are prepared and accepting during this process demonstrate a great deal of empathy to the caregiver. By using OARS skills, you also provide an essential opportunity for clients and caregivers to consider reasons for therapy and for maintaining the status quo. When they are feeling understood, clients and caregivers will begin to challenge their own ambivalence. This leads to the secondary crucial benefits to OARS. When used intentionally, you are not simply affirming, reflecting, or summarizing any topic discussed by clients and caregivers: each of these skills can be used to strategically draw out and highlight discrepancies and the "edges" of ambivalence.

Development of Discrepancy

When developing discrepancy, therapists help clients explore the differences between where they want to be and where they are. In terms of engagement in treatment, therapists develop caregiver awareness of consequences of missing or delaying the subsequent session or not practicing between sessions. Therapists empathize with both sides of attending therapy—for example, by discussing benefits or expectations as well as concerns or barriers. With reflections and affirmations, the therapist can acknowledge both sides of ambivalence and draw out the discrepancies. Examples could include "Tell me more about your concerns with your son's behaviors," "If things stay the same as they are now, you're not quite sure what you'll do," or reflecting back when you hear discrepancy: such as, "On one hand, you're worried about remembering the appointment; on the other, you're concerned that your daughter's depression could get worse unless you start therapy."

Eliciting, Recognizing, and Responding to Change-Talk

Eliciting change-talk is a subtle and essential component of developing and enhancing motivation and engagement. Given the nonconfrontational approach of MI, therapists rely on their ability to evoke change-talk so the client gives voice to the exact types of statements that lead to change. The degree to which the therapist can recognize, evoke, and effectively respond to these statements greatly contributes to encouraging change. Miller and Rollnick (2012) suggest asking evocative questions, asking clients and caregivers to elaborate and clarify "what else" in terms of concerns or goals, exploring extremes (e.g., What concerns you most about your child's behavior in the long run? or What might be the best results you could imagine if counseling is helpful to your family?), looking back and looking forward, and exploring goals and values. These themes are opened up with greater detail in *Motivational Interviewing: Helping People Change* (Miller & Rollnick, 2012) as well as in MI trainings. We encourage therapists to pursue opportunities to further develop engagement-focused skills using these resources.

Problem Solving Around Barriers

As mentioned earlier in this chapter, the two main types of treatment barriers include concrete and perceptual. Problem solving for each type is unique, though perceptual barriers are often the most influential.

Perceptual Barrier Problem Solving. Commonly, perceptual barriers like "Therapy doesn't help," "You're going to tell me I'm a bad parent," or "You're just going to play with my child" are based on misinformation or miscommunication. Open discussion, psychoeducation, and orienting clients and caregivers to the treatment process often help to alleviate perceptual barriers. The challenging part is eliciting these perceptions. Using the skills described above, you will be likely to identify perceptions or thoughts that impede treatment success. You can then provide information, discuss alternative thoughts, and use the cognitive triangle to help clients or caregivers consider how these barriers are impacting their feelings about treatment and their actions in therapy (refer to the "Cognitive Triangle of Family Disengagement in Therapy" figure shown previously).

Concrete Barrier Problem Solving. The types of concrete barriers can vary by treatment setting; however, they often include transportation, child care, scheduling, or changes in living situations. Once the barriers have been identified, therapist transparency and creativity will be useful, but will primarily support client and caregiver engagement in this process. They are the experts on their lives and are more likely to identify individualized solutions. The therapist should elicit solutions from caregivers and clients while looking for ways in which she can reasonably facilitate the solutions. The therapist can sometimes make suggestions the caregiver or client has not considered or that may expand the misperceived limited options (e.g., "Some people have neighbors or friends who might be able to help drive," "I am here until 7:00 p.m. two evenings a week. We can start with this time, but as soon as one of those later appointments becomes available, I can offer it to you," "You and I could connect by phone every week for fifteen to twenty minutes to make sure you have a chance to catch up on progress," or "We also offer therapy at the school. Would that location work better?"). These suggestions should be used to help expand the problem-solving process, since the most meaningful solutions will come from the clients and families themselves.

Skills Training

Based on your client and her family's readiness for change, you might offer different types of support. Resistance comes into the session when the therapist offers support that is misaligned with the client's or family's current stage. In the following sections, we provide a summary of the considerations and skills you might cover in the first three stages of change, including activities that may help to either develop skills or increase engagement at each stage.

PRECONTEMPLATION STAGE (DENIAL)

When clients and families are in the precontemplation stage, the goal is to help them begin to think about changing the status quo. In other words, therapists will help clients and families explore topics that will draw out their ambivalence about making positive changes. Questions that may encourage ambivalence include "What would let you know that this is a problem?" or "Have you tried to make a change like this in the past?" Two activities that may help with engagement include the typical day and decisional balance exercises.

Typical Day. This exercise involves asking a client or caregiver to describe a typical day while you gently elicit thoughtfulness of how depression impacts the individual and family in different contexts (i.e., school, community, at home, and so forth). This encourages clients and caregivers to think about how resistance in treatment is connected to their current concerns and the challenges that brought them to therapy.

Typical Day Exercise

- *Can we spend the next five to ten minutes going through a day from beginning to end?*

  - Guide a discussion about the different individuals and settings the client encounters throughout a typical day.

- *What stood out to you?*

- *How did you feel?*

- *Where does your depression fit in?*

  - If the client or caregiver struggles to engage in a specific module, you may query about how that specific aspect of depression poses challenges in the daily life of the client and family.

  - This exercise should rely on the client or family member talking 80 to 90 percent of the time. Therapists can use OARS skills to encourage an open conversation.

Decisional Balance. The decisional balance exercise helps clients and caregivers walk through the pros and cons of a given decision or opportunity. (A worksheet for this activity is provided at the end of this chapter and online at http://www.newhar binger.com/31175.) First, encourage clients and families to completely explore the pros of maintaining the status quo. By starting with this piece, you demonstrate your willingness to have an open, nondefensive, and realistic discussion about the decision. You then move clockwise through the boxes on the worksheet (i.e., cons of maintaining the status quo, cons of changing, pros of changing), summarizing as you go and then discussing overall reactions after completing the worksheet.

CONTEMPLATION STAGE (QUESTIONING)

The goal for clients and families in the contemplation stage is to encourage them to examine the benefits and barriers to change in order to improve their motivation. You may ask questions such as "Why do you want to change at this time?" or "What could keep you from changing at this time?" The decisional balance exercise (described in the "Precontemplation Stage" section) and the change ruler can be useful during this stage.

Change Ruler. The change ruler, like the feeling thermometer, helps caregivers and clients think about motivation for change in terms of a spectrum, or on a scale. The two aspects of motivation that you can encourage clients to consider are importance and confidence. Using the ruler, you can ask on a scale of zero to ten how important the change is and how confident the client or caregiver is that the change can happen. When clients report a number of two or higher, you can ask what makes the importance or their confidence higher than the lower numbers (i.e., "What makes your score x [their answer] instead of y [lower score]?"). You can also ask what might help boost the score one or two points. You can end with a summary statement and elicit commitment to take some action when appropriate.

Change Ruler

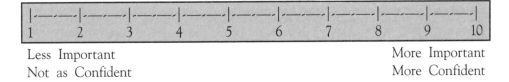

| 1 | 2 | 3 | 4 | 5 | 6 | 7 | 8 | 9 | 10 |

Less Important   More Important
Not as Confident   More Confident

PREPARATION STAGE (STRENGTHS)

During the preparation stage, therapists aim to improve client and caregiver confidence for successful treatment. Adolescents in particular respond to affirmation and validation of their skills and capacity to make changes. Ways to increase confidence during this stage include asking, "When have you changed in the past, and what made it successful?" or "What things (people, skills, strengths) have helped in the past?" The confidence aspect of the change ruler may be useful, along with creating a change plan or completing the Qualities of Success activity.

Qualities of Success. Adapted from Feldstein and Ginsburg's "Characteristics of Successful Adolescents" exercise (2007), this activity offers therapists and clients a chance to identify positive attributes. Create a list of positive characteristics a young person might have and ask the client to read each of the characteristics. The client can mark the traits that describe her. After reading each characteristic and identifying an initial pool of traits that describe her, ask the client or caregiver to pick the top three to five traits that describe her. Once the top traits are identified, ask the individual to describe an experience or example when she used the trait to make a change. This activity is a powerful opportunity to focus on strengths and linking these strengths with a capacity to make changes.

Change Plan. The change plan offers a way to crystallize the preparation steps that have been established and identify aspects that still should be determined. Working through the worksheet provided at the end of the chapter (which is also available online at http://www.newharbinger.com/31175) can be helpful when completed by the client in session with therapist support or at home with caregiver support.

ACTION STAGE (CBT SKILL BUILDING)

The action stage is the stage where CBT skill building is most successful and you can transition to other modules. It will be useful to keep in mind that stages are not discrete and some clients and caregivers move between stages. Unlike other modules, the goal is not necessarily "mastery of engagement." If your clients and their caregivers lose momentum with their engagement, you will have opportunities to refer back to work from previous stages in order to cultivate motivation in treatment and confidence to move forward. Continue to reinforce your client and her caregiver's honest feedback and attempts at engaging in treatment. Recognize and affirm the specific efforts you notice. This is especially crucial for depressed individuals, who may struggle with sustained confidence in their abilities or with accurately interpreting their successes.

Tools for Skill Building

A concrete barrier to completing between-session practices or attending therapy can be disorganization or simply not remembering the appointment. Fortunately, smartphones provide access to reminders for appointments or tasks. Setting up midweek reminders to prepare for the next session is an easy step that can help set up your clients for success. It may also be helpful to provide checklists for the week, to schedule midweek check-in calls, and to involve other adults in the process, such as teachers or other family members.

Between-Session Practice

Since the goal of this module is to boost engagement in treatment, between-session practices can take different forms. These practices will emerge as you identify the barriers and problem solve around solutions. For example, if this module is focused on increasing participation in homework from other modules, that will be the emphasis. If this module is intended to increase more consistent session attendance, the practices can include a plan of the client calling a support person the day before to make sure she has transportation to the session. Assigning between-session practices with this module can also be useful to gauge the client's commitment to treatment. Starting with fairly simple homework might help your client get in the habit of taking responsibility for her treatment. You can gradually increase her responsibility until you're ready to proceed with other modules. The goal is for the between-session practices for this module to gradually taper off and be replaced with between-session practices from other modules.

Summary, Feedback, and Next Steps

It is appropriate in this module to set up plans and specific strategies to avoid future barriers. Connect the engagement and motivation you've elicited in this module with the skill building, practicing, and mastery of other modules. Summarizing the client's and caregivers' reasons for engaging in treatment and keeping those reasons in mind will help all involved make use of their own capacity to overcome challenges as treatment moves forward. Discuss this process openly, and let your clients and their families know that you will continue to remind them of the themes from this module to help them reach the goals they've told you are important to them.

Common Hurdles and Solutions for Therapists

Even after becoming familiar with and using an engagement-focused lens and the skills described in this module, you will probably encounter clients and caregivers who challenge your own engagement or who frustrate you. Seek consultation or supervision for these cases. Identify the sources of frustration or your engagement "blind spots." As mentioned previously in this chapter, engagement skills, like a guitar, need constant retuning and adjustment. Therapists who feel as though they've "mastered" treatment engagement are at risk for missing areas of growth. Even the most experienced and skilled therapists will continuously find ways to engage themselves and their clients in treatment.

Summary

While the modular CBT tools and skills offered in this guide have been developed to help reduce the impact of depression in the lives of young people, clients and families must be actively engaged in the treatment process for these tools and skills to be effective. Conceptualizing cases with an engagement-focused lens and using engagement-focused skills when appropriate will help resistant or disengaged clients and families have more success in modular CBT. Focusing on engagement can supplement the success of treatment by increasing client and family motivation and capacity for change, identifying stages of change, and addressing barriers. An engagement-focused treatment can often be necessary for the success of modular CBT.

Decisional Balance

Possible Change: _____

_____

Benefits (pros) of things staying the same:	*Losses (cons) of things staying the same:*
Benefits (pros) of making a change:	*Losses (cons) of making a change:*

Downloadable copies of this form are available online at http://www.newharbinger .com/31175. (See the very back of this book for more details.)

Change Plan

The changes I want to make are:
The reasons why I want to make these changes are:
The steps I plan to take in changing are:
The ways other people can help me are:
I will know that my plan is working if:
Some things that could get in the way of my plan working are:
What I will do if the plan isn't working:

Downloadable copies of this form are available online at http://www.newharbinger .com/31175. (See the very back of this book for more details.)

Chapter 13

Problem-Solving Skills

In a study on learned helplessness, Hiroto (1974) divided college students into three groups. Two groups were exposed to loud and unpleasant noises. The first group was able to turn off the loud noises by pressing a button four times, so they learned that their actions led to a solution. When presented with a subsequent problem-solving task, the students were able to solve it. On the other hand, the second group was exposed to noises that turned off and on at intermittent times, regardless of how many times the students pressed the button. The second group learned that their attempts at solving the problem were fruitless, so when they were presented with a subsequent solvable task, they failed. The third group of students, which was not exposed to any noise, performed like the first group and was able to solve the problem on the second task.

Hiroto's experiment was based on Martin Seligman's (1972) seminal work on learned helplessness in dogs. Hiroto was able to elicit learned helplessness behavior in human participants and determined that when the students learned that their efforts did not impact the environment, they stopped trying, even when they were presented with a solvable situation. This cognitive representation of uncontrollability can manifest in depression with symptoms of difficulty concentrating, clouded thinking, and difficulty making decisions. Like Hiroto's college students, when depressed children have difficulty solving problems in their lives, they may give up trying.

Preparing the Module

While problem-solving skills training has not been a core component of traditional cognitive behavioral therapy and is considered a supplementary module, it tends to be an essential module to offer in modular CBT for many children and adolescents. This chapter highlights a framework for the problem-solving skills training. We discuss the background and clinical rationale for problem-solving skills training. The background is intended to help therapists understand the reason and context for problem-solving skills and to decide whether to use this module with a given client. We describe the basics of problem-solving skills training and highlight how to implement this module effectively.

Background

Problem solving is defined as the process by which an individual cognitively identifies potential solutions to a real-life problem and behaviorally engages in adaptive activities that enable him or her to attempt to effectively cope with the problem. Problem-solving skills refer to the set of cognitive behavioral skills that an individual can learn in order to cope effectively.

In 1971, psychologists D'Zurilla and Goldfried proposed that individuals who did not have adequate problem-solving skills encountered significant deficits in coping effectively with stress. Based on this initial concept, A. M. Nezu (1987) developed a depression model that linked deficits in problem-solving skills with development of depression. In the Nezu model, depression occurs when an individual lacks the necessary skills to cope with the problems that arise throughout life. In 2000, Garland, Harrington, House, and Scott conducted a preliminary study of individuals with unipolar depression and found that baseline deficits in problem-solving skills were significantly associated with prognosis. Since then, numerous studies have implicated the role of problem-solving skills in depressive disorders. For an overview of this literature, please refer to House and Scott's (1996) review paper.

Clinical Rationale for the Module: Solving Life's Problems

Based on the empirical literature, there is a correlation between inadequate problem-solving skills and depression. Depressed (and suicidal) individuals tend to have an inefficient or ineffectual ability to apply problem-solving skills when confronted with stressful situations; furthermore, they tend to have little confidence in their ability to solve problems while also anticipating that the solutions they do propose will be ineffectual (Gotlib & Asarnow, 1979; Schotte & Clum, 1987). For a meta-analytic review on the role of problem-solving skills interventions in ameliorating depression, please refer to A. C. Bell and D'Zurilla (2009). These authors reviewed problem-solving therapy (PST) specifically and found that the most effective treatment incorporated both a positive problem orientation and problem-solving skills. Notably, they found that problem-solving skills training should address the client's view of himself as an effective problem solver, as well as a positive perspective about the problems (e.g., viewing the problem as an opportunity rather than a burden). These views relate to the positive problem orientation.

Because children and adolescents who are depressed tend to hold a negative view of themselves, the world, and their future, this perspective can lead them to have poor problem-solving skills. In turn, this deficit in problem-solving skills may cause a burgeoning of unsolved problems in the child's life, which may then contribute to the child's entrenched depression. The clinical rationale for teaching children and adolescents effective problem-solving skills is to break this pattern so (1) the frequency and severity of their problems decrease and (2) clients can improve their view on themselves and the world, and be more optimistic about their ability to solve problems.

Fit of Topic with Overall Treatment

Problem-solving skills training is considered a supplementary module in modular CBT. This is primarily because impaired problem-solving skills are not a core feature of depression. Depressed children and adolescents who have intact problem-solving skills do not need to complete this module. However, this module is strongly recommended for inclusion when treating individuals who have a history of suicidal ideations. Schotte and Clum (1987) found that suicidal individuals have deficits in interpersonal problem solving, experience more stress, and endorse feeling more hopeless. This collection of impaired skills, coupled with hopelessness and increased stress, can lead to elevated suicide risk; thus, if you have a client who is currently having suicidal ideations or has a history of suicidal thoughts, this module should be administered alongside the safety plan and crisis management module.

Using the Module

Equipped with the information from the "Preparing the Module" section, the various pieces of this module should be purposeful and feel cohesive with the other modules for your client. This section is designed to introduce and teach these skills effectively. We present all the necessary information required to train the child or adolescent in developing problem-solving skills, including structuring the session, using the agenda, and strategies for building the skills. Overall, your goals for this module are trifold: (1) reframe problems as opportunities or challenges that can be overcome, (2) increase the child's or adolescent's sense of self-efficacy in solving problems, and (3) teach effective problem-solving skills (PSS).

When to Include the Module

We recommend sequencing this module in the course of treatment based on the severity of functional impairment directly related to the child's or adolescent's lack of effectual problem-solving skills. Typically, this module may be conducted later in the treatment course, following the core modules; however, if your client is experiencing significant distress due to difficulty coping with his current life stressors (e.g., being bullied, failing a class, fighting with a sibling), you may wish to teach him these skills early in the course of treatment. Doing so may result in the following benefits: increased therapeutic alliance (e.g., as the child and parents see resolution in problem areas, they may experience increased hope and motivation and continue treatment), decreased stress (e.g., reduced frequency of fighting with sibling results in increased calm in the household), increased safety (e.g., improved ability to follow through with the coping strategies outlined on the safety plan), and improved response to other modules (e.g., improved affect regulation due to effective use of coping skills).

Cultural Considerations

PSS are learned skills and are largely affected by one's cultural environment. The extent to which a child develops mastery over problems (e.g., through problem-solving skills) is primarily based on the extent to which the child's culture emphasizes or provides opportunities for the child to practice and engage in those skills. These opportunities can vary widely among differing cultures, which impacts parenting practices. One recent phenomenon that has been debated is whether overinvolved parental behavioral control (also colloquially known as "helicopter parenting," whereby parents "hover" over their children and solve their problems for them) is linked to negative well-being outcomes for adolescents, presumably due to decreased opportunities for the teenagers to practice their problem-solving skills for themselves. One study on college students correlated these overinvolved parenting behaviors with higher levels of depression and lower levels of perceived autonomy and competence in the students, and further found that adolescents who perceived they had less competence were more likely to be depressed (Shriffin et al., 2014).

Involving Parents and Caregivers

The role of parents and caregivers in this module is more limited than in other modules of modular CBT. Parents' involvement is elicited when conducting role-plays, and to support the child's efforts to follow through with skills between sessions. For this module, the overall goal is to teach the child or adolescent mastery in a new set of skills; thus, the client initially meets with the clinician alone for the initial training and development of these skills. Parents may join sessions to participate in role-plays as the clients practice their skills in session. Parents may also be contacted separately outside of the therapy session (e.g., as collateral contact via phone or in person) in order to elicit their help in supporting the client's efforts to use his problem-solving skills at home. This ongoing communication with parents is critical, as without knowledge and understanding of the child's efforts to use his problem-solving skills, there is a risk of the parent or caregiver inadvertently interfering with that learning process.

Cole, an experienced therapist, just completed a problem-solving skills session with his precocious ten-year-old client, Sophia. Today's problem-solving skills training session proved fruitful. In brainstorming potential alternative options to arguing with her mother during in-home altercations, Sophia identified taking a "chill-out" in her bedroom as a coping skill to help her calm down and a way to decrease escalation of the argument with her mother in a given situation. At the end of the session Sophia agreed to practice this coping skill when she is faced with a problem situation with her mother. However, Sophia's grandmother (who does not live with her) had transported her to therapy, and despite attempting to call the mother, Sophia's therapist wasn't able to talk to the mother over the subsequent week. Over the next few days, on several occasions, Sophia attempted to practice her newly learned problem-solving skills, but when she tried using her chill-out option of taking a self-time-out in her bedroom, her mother (unaware that this response strategy was developed with approval of the therapist) was offended that Sophia walked away during their heated arguments. At the next therapy session, Sophia's mother expressed concern to Cole that Sophia was trying to isolate herself in her bedroom. In the absence of knowledge about the problem-solving skills training session that had occurred the previous week, her mother had interpreted Sophia's efforts to take a chill-out during their arguments as a sign of an increasing depression level with isolative behaviors. This misunderstanding of Sophia's behaviors and efforts to use her problem-solving skills is a good example of the importance of providing timely psychoeducation to parents (and other support people, such as teachers) about the skill set that is being taught to the adolescent.

Structuring the Session

Like other modules, the general structure of the first problem-solving skills intervention session is to start with a check-in, then move to a review of homework (from previous modules), setting the agenda, a brief introduction to put the module in context of the broader course of treatment, psychoeducation, skills training with feedback, and finally, a discussion of next steps.

Example:

- *Check-In and Agenda Setting (5–10 minutes)*

- *Homework Review: Relaxation Training (5 minutes)*

- *Skills Training: Problem-Solving Skills (20 minutes)*

- *Current Concerns (5–10 minutes)*

- *Assigning Between-Session Practice (5 minutes)*

- *Summary, Feedback, and Next Steps (5 minutes)*

First Steps

Check-In. The first few minutes of the session may be spent checking in with the client. Refer to the dry-erase board and prime the client for the session structure.

Therapist: As you can see on the dry-erase board, we will be checking in on how you've been doing, reviewing how the between-session practice has been going for you, and then learning how to solve problems. Now, are there certain things that you'd like to make sure that we talk about today?

Agenda Setting. Any concerns or situations that were brought up during the check-in process may be placed on the agenda for later discussion. As a reminder, an effective way to address any "crisis of the week" incidents is to incorporate the discussion into the skills-building exercise that is on the agenda for each particular week. For instance, an adolescent may wish to discuss an argument with his mother that just occurred on the way to the therapy session. You may incorporate this discussion in the skills-building section of problem-solving skills training by using the situation as an example as you're teaching the skills.

Therapist:	Are there any issues or concerns that you would like to put on the agenda for today?
Client:	Yeah, I just got into a huge fight with Mom on the way here today. It annoys me so much when she nags at me; I just can't help but yell at her to shut up. It's not my fault—if she didn't nag me, I wouldn't get so mad at her.
Therapist:	Okay, let's put that on our agenda for today. We will talk about that argument with your mother when we talk about problem-solving skills.

Homework Review. The next few minutes should be spent reviewing the client's homework assignment from the previous session. It is important to hold the child or adolescent accountable by checking in with him regarding whether he has completed his therapy homework. If the adolescent did not complete his homework assignment, then it is recommended that you spend a little more time at this point in the session to help the client complete his homework assignment. You can engage parents in reminding the child every evening to complete his therapy homework.

Skills Training

PROVIDING A RATIONALE FOR PROBLEM-SOLVING SKILLS TRAINING

As with all modules, you always provide a rationale for the skills you are teaching your client. This psychoeducation is often key in eliciting motivation from your client. If the child or adolescent and parents do not understand why a particular skill set is important to learn, you may encounter resistance from the client to learn the behaviors and lack of follow-through from the parents in supporting your client's efforts to practice the skills at home. Be sure to link the skill set with the client's identified goal for therapy.

Therapist:	Remember how you said you wanted to get along with your mother better—that you were tired of fighting with her all the time? Well, today, we are going to be learning problem-solving skills, which is one of the best ways to make those arguments happen less often.

Another example:

Therapist: Remember how you said you wanted to make more friends but your mom kept grounding you so you couldn't go out? Well, today, we are going to be learning problem-solving skills, which is one of the best ways to make those groundings happen less often, so you will be able to go out with your friends more often.

ACTIVE LEARNING SEQUENCE

When teaching a new skill set that involves a practical skill, you want to use the model–practice–corrective feedback process. After providing the rationale for problem-solving skills in general, you demonstrate the steps of using a particular skill. First, you model the application of the skill, then you engage the client in practicing the skill, and finally, you provide praise, reinforcement, and any needed corrective feedback so the client may learn to use the skill effectively. In problem-solving skills training, you begin by describing the step-by-step process. The aim is for the therapist to teach the client the following problem-solving skills steps using the acronym *CAREFUL.*

Challenge: What is the challenge (problem)?

Affirm: A positive self-statement: "I can do this."

Realistic choices for action

Evaluate consequences of each choice

Fix it. Make a choice

Understand what happened

Like it?

Instructional methods for problem-solving skills may vary; for instance, the client can write this acronym on a dry-erase board, write it on the provided worksheet at the end of this chapter, or even use a smartphone app to remind him of the steps. The key aspect is that the teaching method should be action oriented and interactive in nature.

Therapist: Would you like to write on the white board?

Client: Yes, I'll write CAREFUL on the board.

Therapist: Okay, so what does C stand for?

Client: Um, I don't remember. *(looks at his worksheet)* It means challenge.

Therapist: That's right—nice job checking your worksheet. Yes, the first step in problem-solving skills is to identify the challenge. Ask yourself, "What is the issue?" What is the second step?

Client: *(looks down at worksheet, then writes on dry-erase board)* A, for affirm.

Therapist: That's right. For this step, you are reminding yourself that you can do it.

EXPLAINING THE SEVEN STEPS TO PROBLEM SOLVING

1. Challenge: What is the challenge presented? What is the problem? When the adolescent initiates this first step, it is allowing him to slow down, pause, and ask himself what the issue at hand is. For instance, in arguing with his mother over a chore left undone, the argument may start small but quickly escalate to yelling and screaming if neither party pauses to consider the issue and alternatives. For this first step, the main goal is to get the adolescent to slow his response (e.g., yelling louder and louder) down and to identify the problem. This first step is called a "challenge" rather than a "problem" to encourage the adolescent to reframe the situation as a challenge that he can overcome.

2. Affirm: "I can do this." This step encourages the adolescent to feel self-efficacy. Depressed adolescents may feel hopeless and engage in negative automatic thoughts. This step counters those negative thoughts by reminding the adolescent that he can confront the challenge.

3. Realistic choices for action: This step teaches the adolescent to identify realistic options and realize that these options are choices that he can make actively. In this third step of problem-solving skills, the adolescent learns how to identify realistic alternatives to his behavior (e.g., rather than yelling louder and louder in the argument with his mom, what can he choose to do instead?). These choices for action may include both constructive and maladaptive coping strategies. Ideally, you want to have at least three choices that the adolescent can select for action (e.g., keep yelling at Mom; take some deep breaths and ask to take a chill-out; walk away, and use progressive muscle relaxation).

4. Evaluate consequences of each choice: In this step, the adolescent is encouraged to evaluate the consequences of each identified realistic choice for action. For instance, one of the choices that the adolescent can make is to keep yelling at his mom. In this step, ask the adolescent, "What might happen if you continue to yell louder and louder at your mom?" This allows the adolescent to consider the consequences of his actions and to change the course of action for an improved outcome.

5. Fix it. Make a choice: In this step, the adolescent has already identified the range of choices and consequences for each choice, and now he needs to make a choice. What choice will he pick in order to "fix" the problem? For instance, the adolescent may choose to take some deep breaths and ask to take a chill-out in his room to help him refrain from arguing.

6. Understand what happened: Sometimes clients will make a good choice, and sometimes they will make a maladaptive choice. After the adolescent selects his choice, he should always consider whether he selected an adaptive action.

7. Like it? This last step is a nod to social media. It allows the adolescent to give himself corrective feedback, or if an adaptive choice was made, to praise himself and increase feelings of self-efficacy and hopefulness.

ROLE-PLAY WITH FEEDBACK

After modeling the problem-solving skills steps, elicit the child to practice the problem-solving skills. Role-plays should always begin with the therapist modeling the steps, then the roles are switched and the child practices the steps. The clinician should always provide specific and labeled praise, as well as any needed corrective feedback.

Working on Current Concerns

Any topics that were brought up by the child or caregiver at the beginning of the session may be discussed in this section of the session. In this module, there is a high likelihood that many of the concerns, issues, or incidents that the adolescent (or parent) wants to talk about can be addressed during skills building because problem-solving skills can be generalized to nearly all problems. For instance, let's consider the wide range of issues that the client may have brought up during initial check-in: fight with his best friend, cheating on his boyfriend, failing a class, having difficulty with doing a class presentation, arguing with his sister, being bullied in dance class, and so on. You can use all of these presenting issues as examples while teaching problem-solving skills steps.

Between-Session Practice

The key aspect to learning how to use problem-solving skills effectively is to practice, practice, practice. The child should practice these problem-solving skills steps as frequently as possible so the behaviors become habitual. To aid in helping the adolescent develop these skills, you can make copies of the completed CAREFUL worksheet (available at the end of this chapter and online at http://www.newharbinger .com/31175) so the client can post it in visible areas around his home (e.g., in his bedroom, on the refrigerator). You might ask him to input the acronym CAREFUL into his smartphone or take a picture of it with the device so he can easily access it in different settings, or print it on a card and laminate it so he can keep the card in his pocket, backpack, or school binder. Both you and the client can be creative in finding ways that can help him remember and practice problem-solving skills steps. For instance, if the adolescent is interested in superheroes, you can identify storylines in which the superhero engages in these steps to beat the villain. If an adolescent is interested in movie making, you can use a video camera and engage the client in making a mini-movie about a character who uses the steps to overcome a challenge. These creative ways to teach the skills will enhance your client's motivation, interest level, and eventual follow-through on learning problem-solving skills steps.

As mentioned earlier in this chapter, it is very important to conduct at least a collateral contact with the adolescent's parent (as well as any other support individuals) to review problem-solving steps, discuss the potential coping strategies that the client may select (e.g., take a chill-out in his room), and assess whether the parent is in agreement with the potential coping strategies. You can collaborate with the parents and elicit their support in identifying additional coping strategies that may be strength-based for the client (e.g., parents may create a small chill-out space in the home for the client to use if he doesn't have his own bedroom).

Summary, Feedback, and Next Steps

Have the client summarize the session highlights to you.

Therapist: Today, we learned how to use some problem-solving skills. In what kinds of situations might you use these skills?

Ask the adolescent for feedback regarding the session. This feedback allows you to know what is working in real time and what is not working as well.

Therapist: How do you think today's session went? Which strategy was most helpful to you? Which one was least helpful?

The final step to the session is to prime the child or adolescent as to the next steps in therapy. You may be covering problem-solving skills again at the next session, or you may be moving on to another module. It is helpful to prime the child as to which next step is likely.

Therapist: Okay, so we just started learning problem-solving skills steps and how these steps might help us make better decisions when we have challenges. Just like when you first learned how to ride a bike or play a new video game, it takes time and repetition to really learn how to use these new skills. We are going to practice them again at the next session. I know that you like using the computer, so we can use the computer next time to write out the steps and print out the sheets for you to take home. How does that sound?

Common Hurdles and Solutions for Therapists

In this module, the most common hurdle is having the child or adolescent generalize his problem-solving skills outside of the therapy office. Parents (and clients) may feel discouraged when they observe that the child is able to use his problem-solving skills when discussing problems during therapy sessions, but has not yet generalized the skills to real-world problems (e.g., an argument with sibling, a fight with another student). The therapist may help prevent this discouragement by providing realistic expectations at the beginning of the module. When providing the rationale for the skills, the therapist should inform the child and parent of the challenge with generalizing the skills, and that the key way to overcome that challenge is with repetition and practice outside of the therapy session. It may also be beneficial to instill realistic hope by providing the child and parents with de-identified examples of other children who have successfully learned to use their problem-solving skills in other arenas. Furthermore, it may be helpful to reiterate to them that problem-solving skills are worthwhile skills to learn because even adults need to use problem-solving skills in order to have a successful life. You may remind them that the adolescent has learned poor problem-solving skills over many years, so it will likely take many sessions and some time for them to learn more adaptive skills and to use them at home and school. Clients who would benefit from a more intensive and comprehensive problem-solving skills training program should be referred to Kazdin's evidence-based Problem Solving Skills Training (PSST) program (2003).

Summary

This supplementary module is designed to help depressed children and adolescents who do not have healthy problem-solving skills. They may be in a family environment wherein adaptive problem-solving skills were not modeled adequately for them. Or they may have attempted but, like Hiroto's students, they developed learned helplessness. The good news is that problem-solving skills are *skills*, and can be learned with effort, repetition, and practice.

CAREFUL:
Seven Steps to Problem-Solving Skills

Challenge: What is the challenge? _____

_____

Affirm: A positive self-statement: "I can do this." _____

_____

Realistic choices for action: _____

_____

_____

_____

Evaluate consequences of each choice: _____

_____

_____

_____

Fix it. Make a choice: _____

Understand what happened: What happened after I made my choice? _____

_____

Like it? _____

Downloadable copies of this form are available online at http://www.newharbinger .com/31175. (See the very back of this book for more details.)

Chapter 14

Relapse Prevention

Paul and his family were on a road trip in Colorado, heading to the small ski town of Telluride. The town is tucked away in the San Juan Mountains in southern Colorado, far away from the state capitol. Telluride sits in a box canyon, with steep forested mountains and cliffs surrounding it. Coming from Durango on the southern route, the three-hour drive to Telluride is on a long, narrow, and at times windy road that goes through a mountain pass, which can be susceptible to avalanches and road closures in the winter. At the start of the narrow, windy mountain road, the weather was sunny and the skies were clear. It was a day with ideal driving conditions. As they neared the midway point of the drive to Telluride, clouds had spread across the sky. The sun had disappeared behind them, and on the horizon in the distance, more dark, swirling clouds appeared. But those clouds were off in the far distance, and the family ignored them as the weather was still good. As they continued along the windy road, the air coming in through the car vents became noticeably chillier. Paul turned on the heater; the cold air disappeared as the temperature quickly became warm and comfortable in the car again. However, after about another twenty minutes, snow fluries suddenly appeared. The skies quickly changed to an opaque white. Despite this change in driving conditions, Paul continued along the narrow road. Within five minutes, the family found themselves in the midst of a snowstorm. Surprised at the sudden and severe turn of the weather, Paul realized that his family was unprepared for the road conditions. They had to pull over to the side of the road because the white-out conditions made it impossible to see the road.

Sitting by the side of the road in the midst of the snowstorm, Paul realized that he had missed a number of weather signs that could have warned him of the impending snowstorm. If he had wanted to avoid the dangerous road conditions of the snowstorm, what could he have done differently? For one thing, if he had paid attention to the initial, subtle signs of impending bad weather (e.g., dark and swirling clouds, cold air coming in the car vents, snow flurries), he could have picked up snow chains, considered driving on other roads, or stopped at the hotel in the last little town they had passed. These steps may have helped Paul avoid the dangerous predicament of suddenly finding himself and his family in the center of a white-out snowstorm while on a narrow mountain road.

For depressed children and adolescents who have graduated from treatment and are no longer in therapy, they can learn from Paul's situation. By noticing red flags (e.g., increased days of feeling down, feeling tired, change in appetite or sleep), they can identify if a depressive episode may be imminent and take preventative actions or seek appropriate treatment at early onset.

Preparing the Module

Relapse prevention is the final core module of modular CBT. If you are implementing this module, then congratulations! You and your client have successfully progressed through the essential modules for your client's treatment, and you are reading this module now because you are ready to prepare your client for concluding treatment.

Background

For individuals with depressive disorders, depressive episodes are highly recurrent. Over 50 percent of adolescents who have a depressive episode will have a reoccurrence within seven years. Eighty percent of those who have two episodes will have a reoccurrence. One of the more sobering statistics about depression is that, on average, individuals with a history of depression will have five to nine separate depressive episodes in their lifetime (Kessler & Walters, 1998; Kessler, Zhao, Blazer, & Swartz, 1997).

Clinical Rationale for the Module

Individuals with recurrent depression experience significant functional impairment. Each subsequent reoccurrence may negatively impact the depressed child's or adolescent's view of herself, the world, and the future. Repeated depressive episodes may increase the child's feelings of hopelessness, especially with regard to the future. In a study of more than 3,000 adolescents and young adults, 90 percent of individuals with recurrent depression reported strong impairment in social and occupational functioning (Wittchen, Nelson, & Lachner, 1998). Only 40 percent of those individuals sought out mental health treatment again.

Fit of Topic with Overall Treatment

Relapse prevention is a mandatory, core module in modular CBT. This module is used to help children and adolescents solidify the knowledge and skills that they have learned over numerous sessions. Typically, this module requires only one session to complete.

When to Include the Module

It is recommended that all participants in this modular CBT intervention conclude their treatment with the relapse prevention module. At times, you may have a client who needs to terminate treatment prematurely for a variety of reasons (e.g., due to relocation to another town) and has not completed all of her core or needed supplementary modules. Regardless of missing any core modules, you should plan your last session to conclude with the relapse prevention module.

Using the Module

This module is designed to encourage children and adolescents to feel well prepared for potential future challenges that may occur. In this section, we provide you with relevant psychoeducation material to provide as well as relapse prevention–oriented worksheets (all located at the end of the chapter and available for download at http://www.newharbinger.com/31175).

Cultural Considerations

Because many children and adolescents, including those from various ethnic and racial backgrounds, present their depressive symptoms as physical symptoms (e.g., stomachaches, headaches), these types of symptoms should be included when discussing symptom monitoring. Also, because children and adolescents are often brought to treatment by their parents or caregivers, they may be reticent to participate or continue in treatment. Of particular concern with regard to relapse prevention is that clients may view a reoccurrence as a significant failure on their part. They may feel ashamed to seek treatment again. As eloquently described in the NICE guidelines for identification and management of depression in young children and adolescents (Depression in Children Guideline Development Group & National Collaborating Centre for Mental Health, 2005, p. 76), clients often "think that they *are* the problem, rather than thinking that they *have* a problem with which they may be able to get help." Thus, when reoccurrence occurs, the child or adolescent may have an acute sense that she has failed the treatment. It is important to address this issue with the child and parents, and particularly to provide psychoeducation that reoccurence does not mean failure.

Involving Parents and Caregivers

The role of parents and caregivers in this module is to learn how to support their child or adolescent in preventing a reoccurrence. They may join part of the relapse prevention module session to learn specific skills or steps to help their child (alternatively, this may be done as a collateral contact without the child present if needed). Ideally, it is optimal if parents or caregivers can join the last session for the graduation ceremony section of the session in order to provide praise and reinforcement to their child. Additionally, parents should also be praised and reinforced by the therapist for their role in supporting their child in treatment.

224

Structuring the Session

While the structure of the relapse prevention module is similar to other sessions in modular CBT, there is an addition of a "graduation" celebration at the conclusion. That said, the general structure with the components of checking in, agenda setting, and active skills building remain stable.

Example:

- *Check-In and Agenda Setting (5 minutes)*

- *Homework Review: Problem-Solving Skills (5 minutes)*

- *Skills Training: Relapse Prevention (20 minutes)*

- *Summary and Feedback (10 minutes)*

- *Graduation Celebration (10 minutes)*

First Steps

Check-In. The first few minutes of the session may be spent checking in with the client, as well as the parent or caregiver if he or she is present. At this session, you should directly ask about the child's and family's feelings and thoughts about concluding treatment. While you may have inquired about and addressed these issues at a prior session, those feelings and concerns should be addressed again in this final session.

Agenda Setting. Some children and families may have specific concerns about concluding treatment, and these questions should be placed on the agenda to ensure thorough follow-through on these questions.

Homework Review. The next few minutes may be spent reviewing the client's homework assignment from the previous session. This may be related to skills that the client is practicing from a previously completed module; it may also be a combination of the skills (e.g., affect-regulation and problem-solving skills).

Skills Training

PROVIDING A RATIONALE FOR RELAPSE PREVENTION

As with all modules, you always provide a rationale for the skills you are teaching your client. In this section, you want to provide psychoeducation about reoccurrence rates and normalize that the client may experience some increased symptoms from time to time. This information allows the client to anticipate setbacks and to decrease the level of disappointment and hopelessness she may experience when symptoms arise in the future. You will also want to link relapse-prevention skills to the goals that were initially identified by the client and family from the initial treatment-planning session. For instance, if the client had identified a goal of wanting to have more friends, you want to highlight the reason why relapse-prevention skills can help the client maintain and develop more peer relationships. Making these connections clear to the client and family will help to motivate them to develop and continue their relapse-prevention efforts. Be as specific as you can about their achievements, including any improvement in frequency and severity of behaviors.

Therapist: Remember how you said you wanted to get along with your mother better—that you were tired of fighting with her all the time? Well, you have done a great job of learning how to control your emotions better and using your coping skills. When we first started therapy, you were arguing with her ten to fifteen times per week, and those arguments sometimes resulted with you using a pin to cut yourself. Now, you are arguing with your mom about one to two times per week, which is quite normal for teenagers in general, and you haven't cut yourself for nearly two and a half months! You must be so proud of yourself for putting in hard effort over the past three months! Today, we're going to talk about relapse prevention. Remember that we talked about how one of the goals for your therapy is for you to become your own therapist? Well, you have learned and practiced many skills, and today we will talk about how you can use your new knowledge and skills to be your own therapist when challenging situations come up in the future.

REVIEW OF THERAPY BINDER

You have compiled a binder (or for clients who prefer digital paperwork, you may offer them the electronic forms or give them a list of the materials available online) of the work that your client has completed since the beginning of treatment. You may wish to briefly review the work with the client while highlighting her successes and efforts along the way. It may be helpful (and rewarding) for the child to bring her therapy binder home so that she may review the learned strategies as needed, as part of relapse prevention.

SYMPTOM MONITORING

After normalizing potential reoccurrence of symptoms, describe the rationale for why symptom monitoring may prevent reoccurrence. In the narrative at the beginning of this module, there were many instances in which Paul and his family could have avoided being out on the road in white-out weather conditions. If he had been aware of the initial signs of bad weather, monitored for increasing severity of weather, and took action in order to keep his family safe, then he could have avoided being stuck in a snowstorm with white-out conditions. Likewise, during relapse prevention, explain to the client that symptom monitoring helps her be aware of the initial signs of possible reoccurrence (e.g., increased social withdrawal), which then allows her to take action (e.g., behavioral activation) to prevent eventual reoccurrence of a depressive disorder. As with the other modules, you can be creative in the way you facilitate this skill. For instance, you can use the symptom-monitoring worksheet at the end of this chapter, or you can help the client identify a helpful website or smartphone app. You want to use whichever method is most motivating and aligned with your client's interests and strengths.

Action Plan

In this part of the session, you will collaborate with the client and parent on developing an action plan that they can take with them and use for future challenges. An action plan worksheet is provided at the end of this chapter and available online at http://www.newharbinger.com/31175. This action plan sends a reinforcing message to the client that she can self-engage in therapeutic activities and that she can be self-efficacious and use her available resources to maintain positive mental health. Provide her with examples of how she might do this. For instance, if she noticed during symptom monitoring that she was starting to withdraw from social activities and isolate in her bedroom, then she may open up her therapeutic binder (or pull up the website or app) and review the module on behavioral activation. This way, she can be reminded as to why behavioral activation is effective in decreasing social withdrawal and further depressive symptoms. Putting on her own "therapist cap," she can assign herself tasks to engage in behavioral activation. This action plan should also include ways she can access more intensive help if needed. For instance, it may include telephone numbers to mental health providers and crisis hotlines and chatlines.

Summary and Feedback

Summary. Have the client summarize the session highlights to you.

Therapist: Today, we learned ways to help you decrease the chance of getting really depressed again in the future. Can you tell me some strategies that we've planned to help you be your own therapist?

Feedback. Ask the adolescent for feedback regarding the session and overall treatment. This is also a good opportunity to review the client's completed outcomes measures (e.g., Child Depression Inventory) and describe her improved depression scores using objective data. You may compare her scores from the depression measure she completed when she first began treatment to the most recent one to highlight her significant improvement.

Graduation Celebration. The final step to the session is to have a "graduation" celebration. You may present the client with an individualized certificate with a list of her specific strengths (a sample certificate is provided at the end of this chapter and online at http://www.newharbinger.com/31175). If developmentally appropriate and there are available resources, treats or small rewards may accompany the graduation certificate.

Common Hurdles and Solutions for Therapists

The most common hurdle in this module is the client and parents' wariness about concluding treatment. Parents may be concerned that their child will no longer have therapeutic support to aid in issues that arise. Sometimes clients (or parents) have the misconception that they should be symptom free in order to graduate from treatment. The best way to address these hurdles is through good communication and comprehensive psychoeducation. More specifically, the therapist assures the client and parents that they have learned the skills necessary to cope with issues that may arise from time to time. They should also be aware of normal mood shifts versus worrisome mood shifts that indicate a burgeoning depressive episode. Over the course of therapy, as per the chapters on case conceptualization and treatment planning (chapters 1 and 2), the therapist has continually revisited the realistic treatment goals that the client and parents developed in collaboration with the therapist. The therapist may reiterate to the client and parents that the primary focus of treatment is for the child or adolescent to develop adaptive skills, rather than a narrow focus on symptom elimination.

Summary

In this module, you have effectively navigated the myriad clinical problems that can arise when treating children and adolescents with depression. As you may have already experienced in your clinical practice, children and adolescents who have depression may also present with the following: anxious thoughts, avoidance of social situations, conflicts with peers and adults, noncompliance with adult directions, poor social skills, family problems, parent-child relational issues, poor school performance, school suspensions, and more. In using our modular CBT treatment, you have used an evidence-based approach in tackling depressive symptoms, as well as the clinical problems that typically arise when treating children and adolescents in real-world clinical settings.

Conclusion: Treating Depression with Modular CBT

In developing this treatment manual, we were guided by the transdiagnostic approach to assessment and treatment. This guidance is supported by cutting-edge clinical research. For instance, Barlow and colleagues (2008) developed the Unified Protocol, which incorporates known treatment techniques such as relaxation training and exposures, and demonstrated efficacy for the treatment of comorbid depression and anxiety disorders. While we do not intend our treatment manual to replace comprehensive treatments for anxiety and other childhood disorders (we refer you to Chorpita's *Modular CBT for Anxiety*, Chorpita and Weisz's *MATCH-ADTC* [2009], and the PracticeWise website), our treatment manual is designed to serve a significant population of your real-world clinical practice. We hope that your depressed child or adolescent client with complex clinical presentations will be effectively treated using our modular CBT treatment manual. Looking ahead, we expect to see the transdiagnostic approach to assessment, treatment planning, and treatment as the future of evidence-based mental health treatment.

Symptom Monitoring

	Day 1	Day 2	Day 3	Day 4	Day 5
(1) THINKING. Are you having difficulty today with:					
• Concentrating					
• Making decisions					
• Completing school work					
• Maintaining grades					
(2) PHYSICAL. Did you experience these today?					
• Headaches					
• Stomachaches					
• Joint- or backaches					
• Lack of energy					
• Sleeping problems					
• Weight or appetite changes (gain or loss)					
(3) BEHAVIORAL. Have you felt or done these today?					
• Restless					
• Irritable					
• Not wanting to go to school					
• Wanting to be alone most of the time					
• Having difficulty getting along with others					
• Cutting classes or skipping school					
• Dropping out of sports, hobbies, or activities					
• Drinking or using drugs					
(4) SUICIDE RISK. Have you been thinking about?					
• Self-harm					
• Suicide					
• Death					

Downloadable copies of this form are available online at http://www.newharbinger.com/31175. (See the very back of this book for more details.)

Relapse Prevention Action Plan

1. When I notice that I am getting more symptoms, what should I do? _____

_____

2. What are my resources that I feel comfortable using? _____

_____

_____

3. Client's Family and Support Persons' Actions to Support the Child ("What can I, as the support person, do to help my child use his or her coping strategies and reduce symptoms?"):

_____

_____

4. In the case that I want to see a therapist again, whom do I call? _____

5. In the case of an emergency or high-risk situation (list some past examples of these situations)

_____

_____ ,

I will contact the following resources*:

911 / Police Department (telephone number): _____

County Mental Health Crisis Hotline: _____

Suicide Prevention Hotline or Crisis Chatline: _____

On-Call Hospital Psychiatrist: _____

* These telephone numbers should be saved on my smartphone when possible.

Downloadable copies of this form are available online at http://www.newharbinger .com/31175. (See the very back of this book for more details.)

Graduation Certificate

Great job on successfully working on your coping skills and learning effective skills! Congratulations on keeping up with your hard work and excellent effort!

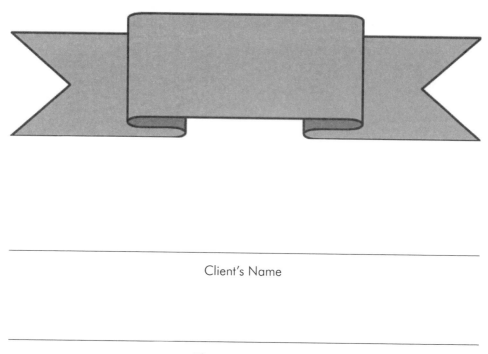

_____

Client's Name

_____

Therapist's Name

Downloadable copies of this form are available online at http://www.newharbinger .com/31175. (See the very back of this book for more details.)

References

Ackerman, S. J., & Hilsenroth, M. J. (2003). A review of therapist characteristics and techniques positively impacting the therapeutic alliance. *Clinical Psychology Review, 23*(1), 1–33.

American Academy of Pediatrics. (1998). Guidance for effective discipline. *Pediatrics, 101*(4), 723–728.

American Psychiatric Association. (2013). *Diagnostic and statistical manual of mental disorders* (Fifth Edition). Arlington, VI: American Psychiatric Association.

Armstrong, L. (2001). *Louis Armstrong, in his own words: Selected writings.* New York, NY: Oxford University Press.

Asarnow, J. (2010). Practitioner review: Self-harm in adolescents. *Journal of Child Psychology and Psychiatry, 53*(4), 337–350.

Asarnow, J., Carlson, G., & Guthrie, D. (1987). Coping strategies, self-perceptions, hopelessness, and perceived family environments in depressed and suicidal children. *Journal of Consulting and Clinical Psychology, 55*(3), 361–366.

Associated Press. (2005, June 22). Disaster on a stick: Snapple's attempt at Popsicle world record turns into gooey fiasco. *NBCNEWS.com.* Retrieved from http://www.nbcnews.com/id/8321110/ns/us_news-weird_news/t/disaster-stick

Atlas Obscura. (2014, July). Hess' Triangle: New York City's smallest piece of private property. Retrieved from http://www.atlasobscura.com/places/hess-triangle

Bannon, W. M., Jr., & McKay, M. M. (2005). Are barriers to service and parental preferences match for services related to urban child mental health service use? *Families in Society: The Journal of Contemporary Social Services, 86,* 30–34.

Barlow, D. H. (2000). Unraveling the mysteries of anxiety and its disorders from the perspective of emotion theory. *American Psychologist, 55*(11), 1247–1263.

Barlow, D. H., Farchione, T. J., Fairholme, C. P., Ellard, K. K., Boisseau, C. L., Allen, L. B., & Ehrenreich-May, J. T. (2011). *The unified protocol for transdiagnostic treatment of emotional disorders: Therapist guide.* New York, NY: Oxford University Press.

Barlow, D., Gallagher, M. W., Carl, J. R., & Thompson-Hollands, J. (2008). Unified protocol for transdiagnostic treatment of emotional disorders: A randomized controlled trial. *Behavior Therapy, 43,* 666–678.

Baumrind, D. (1967). Child care practices anteceding three patterns of preschool behavior. *Genetic Psychology Monographs, 75*(1), 43–88.

Baumrind, D. (1971). Current patterns of parental authority. *Developmental Psychology,* 4(1p2), 1.

Baumrind, D. (1975). The contributions of the family to the development of competence in children. *Schizophrenia Bulletin, 14,* 12–37.

Beck, A. T. (1976). *Cognitive therapy and the emotional disorders.* Oxford, England: International Universities Press.

Beck, J. S. (1995). *Cognitive therapy.* New York, NY: John Wiley & Sons.

Beck, J. S. (2011). *Cognitive behavior therapy: Basics and beyond.* New York, NY: Guilford Press.

Bell, A. C., & D'Zurilla, T. J. (2009). Problem-solving therapy for depression: A meta-analysis. *Clinical Psychology Review, 29*(4), 348–353.

Bell, C. C., & McBride, D. F. (2010). Affect regulation and prevention of risky behaviors. *JAMA: The Journal of the American Medical Association, 304*(5), 565–566.

Benassi, V. A., Sweeney, P. D., & Dufour, C. L. (1988). Is there a relation between locus of control orientation and depression? *Journal of Abnormal Psychology, 97*(3), 357–367.

Benjamin, C. L., Puleo, C. M., Settipani, C. A., Brodman, D. M., Edmunds, J. M., Cummings, C. M., & Kendall, P. C. (2011). History of cognitive-behavioral therapy (CBT) in youth. *Child and Adolescent Psychiatric Clinics of North America, 20*(2), 179–189.

Birmaher, B., Arbelaez, C., & Brent, D. (2002). Course and outcome of child and adolescent major depressive disorder. *Child and Adolescent Psychiatric Clinics of North America, 11*(3), 619–637.

Birmaher, B., Brent, D., Bernet, W., Bukstein, O., Walter, H., Benson, R. S., ... Medicus, J. (2007). Practice parameter for the assessment and treatment of children and adolescents with depressive disorders. *Journal of the American Academy of Child & Adolescent Psychiatry, 46*(11), 1503–1526.

Blankstein, K. R., & Segal, Z. V. (2001). Cognitive assessment: Issues and methods. In K. S. Dobson (Ed.), *Handbook of cognitive-behavioral therapies,* (Second Edition, pp. 40–85). New York, NY: Guildford Press.

Brådvik, L. (2003). Suicide after suicide attempt in severe depression: A long-term follow-up. *Suicide and Life-Threatening Behavior, 33*(4), 381–388.

Brent, D. A., & Poling, K. (1997). *Cognitive therapy treatment manual for depressed and suicidal youth.* Pittsburgh, PA: University of Pittsburgh Health System Services for Teens at Risk.

Brookman-Frazee, L. I., Haine, R. A., Baker-Ericzen, M., Zoffness, R., & Garland, A. F. (2010). Factors associated with use of evidence-based practice strategies in usual care youth psychotherapy. *Administration and Policy in Mental Health and Mental Health Services Research, 37,* 254–269.

Broome, K. M., Flynn, P. M., Knight, D. K., & Simpson, D. D. (2007). Program structure, staff perceptions, and client engagement in treatment. *Journal of Substance Abuse Treatment, 33*(2), 149–158.

Bugental, D. B., & Goodnow, J. G. (2006). Socialization processes. In Eisenberg, N., Damon, W., & Lerner, R. M. (Eds.), *Handbook of child psychology: Social, emotional, and personality development* (pp. 646–718). New York, NY: John Wiley & Sons.

Bui, K. V. T., & Takeuchi, D. T. (1992). Ethnic minority adolescents and the use of community mental health care services. *American Journal of Community Psychology, 20*(4), 403–417.

Burns, D. D. (1989). *The feeling good handbook: Using the new mood therapy in everyday life.* New York, NY: William Morrow & Company.

Cauce, A. M., Domenech-Rodríguez, M., Paradise, M., Cochran, B. N., Shea, J. M., Srebnik, D., & Baydar, N. (2002). Cultural and contextual influences in mental health help seeking: A focus on ethnic minority youth. *Journal of Consulting and Clinical Psychology, 70*(1), 44–55.

Centers for Disease Control and Prevention. (n.d.). Suicide prevention. Retrieved from http://www.cdc.gov/violenceprevention/pub/youth_suicide.html

Chandler, M. J. (1973). Egocentrism and antisocial behavior: The assessment and training of social perspective-taking skills. *Developmental Psychology, 9*(3), 326–332.

Chorpita, B. F. (2006). *Modular cognitive-behavioral therapy for childhood anxiety disorders.* New York, NY: Guilford Press.

Chorpita, B. F., Daleiden, E. L., & Weisz, J. R. (2005). Identifying and selecting the common elements of evidence based interventions: A distillation and matching model. *Mental Health Services Research, 7*(1), 5–20.

Chorpita, B. F., Taylor, A. A., Francis, S. E., Moffitt, C. E., & Austin, A. A. (2004). Efficacy of modular cognitive behavior therapy for childhood anxiety disorders. *Behavior Therapy, 35*, 263–287.

Chorpita, B. F., & Weisz, J. R. (2009). *MATCH-ADTC: Modular approach to therapy for children with anxiety, depression, trauma, or conduct problems.* Satellite Beach, FL: PracticeWise.

Chorpita, B. F., Weisz, J. R., Daleiden, E. L., Schoenwald, S. K., Palinkas, L. A., Miranda, J., ... Research Network on Mental Health (2013). Long-term outcomes for the Child STEPs randomized effectiveness trial: A comparison of modular and standard treatment designs with usual care. *Journal of Consulting and Clinical Psychology, 81*, 999–1009.

Clarke, G. N., Lewinsohn, P. M, & Hops, H. (1990). *Leader's manual for adolescent groups: Adolescent Coping with Depression Course.* Eugene, OR: Castalia Publishing Company.

Cohen, J. A., & Mannarino, A. P. (2008). Trauma-focused cognitive behavioural therapy for children and parents. *Child and Adolescent Mental Health, 13*(4), 158–162.

Cohen, J. A., Mannarino, A. P., & Deblinger, E. (2006). *Treating trauma and traumatic grief in children and adolescents.* New York, NY: Guilford Press.

Cohen, P., & Hesselbart, C. S. (1993). Demographic factors in the use of children's mental health services. *American Journal of Public Health, 83*(1), 49–52.

Costello, E. J., Pine, D. S., Hammen, C., March, J. S., Plotsky, P. M., Weissman, M. M., ... Leckman, J. F. (2002). Development and natural history of mood disorders. *Biological Psychiatry, 52*(6), 529–542.

Crick, N. R., & Dodge, K. A. (1994). A review and reformulation of social information-processing mechanisms in children's social adjustment. *Psychological Bulletin, 115*(1), 74–101.

Curry, J. F., Wells, K. C., Brent, D. A., Clarke, G. N., Rohde, P., Albano, A. M., ... March, J. S. (2000). *Treatment for adolescents with depression study (TADS) cognitive behavior therapy manual: Introduction, rationale, and adolescent sessions.* Unpublished manuscript, Duke University Medical Center. Durham, NC.

D'Zurilla, T. J., & Goldfried, M. R. (1971). Problem solving and behavior modification. *Journal of Abnormal Psychology, 78*(1), 107–126. doi:10.1037/h0031360

Damon, W., & Killen, M. (1982). Peer interaction and the process of change in children's moral reasoning. *Merrill-Palmer Quarterly (28)*3, 347–367.

Dattilio, F. M. (1998). Cognitive-behavioral family therapy. In F. M. Dattilio (Ed.), *Case studies in couples and family therapy* (pp. 62–84). New York, NY: Guilford Press.

Dattilio, F. M. (2001). Cognitive behavior family therapy: Contemporary myths and misconceptions. *Contemporary Family Therapy, 23*(10), 3–18.

Dattilio, F. M. (2002). Homework assignments in couple and family therapy. *Journal of Clinical Psychology, 58*(5), 535–547.

Dattilio, F. M. (2014). Techniques and strategies with couples and families. In G. Simons (Ed.), *Cognitive behaviour therapy: A guide for the practising clinician, Volume 1* (pp. 242–274). London, England: Routledge.

Dattilio, F. M., Epstein, N. B., & Baucom, D. H. (1998). Introduction to cognitive-behavior therapy with couples and family. In F. M. Dattilio (Ed.), *Case studies in couple and family therapy: Systemic and cognitive perspectives* (pp. 1–36). New York, NY: Guilford Press.

David-Ferndon, C., & Kaslow, N. (2008). Evidence-based psychosocial treatments for child and adolescent depression. *Journal of Clinical Child & Adolescent Psychology, 37*(1), 62–104.

Davies, M., Raveis, V. H., & Kandel, D. B. (1991). Suicidal ideation in adolescence: Depression, substance use, and other risk factors. *Journal of Youth and Adolescence, 20*(2), 289–309.

Dawes, R. M., Faust, D., & Meehl, P. E. (1989). Clinical versus actuarial judgment. *Science, 243*(4899), 1668–1674.

Deacon, B., & Maack, D. (2007). The effects of safety behaviors on the fear of contamination: An experimental investigation. *Behaviour Research and Therapy, 46*(4), 537–547.

Depression in Children Guideline Development Group and National Collaborating Centre for Mental Health. (2005). *Depression in children and young people: Identification and management in primary, community and secondary care.* Leicester, England: The British Psychological Society.

DeRubeis, R. J., Tang, T. Z., & Beck, A. T. (2009). Cognitive therapy. In K. S. Dobson (Ed.), *Handbook of cognitive-behavioral therapies* (pp. 277–316). New York, NY: Guilford Press.

DiClemente, C. C., Prochaska, J. O., Fairhurst, S. K., Velicer, W. F., Velasquez, M. M., & Rossi, J. S. (1991). The process of smoking cessation: An analysis of precontemplation, contemplation, and preparation stages of change. *Journal of Consulting and Clinical Psychology, 59*(2), 295–304.

Dimidjian, S., Hollon, S., Dobson, K., Schmaling, K., Kohlenberg, R., Addis, M., … Jacobson, N. (2006). Randomized trial of behavioral activation, cognitive therapy, and antidepressant medication in the acute treatment of adults with major depression. *Journal of Consulting and Clinical Psychology, 74*(4), 658–670.

Drew, B. L. (2001). Self-harm behavior and no-suicide contracting in psychiatric inpatient settings. *Archives of Psychiatric Nursing, 15*(3), 99–106.

Edwards, B. H. (2002). Louis Armstrong and the syntax of scat. *Critical Inquiry, 28*(3), 618–649.

Eisen, A. R., & Silverman, W. K. (1998). Perspective treatment for generalized anxiety disorder in children. *Behavior Therapy, 29,* 105–121.

Eisenberg, N., & Fabes, R. A. (1992). Emotion, regulation, and the development of social competence. In M. S. Clark (Ed.), *Emotion and social behavior: Review of personality and social psychology, Volume 14,* (pp. 119–150). Thousand Oaks, CA: Sage Publications.

Epstein, N., & Schlesinger, S. E. (1996). Treatment of family problems. In M. Reinecke, F. M. Dattilio, & A. Freeman (Eds.), *Cognitive therapy with children and adolescents: A casebook for clinical practice* (pp. 229–326). New York, NY: Guilford Press.

Faulstich, M. E., Carey, M. P., Ruggiero, L., Enyart, P., & Gresham, F. (1986). Assessment of depression in childhood and adolescence: An evaluation of the Center for Epidemiological Studies Depression Scale for Children (CES-DC). *American Journal of Psychiatry, 143,* 1024–1027.

Feldstein, S. W., & Ginsburg J. I. D. (2007). Sex, drugs, and rock 'n' rolling with resistance: Motivational interviewing in juvenile justice settings. In D. W. Springer & A. R. Roberts (Eds.), *Handbook of forensic mental health with victims and offenders: Assessment, treatment, and research* (pp. 247–271). New York, NY: Springer Publishing Company.

Ferster, C. B. (1973). A functional analysis of depression. *American Psychologist, 28*(10), 857–870. doi:10.1037/h0035605

Feske, U., & Chambless, D. L. (1995). Cognitive behavioral versus exposure only treatment for social phobia: A meta-analysis. *Behavior Therapy, 26,* 695–720.

Figley, C. R. (2002). Compassion fatigue: Psychotherapists' chronic lack of self-care. *Journal of Clinical Psychology, 58*(11), 1433–1441.

Foa, E. B., & Kozak, M. J. (1986). Emotional processing of fear: Exposure to corrective information. *Psychological Bulletin, 99*(1), 20–35.

Fritsch, S., Donaldson, D., Spirito, A., & Plummer, B. (2000). Personality characteristics of adolescent suicide attempters. *Child Psychiatry & Human Development, 30*(4), 219–235.

Garber, J., Braafladt, N., & Weiss, B. (1995). Affect regulation in depressed and nondepressed children and young adolescents. *Development and Psychopathology, 7*(01), 93–115.

Garland, A. F., Accurso, E. C., Haine-Schlagel, R., Brookman-Frazee, L. I., Roesch, S., & Zhang, J. J. (2014). Searching for elements of evidence-based practices in children's usual care and examining their impact. *Journal of Clinical Child & Adolescent Psychology, 43*(2), 201–215.

Garland, A. F., Bickman, L., & Chorpita, B. F. (2010). Change what? Identifying quality improvement targets by investigating usual mental health care. *Administration and Policy in Mental Health and Mental Health Services Research, 37*, 15–26.

Garland, A. F., Brookman-Frazee, L. I., Hurlburt, M. S., Accurso, E. C., Zoffness, R. J., Haine-Schlagel, R., & Ganger, W. (2010). Mental health care for children with disruptive behavior problems: A view inside therapists' offices. *Psychiatric Services, 61*(8), 788–795.

Garland, A., Harrington, J., House, R., & Scott, J. (2000). A pilot study of the relationship between problem-solving skills and outcome in major depressive disorder. *British Journal of Medical Psychology, 73*(3), 303–309.

Garland, A. F., Hawley, K. M., Brookman-Frazee, L. I., & Hurlburt, M. (2008). Identifying common elements of evidence-based psychosocial treatments for children's disruptive behavior problems. *Journal of the American Academy of Child & Adolescent Psychiatry, 47*, 505–514.

Gayle, G. (2005, June 22). Giant Popsicle melts, floods New York park. *USAToday.com*. Retrieved from http://usatoday30.usatoday.com/news/nation/2005-06-22-popsicle_x .htm?csp=34

Glisson, C. (2002). The organizational context of children's mental health services. *Clinical Child and Family Psychology Review, 5*(4), 233–253.

Glisson, C. (2007). Assessing and changing organizational culture and climate for effective services. *Research on Social Work Practice, 17*(6), 736–747.

Goetz, T. E., & Dweck, C. S. (1980). Learned helplessness in social situations. *Journal of Personality and Social Psychology, 39*(2), 246–255. doi: 10.1037/0022-3514.39.2.246

Goodyer, I. M., Germany, E., Gowrusankur, J., & Altham, P. (1991). Social influences on the course of anxious and depressive disorders in school-age children. *The British Journal of Psychiatry, 158*(5), 676–684.

Goodyer, I. M., Herbert, J., Tamplin, A., Secher, S. M., & Pearson, J. (1997). Short-term outcome of major depression: II. Life events, family dysfunction, and friendship difficulties as predictors of persistent disorder. *Journal of the American Academy of Child & Adolescent Psychiatry, 36*(4), 474–480.

Gortner, E. T., Gollan, J. K., Dobson, K. S., & Jacobson, N. S. (1998). Cognitive-behavioral treatment for depression: Relapse prevention. *Journal of Consulting and Clinical Psychology, 66*(2), 377–384.

Gotlib, I. H., & Asarnow, R. F. (1979). Interpersonal and impersonal problem-solving skills in mildly and clinically depressed university students. *Journal of Consulting and Clinical Psychology, 47*, 86–95. doi:10.1037/0022-006X.47.1.86

Greenberg, M. T. (2007). Commentary on "the role of emotion theory and research in child therapy development." *Clinical Psychology: Science and Practice, 14*(4), 372–376.

Greener, J. M., Joe, G. W., Simpson, D. D., Rowan-Szal, G. A., & Lehman, W. E. (2007). Influence of organizational functioning on client engagement in treatment. *Journal of Substance Abuse Treatment, 33*(2), 139–147.

Griffin, J. A., Cicchetti, D., & Leaf, P. J. (1993). Characteristics of youths identified from a psychiatric case register as first-time users of services. *Hospital & Community Psychiatry, 44*(1), 62–65.

Grove, W. M., Zald, D. H., Lebow, B. S., Snitz, B. E., & Nelson, C. (2000). Clinical versus mechanical prediction: A meta-analysis. *Psychological Assessment, 12*(1), 19–30.

Guarnaccia, P., & Pincay, I. M. (2007). Culture-specific diagnoses and their relationship to mood disorders. In S. Loue & M. Sajatovic (Eds.), *Diversity issues in the diagnosis, treatment, and research of mood disorders* (pp. 32–53). New York, NY: Oxford University Press.

Hamilton, J. D. (2001). Do we under utilise actuarial judgement and decision analysis? *Evidence-Based Mental Health, 4*, 102–103.

Hammen, C., & Rudolph, K. D. (2003). Childhood mood disorders. In E. J. Mash & R. A. Barkley (Eds.), *Child psychopathology* (Second Edition, pp. 233–278). New York, NY: Guilford Press.

Hammen, C., Rudolph, K., Weisz, J., Rao, U., & Burge, D. (1999). The context of depression in clinic-referred youth: Neglected areas in treatment. *Journal of the American Academy of Child & Adolescent Psychiatry, 38*(1), 64–71.

Harrison, M. E., McKay, M. M., & Bannon, W. M., Jr. (2004). Inner-city child mental health service use: The real question is why youth and families do not use services. *Community Mental Health Journal, 40*(2), 119–131.

Hayes, S. C., Wilson, K. G., Gifford, E. V., Follette, V. M., & Strosahl, K. (1996). Experiential avoidance and behavioral disorders: A functional dimensional approach to diagnosis and treatment. *Journal of Consulting and Clinical Psychology, 64*(6), 1152–1168.

Heinrichs, N. (2006). The effects of two different incentives on recruitment rates of families into a prevention program. *Journal of Primary Prevention, 27*(4), 345–365.

Henggeler, S. W., Schoenwald, S. K., Borduin, C. M., Rowland, M. D., & Cunningham, P. B. (1998). *Multisystemic treatment of antisocial behavior in children and adolescents.* New York, NY: Guilford Press.

Hinton, D. E., Rivera, E. I., Hofmann, S. G., Barlow, D. H., Otto, M. W. (2012). Adapting CBT for traumatized refugees and ethnic minority patients: Examples from culturally adapted CBT (CA-CBT). *Transcultural Psychiatry, 49*(2), 340–365.

Hinton, D., Hofmann, S. G., Rivera, E., Otto, M. W., & Pollack, M. H. (2011). Culturally adapted CBT (CA-CBT) for Latino women with treatment-resistant PTSD: A pilot study comparing CA-CBT to applied muscle relaxation. *Behaviour Research and Therapy, 49*(4), 275–280.

Hiroto, D. S. (1974). Locus of control and learned helplessness. *Journal of Experimental Psychology, 102*(2), 187–193.

House, R. & Scott, J. (1996). Problems in measuring problem-solving: The suitability of the means-ends problem-solving (MEPS) procedure. *International Journal of Methods in Psychiatric Research, 6*(4), 243–251.

Hovey, J. D., & King, C. A. (1996). Aculturative stress, depression, and suicidal ideation among immigrant and second-generation Latino adolescents. *Journal of American Academy of Child & Adolescent Psychiatry, 35*(9), 1183–1192.

Hubbard, J. A., & Coie, J. D. (1994). Emotional correlates of social competence in children's peer relationships. *Merrill-Palmer Quarterly, 40*(1), 1–20.

Huey, S. J., Jr., Tilley, J. L., Jones, E. O., & Smith, C. (2014). The contribution of cultural competence to evidence-based care for ethnically diverse populations. *Annual Review of Clinical Psychology, 10*, 305–338.

Ingoldsby, E. M. (2010). Review of interventions to improve family engagement and retention in parent and child mental health programs. *Journal of Child and Family Studies, 19*(5), 629–645.

Jacobson, N. S., Dobson, K. S, Truax, P. A, Addis, M. E, Koerner, K., Gollan, J. K., … Prince, S. E. (1996). A component analysis of cognitive-behavioral treatment for depression. *Journal of Consulting and Clinical Psychology, 64*(2), 295–304.

Jaffari-Bimmel, N., Juffer, F., van Ijzendoorn, M. H., Bakermans-Kranenburg, M. J., & Mooijaart, A. (2006). Social development from infancy to adolescence: Longitudinal and concurrent factors in an adoption sample. *Developmental Psychology, 42*(6), 1143–1153. doi:10.1037/0012-1649.42.6.1143

Jose, A., & Goldfried, M. (2008). A transtheoretical approach to case formulation. *Cognitive and Behavioral Practice, 15*(2), 212–222.

Joshi, N. (2014, January 4). Doctor, shut up and listen. *New York Times.*

Kahneman, D. & Tversky, A. (1972). Subjective probability: A judgment of representativeness. *Cognitive Psychology, 3*, 430–454.

Kahneman, D., & Tversky, A. (1982). On the study of statistical intuitions. *Cognition, 11*, 123–141.

Kaplan, A. (1964). *The conduct of inquiry: Methodology for behavioral science.* San Francisco, CA: Chandler Publishing Company.

Kazdin, A. E. (1997). Parent management training: Evidence, outcomes, and issues. *Journal of the American Academy of Child & Adolescent Psychiatry, 36*(10), 1349–1356.

Kazdin, A. E. (2001). Bridging the enormous gaps of theory with therapy research and practice. *Journal of Clinical Child Psychology, 30*(1), 59–66.

Kazdin, A. E. (2003). Problem-solving skills training and parent management training for oppositional defiant disorder and conduct disorder. In A. E. Kazdin and J. R. Weisz (Eds.). *Evidence-based psychotherapies for children and adolescents* (pp. 241–262), New York, NY: Guilford Press.

Kazdin, A. E. (2008). Evidence-based treatment and practice: New opportunities to bridge clinical research and practice, enhance the knowledge base, and improve patient care. *American Psychologist, 63*(3), 146–159.

Kazdin, A. E., French, N. H., Esveldt-Dawson, K., & Sherick, R. B. (1983). Hopelessness, depression, and suicidal intent among psychiatrically disturbed inpatient children. *Journal of Consulting and Clinical Psychology, 51*(4), 504–510.

Kazdin, A. E., & Wassell, G. (2000). Predictors of barriers to treatment and therapeutic change in outpatient therapy for antisocial children and their families. *Mental Health Services Research, 2*(1), 27–40.

Kearney, C. A., & Silverman, W. K. (1990). Treatment of an adolescent with obsessive-compulsive behavior by alternating response prevention and cognitive therapy: An empirical analysis. *Journal of Behavior Therapy and Experimental Psychiatry, 21,* 39–48.

Kelly, K., & Knudson, M. P. (2000). Are no-suicide contracts effective in preventing suicide in suicidal patients seen by primary care physicians? *Archives of Family Medicine, 9*(10), 1119–1121.

Kendall, P. C. (1994). Treating anxiety disorders in children: Results of a randomized clinical trial. *Journal of Consulting and Clinical Psychology, 62*(1), 100–110.

Kendall, P. C., & Braswell, L. (1993). *Cognitive-behavioral therapy for impulsive children.* New York, NY: Guilford Press.

Kessler, R., & Walters, E. (1998). Epidemiology of DSM-III-R major depression and minor depression among adolescents and young adults in the national comorbidity survey. *Depression and Anxiety, 3–14.*

Kessler, R., Zhao, S., Blazer, D., & Swartz, M. (1997). Prevalence, correlates, and course of minor depression and major depression in the National Comorbidity Survey. *Journal of Affective Disorders, 45*(1–2), 19–30.

Khanna, M., & Kendall, P. C. (2008). Computer-assisted CBT for child anxiety: The Coping Cat CD-ROM. *Cognitive and Behavioral Practice, 15,* 159–165.

Klein, D., Dougherty, L., & Olino, T. (2005). Toward guidelines for evidence-based assessment of depression in children and adolescents. *Journal of Clinical Child & Adolescent Psychology, 34*(3), 412–432.

Kolko, D. J., Brent, D. A., Baugher, M., Bridge, J., & Birmaher, B. (2000). Cognitive and family therapies for adolescent depression: Treatment specificity, mediation, and moderation. *Journal of Consulting and Clinical Psychology, 68*(4), 603–614.

Kovacs, M., Goldston, D., & Gatsonis, C. (1993). Suicidal behaviors and childhood-onset depressive disorders: A longitudinal investigation. *Journal of the American Academy of Child & Adolescent Psychiatry, 32*(1), 8–20.

Kovacs, M., & Yaroslavsky, I. (2014). Practitioner review: Dysphoria and its regulation in child and adolescent depression. *Journal of Child Psychology and Psychiatry, 55*(7), 741–757.

La Roche, M., Batista, C., & D'Angelo, E. (2011). A culturally competent relaxation intervention for Latino/as: Assessing a culturally specific match model. *American Journal of Orthopsychiatry,* 535–542.

La Roche, M., D'angelo, E., Gualdron, L., & Leavell, J. (2011). Culturally sensitive guided imagery for allocentric Latinos: A pilot study. *Psychotherapy: Theory, Research, Practice, Training, 81*(4), 555–560.

Lau, A. S. (2006). Making the case for selective and directed cultural adaptations of evidence-based treatments: Examples from parent training. *Clinical Psychology: Science and Practice, 13*(4), 295–310.

Lewinsohn, P. M. (1974). A behavioral approach to depression. In R. M. Friedman & M. M. Katz (Eds.), *The psychology of depression: Contemporary theory and research* (pp. 157–185). New York, NY: John Wiley & Sons.

Lewinsohn, P. M., Clarke, G. N., Hops, H., & Andrews, J. (1990). Cognitive-behavioral treatment for depressed adolescents. *Behavior Therapy, 21,* 385–401.

Lewinsohn, P. M., Rohde, P., Seeley, J. R., Klein, D. N., & Gotlib, I. H. (2000). Natural course of adolescent major depressive disorder in a community sample: Predictors of recurrence in young adults. *American Journal of Psychiatry, 157*(10), 1584–1591.

MacKenzie, M. J., Nicklas, E., Waldfogel, J., & Brooks-Gunn, J. (2013). Spanking and child development across the first decade of life. *Pediatrics, 132*(5), e1118–e1125.

March, J., Silva, S., Vitiello, B., & TADS team. (2006). The Treatment for Adolescents with Depression Study (TADS): Methods and message at 12 weeks. *Journal of the American Academy of Child & Adolescent Psychiatry, 45*(12), 1393–1403.

Mash, E. J., & Barkley, R. A. (Eds.). (2006). *Treatment of childhood disorders.* New York, NY: Guilford Press.

Matsumoto, D., Yoo, S., & Nakagawa, S. (2008). Culture, emotion regulation, and adjustment. *Journal of Personality and Social Psychology, 94*(6), 925–937.

McDermott, P., & Hale, R. (1982). Validation of a systems-actuarial computer process for multidimensional classification of child psychopathology. *Journal of Clinical Psychology, 38*(3), 477–486.

McKay, M. M. (May, 2013). *Family engagement: What does the evidence suggest?* New York State Parenting Education Partnership Spring 2013 Meeting, Latham, New York.

McKay, M. M., & Bannon W. M., Jr., (2004). Engaging families in child mental health services. *Child and Adolescent Psychiatric Clinics of North America, 13*(4), 905–921.

McKay, M. M., Nudelman, R., McCadam, K., & Gonzales, J. (1996). Involving inner-city families in mental health services: First interview engagement skills. *Research on Social Work Practice, 6,* 462–472.

McKay, M. M., Pennington, J., Lynn, C. J., & McCadam, K. (2001). Understanding urban child mental health service use: Two studies of child, family, and environmental correlates. *The Journal of Behavioral Health Services & Research, 28*(4), 475–483.

McKay, M. M., Stoewe, J., McCadam, K., & Gonzales, J. (1998). Increasing access to child mental health services for urban children and their caregivers. *Health & Social Work, 23*(1), 9–15.

Meehl, P. E. (1954). *Clinical versus statistical prediction: A theoretical analysis and a review of the evidence.* Minneapolis, MN: University of Minnesota Press.

Meichenbaum, D. (2009, May). Psycho-cultural assessment and interventions: The need for a case conceptualization model. Paper presented at the 13th Annual Melissa Institute Conference on Race, Ethnicity and Mental Health. Coral Gables, Florida.

Merikangas, R., He, J., Burstein, M., Swanson, S., Avenevoli, S., Cui, L., … Swendsen, J. (2010). Lifetime prevalence of mental disorders in U.S. adolescents. *Journal of the American Academy of Child & Adolescent Psychiatry, 49*(10), 980–989.

Meyer, G., Finn, S., Eyde, L., Kay, G., Moreland, K., Dies, R., … Read, G. (2001). Psychological testing and psychological assessment: A review of evidence and issues. *American Psychologist, 56*(2), 128–165.

Meyerbröker K., & Emmelkamp, P. M. (2010). Virtual reality exposure therapy in anxiety disorders: A systematic review of process-and-outcome studies. *Depression and Anxiety, 27*(10), 933–944.

Miller, W. R., Moyers, T., & Rollnick, S. (2010). *Motivational interviewing: A beginning workshop.* Training conducted in Albuquerque, New Mexico.

Miller, W. R., & Rollnick, S. (2012). *Motivational interviewing: Helping people change.* New York, NY: Guilford Press.

Miller, W. R., Zweben, A., DiClemente, C. C., & Rychtarik, R. G. (1992). *Motivational enhancement therapy manual: A clinical research guide for therapists treating individuals with alcohol abuse and dependence.* Rockville, MD: National Institute on Alcohol Abuse and Alcoholism.

Moos, R. H., & Moos, B. S. (1998). The staff workplace and the quality and outcome of substance abuse treatment. *Journal of Studies on Alcohol and Drugs, 59*(1), 43–51.

Moos, R. H., & Schaefer, J. (1987). Evaluating health care work settings: A holistic conceptual framework. *Psychology & Health, 1*(2), 97–122.

Nezu, A. M. (1987). A problem-solving formulation for depression: A literature review and proposal of a pluralistic model. *Clinical Psychology Review, 7,* 121–144.

O'Donnell, L., O'Donnell, C., Wardlaw, D. M., & Stueve, A. (2004). Risk and resiliency factors influencing suicidality among urban African-American and Latino Youth. *American Journal of Community Psychology, 33,* 37–49.

Ollendick, T. H. (2000, November). Discussant in T. L. Morris (Chair), *Innovative approaches to the treatment of child anxiety: Conceptual issues and practical constraints.* Symposium conducted at the meeting of the Association for Advancement of Behavior Therapy, New Orleans, Louisiana.

Pahl, K. M., & Barrett, P. M. (2010). Interventions for anxiety disorders in children using group cognitive-behavioral therapy with family involvement. In J. R. Weisz & A. E. Kazdin (Eds.), *Evidence-based psychotherapies for children and adolescents* (pp. 61–79). New York, NY: Guilford Press.

Palinkas, L. A., Weisz, J. R., Chorpita, B. F., Levine, B., Garland, A., Hoagwood, K. E., & Landsverk, J. (2013). Continued use of evidence-based treatments after a randomized controlled effectiveness trial: A qualitative study. *Psychiatric Services, 64,* 1110–1118.

Patterson G. R., & Forgatch, M. S. (1985). Therapist behavior as a determinant for client noncompliance: A paradox for the behavior modifider. *Journal of Consulting and Clinical Psychology, 53*(6), 846–851.

Persons, J. B. (2012). *The case-formulation approach to cognitive-behavior therapy.* New York, NY: Guilford Press.

Pfaff, J. J., Acres, J., & Wilson, M. (1999). The role of general practitioner's in parasuicide: A Western Australia perspective. *Archives of Suicide Research, 5,* 207–214.

Poston, J., & Hanson, W. (2010). Meta-analysis of psychological assessment as a therapeutic intervention. *Psychological Assessment, 22*(2), 203–212.

Puig-Antich, J., Lukens, E., Davies, M., Goetz, D., Brennan-Quattrock, J., & Todak, G. (1985). Psychosocial functioning in prepubertal major depressive disorders: I. Interpersonal relationships during the depressive episode. *Archives of General Psychiatry, 42*(5), 500–507.

Rachman, S. (1977). The conditioning theory of fear-acquisition: A critical examination. *Behaviour Research & Therapy, (15)*5, 375–387.

Rao, U., & Chen, L. A. (2009). Characteristics, correlates, and outcomes of childhood and adolescent depressive disorders. *Dialogues in Clinical Neuroscience, 11*(1), 45–62.

Ray, S. L., Wong, C., White, D., & Heaslip, K. (2013). Compassion satisfaction, compassion fatigue, work life conditions, and burnout among frontline mental health care professionals. *Traumatology, 19*(4), 255–267.

Rubin, K. H., & Asendorpf, J. B. (1993). *Social withdrawal, inhibition, and shyness in childhood.* Hillsdale, NJ: Lawrence Erlbaum Associates, Inc.

Rubin, K. H., Bukowski, W. M., & Parker, J. G. (1998). Peer interactions, relationships, and groups. In N. Eisenberg (Ed.), *Handbook of child psychology* (pp. 571–645). New York, NY: John Wiley & Sons.

Rubin, K. H., Burgess, K. B., Kennedy, A. E., & Stewart, S. L. (2003). Social withdrawal in childhood. In E. J. Mash & R. A. Barkley (Eds.), *Child psychopathology* (Second Edition, pp. 372–406). New York, NY: Guilford Press.

Rudolph, K. D., & Hammen, C. (1999). Age and gender as determinants of stress exposure, generation, and reactions in youngsters: A transactional perspective. *Child Development, 70*(3), 660–677.

Ryan, N. D., Puig-Antich, J., Ambrosini, P., Rabinovich, H., Robinson, D., Nelson, B., ... Twomey, J. (1987). The clinical picture of major depression in children and adolescents. *Archives of General Psychiatry, 44*(10), 854–861.

Schaefer, J. A., & Moos, R. H. (1996). Effects of work stressors and work climate on long-term care staff's job morale and functioning. *Research in Nursing & Health 19*(1), 63–73.

Schmidt, N. B., Woolaway-Bickel, K., Trakowski, J., Santiago, H., Storey, J., Koselka, M., & Cook, J. (2000). Dismantling cognitive-behavioral treatment for panic disorder: Questioning the utility of breathing retraining. *Journal of Consulting and Clinical Psychology, 68*(3), 417–424.

Schoenwald, S. K., & Hoagwood, K. (2001). Effectiveness, transportability, and dissemination of interventions: What matters when? *Psychiatric Services, 52*(9), 1190–1197.

Schotte, D., & Clum, G. (1987). Problem-solving skills in suicidal psychiatric patients. *Journal of Consulting and Clinical Psychology, 55*(1), 49–54.

Schwarz, Joyce. (2005, June 29). Snapple Popsicle is flopsicle. *Hollywood 2020.* Retrieved from http://hollywood2020.blogs.com/hollywood2020/2005/06/snapple_popsicl.html

Seligman, M. E. (1972). Learned helplessness. *Annual Review of Medicine, 23,* 407–412. doi: 10.1146/annurev.me.23.020172.002203

Selman, R. L., & Schultz, L. H. (1998). *Making a friend in youth: Developmental theory and pair therapy.* New Brunswick, NJ: Transaction Publishers.

Shriffin, H. H., Liss, M., Miles-McLean, H., Geary, K. A., Erchull, M. J., & Tashner, T. (2014). Helping or hovering? The effects of helicopter parenting on college students' well-being. *Journal of Child and Family Studies, 23*(3), 548–557.

Southam-Gerow, M. A., & Kendall, P. C. (2000). Cognitive-behaviour therapy with youth: Advances, challenges, and future directions. *Clinical Psychology & Psychotherapy, 7*(5), 343–366.

Sperry, L., & Sperry, J. (2012). *Case conceptualization: Mastering this competency with ease and confidence.* New York, NY: Routledge.

Sprang, G., Clark, J. J., & Whitt-Woosley, A. (2007). Compassion fatigue, compassion satisfaction, and burnout: Factors impacting a professional's quality of life. *Journal of Loss & Trauma, 12*(3), 259–280.

Stamm, B. H. (2002). Measuring compassion satisfaction as well as fatigue: Developmental history of the compassion satisfaction and fatigue test. In C. R. Figley (Ed.), *Treating compassion fatigue* (pp. 107–119). New York, NY: Brunner-Routledge.

Stanley, B., Brown, G., Brent, D., Wells, K., Poling, K., Curry, J., ... Hughes, J. (2009). Cognitive-behavioral therapy for suicide prevention (CBT-SP). *Journal of the American Academy of Child & Adolescent Psychiatry, 48*(10), 1005–1013.

Steinberg, L., Fletcher, A., & Darling, N. (1994). Parental monitoring and peer influences on adolescent substance use. *Pediatrics, 93*(6), 1060–1064.

Stoddard, J. A., & Williams, K. N. (2012). CBT for mood disorders in children and adolescents. *Rady Children's Outpatient Psychiatry Seminar Series.* Lecture conducted in Oceanside, California.

Swinkels, A., & Giuliano, T. A. (1995). The measurement and conceptualization of mood awareness: Monitoring and labeling one's mood states. *Personality and Social Psychology Bulletin, 21*(9), 934–949.

Teichman, Y. (1992). Family treatment with an acting-out adolescent. In A. Freeman & F. M. Dattilio (Eds.), *Comprehensive casebook of cognitive therapy* (pp. 331–346). New York, NY: Springer Publishing Company.

Tversky, A., & Kahneman, D. (1973). Availability: A heuristic for judging frequency and probability. *Cognitive Psychology, 5,* 207–232.

Tversky, A., & Kahneman, D. (1974). Judgment under uncertainty: Heuristics and biases. *Science, 185*(4157), 1124–1131.

Warner, V., Weissman, M. M., Fendrick, M., Wickramaratne, P., & Moreau, D. (1992). The course of major depression in the offspring of depressed parents. *Archives of General Psychiatry, 49*(10), 795–801.

Weersing, V. R., & Weisz, J. R. (2002). Community clinic treatment of depressed youth: Benchmarking usual care against CBT clinical trials. *Journal of Consulting and Clinical Psychology, 70,* 299–310.

Weisman, C. S., & Nathanson, C. A. (1985). Professional satisfaction and client outcomes. *Medical Care, 23,* 1179–1192.

Weisz, J. R., & Chorpita, B. F. (2012). Mod squad for child psychotherapy: Restructuring evidence-based treatment for clinical practice. In P. C. Kendall (Ed.), *Child and adolescent therapy: Cognitive-behavioral procedures* (Fourth Edition, pp. 379–397). New York: Guilford Press.

Weisz, J. R., Chorpita, B. F., Palinkas, L. A., Schoenwald, S. K., Miranda, J., Bearman, S ... Research Network on Youth Mental Health (2012). Testing standard and modular designs for psychotherapy treating depression, anxiety, and conduct problems in youth: A randomized effectiveness trial. *Archives of General Psychiatry, 69*(3), 274-282. doi:10.1001/archgenpsychiatry.2011.147

Whong, C. (2014, September 14) In search of Hess' Triangle—Part 2. Retrieved from http://chriswhong.com/local/in-search-of-hess-triangle-part-2

Wittchen, H., Nelson, C., & Lachner, G. (1998). Prevalence of mental disorders and psychosocial impairments in adolescents and young adults. *Psychological Medicine, 28*(1), 109–126.

World Health Organization. (2012, October). Depression factsheet. Retrieved from http://www.who.int/mediacentre/factsheets/fs369/en/

Yap, M. B. H., Pilkington, P. D., Ryan, S. M., & Jorm, A. F. (2014). Parental factors associated with depression and anxiety in young people: A systematic review and meta-analysis. *Journal of Affective Disorders, 156,* 8–23.

Katherine Nguyen Williams, PhD, is a licensed supervising psychologist, professor, and clinical faculty member in the department of psychiatry at the University of California, San Diego (UCSD). She is clinical training director of child and adolescent psychology, and director of the anxiety and OCD clinic at Rady Children's Hospital Outpatient Psychiatry in San Diego, CA, where she provides child and adolescent therapy, and specializes in child and adolescent psychological assessments. She is also founding director of the Center for Child and Adolescent Testing (C-CAT). Nguyen Williams frequently provides clinical trainings, hospital workshops, and university courses on the topics of evidence-based practices, clinical research, and childhood disorders, both locally and nationally. In addition to an active clinical practice, she teaches and clinically supervises psychology students, marriage and family therapists, social workers, psychiatry fellows, and medical students about the application of modular cognitive behavioral therapy (CBT) for child and adolescent depression and anxiety.

Brent Crandal, PhD, is a clinical psychologist and research investigator at the Chadwick Center for Children and Families at Rady Children's Hospital in San Diego, CA. As a clinician, he has offered evidence-based treatments for children, youth, and families in outpatient, inpatient, pediatric, military, and community mental health settings, and supervises and trains therapists. As a research investigator, he developed strategies to promote family engagement in services, screen and assess mental health needs, and measure treatment outcomes. He also advances access to care for children and youth in California's Child Welfare and Behavioral Health systems as part of the California Assessment, Screening, and Treatment Initiative.

Index

46–48; resources on depression, 54, 65; role of parents/families, 47–48; session summary, 63; skills training and, 48–49, 61–62; treatment overview, 49–50

psychotropic treatments, 2, 54–55

punishment, 181, 183

Q

Qualities of Success activity, 205–206

questionnaires, assessment, 14–15

questions: about depression, 51–53; open-ended, 73, 200; three-questions technique, 113–114

R

rapport building, 12

rating scales, 16

recording out-of-session interactions, 186

reflective listening, 193–194, 200–201

reinforcement, 181, 185

relapse prevention module, 222–232; action plan, 227, 231; background for, 223; clinical rationale for, 223; common hurdles and solutions in, 228; cultural considerations, 224; explaining the rationale for, 225–226; graduation certificate, 228, 232; overall treatment and, 223; parent/ caregiver involvement in, 224; preparation process, 223–224; session summary and feedback, 227; skills training, 225–227; structuring the session, 225; symptom monitoring and, 226–227, 230; therapy binder review, 226; when to include, 223–224; worksheets, 230–231

relaxation training module, 119–137; agenda setting, 125–126; background for, 120–121; between-session practice, 131; clinical rationale for, 121–123; common hurdles and

solutions in, 131–132; cultural considerations, 123–124; current concerns discussed in, 130; developmental considerations, 121; explaining the rationale for, 126–127; modeling and role-playing in, 127; overall treatment and, 122–123; parent/caregiver involvement in, 124; preparation process, 119–123; relaxation strategies/scripts, 128–130, 136–137; session summary, 131; skills training, 126–127; structuring the session, 124–126; when to include, 123; worksheets, 133–137

religious practices, 123–124

resistance, 189, 190, 194, 203

resources: depression, 54, 65; relaxation training, 122; suicide prevention, 39. *See also* worksheets

reward charts, 182

risk assessment, 29, 39

role-playing: affect regulation, 164–165; behavioral activation, 94; problem-solving skills, 218; relaxation exercises, 127; social skills, 147, 148

S

safety behaviors, 130

safety considerations, 29, 37–39

safety plan and crisis management module, 37–44; background for, 38; between-session practice, 41; clinical rationale for, 38–39; common hurdles and solutions in, 42; plan development, 39–41; preparation process, 37–39; resources related to, 39; session summary, 42; worksheets, 43–44

scaling emotions, 68, 78–79

screening measures, 14–15

scripts, relaxation, 136–137

selective attention, 183–185

self-harm risk, 40

self-injurious behaviors, 38

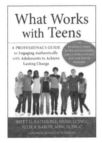

Register your **new harbinger** titles for additional benefits!

When you register your **new harbinger** title—purchased in any format, from any source—you get access to benefits like the following:

- Downloadable accessories like printable worksheets and extra content

- Instructional videos and audio files

- Information about updates, corrections, and new editions

Not every title has accessories, but we're adding new material all the time.

Access free accessories in 3 easy steps:

1. Sign in at NewHarbinger.com (or **register** to create an account).

2. Click on **register a book**. Search for your title and click the **register** button when it appears.

3. Click on the **book cover or title** to go to its details page. Click on **accessories** to view and access files.

That's all there is to it!

If you need help, visit:

NewHarbinger.com/accessories

new harbinger
CELEBRATING
40 YEARS